P9-DEU-824

3 1192 01420 2350

612.82 Horne.T
Horne, Terry.
Teach yourself training your
brain for the over 50s /

training your brain
for the over 50s

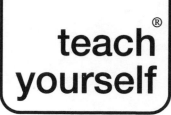

training your brain
for the over 50s
terry horne and
simon wootton

EVANSTON PUBLIC LIBRARY
1703 ORRINGTON AVENUE
EVANSTON, ILLINOIS 60201

Launched in 1938, the **teach yourself** series grew rapidly in response to the world's wartime needs. Loved and trusted by over 50 million readers, the series has continued to respond to society's changing interests and passions and now, 70 years on, includes over 500 titles, from Arabic and Beekeeping to Yoga and Zulu. What would you like to learn?

be where you want to be with **teach yourself**

Orders: please contact Bookpoint Ltd, 130 Milton Park, Abingdon, Oxon OX14 4SB. Telephone: +44 (0) 1235 827720. Fax: +44 (0) 1235 400454. Lines are open 09.00–17.00, Monday to Saturday, with a 24-hour message answering service. You can also order through our website www.hoddereducation.co.uk

British Library Cataloguing in Publication Data: a catalogue record for this title is available from the British Library.

First published in UK 2008 by Hodder Education, part of Hachette Livre UK, 338 Euston Road, London NW1 3BH

This edition published 2008.

Copyright © 2008 Simon Wootton and Terry Horne

All rights reserved. Apart from any permitted use under UK copyright law, no part of this publication may be reproduced or transmitted in any form or by any means, electronic or mechanical, including photocopy, recording, or any information, storage and retrieval system, without permission in writing from the publisher or under licence from the Copyright Licensing Agency Limited. Further details of such licences (for reprographic reproduction) may be obtained from the Copyright Licensing Agency Limited, of Saffron House, 6–10 Kirby Street, London EC1N 8TS.

Typeset by Transet Ltd, Coventry, England.
Printed in Great Britain for Hodder Education, an Hachette Livre UK Company, 338 Euston Road, London NW1 3BH, by CPI Cox and Wyman, Reading, Berkshire, RG1 8EX.

The publisher has used its best endeavours to ensure that the URLs for external websites referred to in this book are correct and active at the time of going to press. However, the publisher and the author have no responsibility for the websites and can make no guarantee that a site will remain live or that the content will remain relevant, decent or appropriate.

Hachette Livre UK's policy is to use papers that are natural, renewable and recyclable products and made from wood grown in sustainable forests. The logging and manufacturing processes are expected to conform to the environmental regulations of the country of origin.

Impression number   10 9 8 7 6 5 4 3 2 1
Year   2012 2011 2010 2009 2008

v

contents

dedication

This book is dedicated to Carolyn Horne. Carolyn's life is testimony to the way personal choices can produce eminence and expertise at work, and closeness and intimacy in relationships at 50+.

As a tomboy teenager, Carolyn did not consider herself good at books, or good at boys. She studied pottery and drama and became an accomplished actress and, eventually, an inspiring teacher. Ever curious about what went on in the heads of her children, Carolyn took time out to study for a degree in psychology at Bedford College, London. Later she switched from educational psychology to teacher training. Again, she took time out to study for a Masters in Education, producing seminal research on 'the match' in early years' development.

At 50+, as Director of Education at the now University of Cumbria, Carolyn built the UK's largest single campus programme of primary education in the UK. Her innovative programmes were characterized by creative thinking on early years' child development, novel forms of in-service training and new, accelerated forms of full time study.

At 50+, Carolyn agreed to take on a UK college that was faced with imminent closure by inspectors. She and her team turned the college around in less than six months. The day after she got the good news about her college, Carolyn was hit by a car and killed, while training for her second London marathon.

At 50+, Carolyn's death was a tragic loss for her husband, her family and her many close friends. Her death also deprived the world of the burgeoning benefits of her 50+ brain, which would have continued to add life to all our years for at least another 30 years!

acknowledgements

We are indebted to so many brain researchers (biologists, biochemists, neurologists, neuroscientists, dieticians, social workers and cognitive psychologists) and so many brain research centres specializing in ageing, that it is iniquitous to name only five individuals and three centres.

That said, we especially acknowledge that much of our material was first researched with Roger Armstrong at LBS, University of Central Lancashire; Peter Checkland, Department of Systems Thinking and Practice, University of Lancaster; Tony Doherty, at the Centre for Social Enterprise, University of London; P.J. Howard at the Centre for Cognitive Studies in Carolina, USA; Sayaka Mitsuhashi of the Okinawa Centenarian Centre; and David Gamon, Allen Bragdon, Ian Robertson, Guy Brown, Susan Greenfield, Jeff Victoroff, James Fixx, Rosemarie Janski, Zak Tan, Pam Ayres, Felix Dennis, Ian Deary, David Snowden, Paul McKenna, Richard Templar, Sally Moon and Nathan Haselbayer of the International High IQ Society. We are grateful to their publishers, where they have given help with tracing sources or have given permissions to reproduce diagrams or tables. We are especially indebted to the Saunders Brown Centre for Ageing in Kentucky, USA, Members of the Noetic Institute, UK, and the Institute of Brain and Ageing at the University of California, Irvine. This book is part of a long journey with many companions, usually for only part of the way. Part way companions have included many research students, too many to mention. We thank them for their legacy of findings and good questions.

Frances, of Age Concern, stands out. As a part time student on an MBA programme, many years ago, it was Frances who first challenged our view of the elderly as needing help. She said the elderly needed opportunity. She was right.

We thank our families finally: Fakhrun Nisa and Danya Horne; and Gillian, Ellis, James and Holly Wootton, for their sacrifices and support in this, our joint endeavour.

preface

Adding years to life and life to later years

Rage, rage, against the dying of the light

(Dylan Thomas)

This book is for everyone. Which of us will not, one day, be older? If you have ever wondered what goes on in the head of a parent, a grandparent, an older friend or your own head as you get older, then this book is for you.

There are many other books on brain training, but few acknowledge that the brains they train are ageing. When ageing is acknowledged, it is usually as a problem to be lived with, like amnesia, or slower reactions. Yet the neuroscience research underpinning our first book showed that your brain gets better and better at thinking as you get older.

> *The research is up to date and very readable. It contains some of the world's most advanced models of the way the brain thinks.*

(Professor Susan Greenfield)

Nine out of ten of the components of good applied thinking improve with age. The 50+ can exploit this advantage over younger brains. New memories form more slowly, but this can be overcome.

For example, verbal thinking, visual thinking, ethical thinking, critical thinking, predictive thinking, creativity, problem solving and learning from experience all improve with age. If these particular skills are exploited, the problems caused by a slower speed of new memory formation can be avoided or side stepped.

Provided that you do not suffer from a degenerative brain disease (and you can minimize the chances that you will), the loss of speed can be delayed, diminished and reversed in later years. The ongoing development of intellectual power, until you are at least 90, is a realistic goal for readers of this book. Protecting that power from disease becomes a lifestyle choice and the book explains how to make that choice.

Other books will exhort you to 'use it or lose it'. We have researched and evaluated different possible uses of the brain, in order to discover which uses most enhance the power of the brain to think. In four earlier books on thinking skills for planners, strategists, managers and public service professionals, we isolated 12 components of thinking. By exercising each component separately, or in more advanced combinations, you can improve your ability to think clearly and to clearly express what you think. You can exploit the components of applied thinking which improve with age.

This will give you a choice about whether or not to carry on working. Sometimes people retire because they find the problems too complex or too confusing. But the confusion is not often caused by complex problems. Confusion is caused by trying to solve complex problems too quickly. You need to start earlier. Fortunately, in later years, enhanced skills in predictive thinking can help to anticipate some problems, avoid others, and to make an earlier start on solving the rest.

When you anticipate problems and refuse to be rushed, you will calm the panic of those around you. Your ability to keep your head, when younger ones around you are losing theirs, is characteristic of strong leaders.

Of all the improvements with age that we have uncovered, none are more dramatic than the way IQ and intelligence improve as you get older. The gains in IQ shown by the Scottish 70 and 80-year-olds returning to re-sit tests they sat when they were 11-years-old astonished them, but did not surprise those of us who have experience of working with mature learners. Deeper analysis of the diets and lifestyles of the 50+ with high gains in IQ is revealing - your IQ is not determined by your genes or your age, but by things over which you have control. Even your risk of degenerative disease, or dementia, is now down to choices you can make (see Chapters 03 and 04). Perhaps not genius but eminence, or at least expertise, is a realistic goal for people who choose to carry on working well into their later years (Chapters 02 and 05).

In later years, we often prefer relationships characterised by reasonableness and thoughtfulness. But we cannot be reasonable if we cannot reason. We cannot be thoughtful if we cannot think reflectively (Chapter 06).

In earlier work with Tony Doherty, at the University of London, we established that the inability to work and the inability to form close relationships were two major obstacles to human health and happiness (Chapter 01). This book can help you to achieve both. It can help you continue to work and continue to form close relationships in later life.

With this book, you can 'add years to your life as well as life to your later years'.

(American Society of Gerontologists)

introduction

The superior thinking skills of the 50+ brain

On 8 November 2007, the comedian Ken Dodd was 80 years old. The BBC programme 'Songs of Praise' arranged a surprise party for him. His repartee was light and quick. His memory of his lines was faultless. 'I don't mind getting older,' he quipped, 'as long as I don't get to be old!' However old Ken's body will one day become, barring disease his brain is likely to get better and better the older he gets.

Mae West used to say that she was never too old to become younger. In a way she was right. Her older brain would have become better at critical thinking, creative thinking and reflective thinking and at making predictions. Her verbal and numerical IQ would already have been higher than when she was younger, and her long-term memory would also have been better. True, she would have been slower to process new information and form new memory, but her experience, street wisdom and powers of prediction would have taught her to start sooner and to make notes. As long as you are not under time pressure, your experiential learning and your creative problem solving will get better as you get older. This might help to explain why your IQ is 10–25 per cent higher than when you were 11 years old (see Chapter 02). Experiential learning and creative problem solving benefit from experience and broader general knowledge, and the only way to acquire experience and general knowledge is to become older! Your memory of what you already know will get better, not worse, because your recollection improves with the number of times you make a given recall. The older you are the more likely you are to have made a recall.

Einstein also resolved never to grow old, no matter how long he lived. Einstein resolved to remain a child – a curious child – in the face of the mysteries of the world in which he found himself. He bequeathed his brain to science. Einstein's brain looks much like yours or mine. What seems to matter is how you use your brain. When you do the kinds of things described in this book, your brain will develop better myelin insulation on its neural pathways – enabling it to think faster with less error. When you do the kinds of things described in this book, your brain can also develop more cognitive capacity than it currently needs. This can help you to preserve your mental performance even if you contract a disease that damages your brain. In Chapters 01 and 03 we will discover that nuns who had remained academically very able until they died were found, on autopsy, to have brains that were riddled with Alzheimer plaques, but because they still had more than enough cognitive capacity left intact, no one, themselves included, ever knew that they had Alzheimer's disease.

The physical state of your brain as you age is not determined by your genes – it is a lifestyle choice (Chapters 01 and 04). If earlier lifestyle choices have damaged your brain, the advice and exercises in this book can reverse the damage – whatever your age.

Death is not what it used to be

Writing in the *Guardian* newspaper in November 2007, Dr Guy Brown, winner of the Welcome Trust Prize, claimed that 'death is not what it used to be'. The nature of death is set to change markedly for the 50+. We think that the decline in acute deaths by, for example, infection, violence, stroke or heart disease (see Figure 0.1), will lead to a rise in slower deaths from neurodegenerative diseases like dementia, Parkinson's or Alzheimer's. The 50+ generation will be stalked by Three Deadly Ds – Disability, Dementia and Degenerative disease. Any of these could turn the last 20 years of your life into a living death. It must be a kind of living hell to wake up every morning, feeling afraid, in a place you do not recognize, to have things done to you, for no reason, by people you do not know (albeit they might be your own children). Yet this prospect is not inevitable. Barring physical illness, and in some cases in spite of physical illness, the 50+ should expect to remain mentally fit and sharp well into their nineties (Figure 0.2).

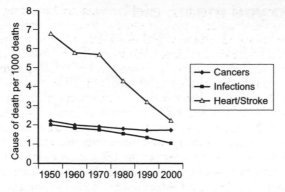

Figure 0.1: Early twentieth-century 'killer' diseases now accounting for only about 0.6% of deaths (based on England & Wales, ONS 2004)

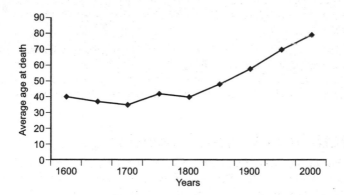

Figure 0.2: Rising life expectancies of Western women, 1600–2000 (based on Deppan, H. (2002) *Science*, 296, p1030)

What matters is what you do in order to train and maintain the fitness of your brain. There are many exciting and enjoyable things that you can do, both to exploit the growing power of your brain and to defend if from disease. You can add life to your years, and not just years to your life.

You should resist the idea of retirement. (Unless it entitles you to a lump sum which you want to use to start your own business – see Chapter 05. Colonel Sanders started KFC when he was 67. Last year 40 per cent of successful new business start-ups in the UK were started by people over 50.)

What do you mean, old?

If you have survived to be 50 years old, you will now need to reframe what you think of as 'old'. For you, now, 60 is no longer old, 100 is old. You can no longer justify a pension at 65 on account of 'old age'. It is a supplementary income for which you have saved or invested. You will be more able, not less able, to work than a younger person – as long as the work is mental not physical (Chapter 05).

At the moment, according to the UK Government Actuary, there are only about 10,000 old people in the UK, i.e. people who are more than 100 years old. By 2070, this number will probably have risen to about half a million people.

You need to make sure that your physical lifespan is matched by an extension in your healthy lifespan, otherwise you can expect to suffer from disability, dementia or degenerative disease – the 3Ds.

The dreaded DDDs

During the 1990s, the life expectancy of the 50+ increased by an extra 2.2 years, but 'healthy' life expectancy increased by only 7 months. Because the increase in your lifespan is linear, and the chance of brain disease is exponential, the baby boom generation is increasingly likely to die from degenerative brain disease, and unnecessarily so, given that there are relatively simple means of defending yourself against this (see Chapter 04 and Part Two). By 2008, 700,000 people in the UK had already succumbed to dementia. If the advice in this book goes unheeded, by the time you are 90 nearly 2 million people in the UK alone will be suffering from dementia. The suffering of the families of the demented will be pervasive. The social cost of caring for 2 million demented people will be hard to finance. National and local governments, and social and medical agencies, as well as the 50+ themselves, need to take this book seriously.

Are you heading in that direction?

In 2007, the Institute of Public Health in Cambridge, UK, reported on people's health in the year before death and they found that nearly half suffered from a moderate to severe cognitive deficit in the year before they died. Around 30 per cent had full-blown dementia. Yet there is no necessity for the present 50+ generation to become part of these statistics. Would your life be worth living if your head went in that direction? We are in danger of merging and confusing living and dying. In the UK, death is already preceded by 10 years of chronic ill health. At the moment, perhaps being out of your mind is the only way to escape a life not worth living. It does not have to be this way. It is not necessary for the years between 80 and 100 to be accompanied by loss of mood, loss of memory or loss of marbles.

The road to hell

Perhaps this road to hell has been paved with the good intentions of a health and safety executive that has devoted resources to preventing accidents. Accidents may have been a better way to die than from protracted brain disease. Perhaps we would not choose, if choose we could, to spend our last remaining year in a care home for the mentally impaired. At the moment, research resources are devoted primarily to preventing us from dying, instead of encouraging us to live livelier, even riskier lives. If we lived livelier, riskier lives we might be more likely to die suddenly and thereby have a better acute death, as well as live a better life. Unfortunately, acute death is often protracted into chronic death and disability: a heart attack becomes an ongoing heart condition to be managed; a stroke becomes vascular dementia for our families to live with; diabetes, AIDS and some cancers become qualifications for long-term disability and mobility allowances. It becomes more and more profitable to develop drugs that maintain us in chronic ill health, than to develop drugs that either cure us, or help us to die a good death!

Making the end a life worth living

The three goals of this book are to enable you:

1 to exploit, for economic gain for yourself and others, the superior powers of the 50+ brain
2 to maintain and enhance the advantages in mental performance which you acquire as you get older, and to defend them against degenerative diseases by creating spare cognitive capacity
3 to demonstrate how you can add life to your years and not just years to your life, knowing that last 10 years of your life can be the best ten years of your life.

The best is yet to come. Think on! Read on!

Don't retire!

Who decided it was a good idea to retire at 65? The answer is Bismarck – when he himself was over 70 and an extremely effective Chancellor of Germany! Why? Under pressure to introduce a state retirement pension, but not wanting it to cost too much, he asked:

'On average, when do people die?'

On being told 65, he agreed, 'OK, then give them a pension at 65!' Such an arbitrary age for retirement mattered less in those days, when businesses were more likely to need your brawn than your brain. However, in a knowledge-based economy, when competitive advantage comes from how much better you think about what you know, we should be recruiting 65 year olds, not retiring them.

When it comes to problem solving, leadership, decision making, creative thinking or making money, an older brain is better. Because aging was associated with loss of brain size, or brain weight, this was mistakenly assumed to be associated with irreversible loss of brain cells and with inevitable mental decline. Your cognitive capacity is, in fact, determined by the number of interconnections between your neurons, not the number of neurons in your brain. The number of neurons in your brain can increase, as well as decrease, depending on lifestyle choices you make. How you use your brain, and what you choose to use it for, can increase both the number and the quality of the connections in your brain. Consuming excessive alcohol, for example, can accelerate neuron losses to 60,000 cells a day. Unattended grief, unmanaged blood pressure, and the absence of thoughtful conversation, can all impair thinking (Chapters 01, 04, and 06).

Age does not cause brain disease

Mary Haam studied 5,000 50+ citizens, over 10 years, in California. She found that age was not, of itself, a factor in brain deterioration, although physical illnesses and lack of physical and mental fitness sometimes had side effects on brain functioning. Although there is some slowing down of new memory formation and in the speed of new information processing as people get older, it is possible to work around this, as such processing is only one part of one of the ten components that make up effective applied thinking (Chapter 05). As Keith Simonton discovered, creative thinking actually improves with age. Edison, Monet, Picasso and Titian produced their best work in their seventies and eighties.

The more we train our brains, the higher our performance becomes and remains. A well used brain has a higher ratio of synaptic connections to neurons. Neural nerve growth factor (NGF) is released by the process of thinking. This, in turn, promotes the thickening of the myelin insulation around the axons of connected neurons. The neurochemistry of this is described in 'First thoughts' (see page 10), for readers who like to know 'why' as well as 'how' the cognitive capacity of their 50+ brains can increase.

Willis and Schaie have shown than it is never too late to prevent, or reverse, cognitive deterioration and to boost mental performance, even if you have allowed it to decline significantly. Optimism and humour (Chapter 01) and thoughtful conversations (Chapter 06) are important in developing intelligence, as well as in deepening intimate relationships (Chapter 06). Better talking leads to better thinking, which leads to better writing, which leads to better action, which leads to feeling better, which leads to... etc. – it is a virtuous circle (see Figure 0.3).

Carl Cotman also found that certain types of physical and mental exercises can arrest and reverse mental degeneration and promote the growth of new brain cells (Chapter 01).

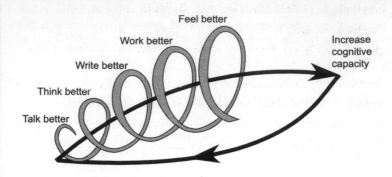

Figure 0.3: The virtuous circle of talking better, thinking better, writing better, working better and feeling better increases cognitive capacity

Minding your own business

Far from considering retiring, you should be pursuing your interests and curiosity and promoting your career horizons. You should consider setting up your own business (Chapter 05). In a brain-based economy, at 50+ you may be only a third of the way through your potential working life! You will need to keep your brain fit, in the same way that you know you need to keep your body fit. This book teaches you the kind of lifestyle you need to lead and the kind of exercises you need to do. There is no need to threaten your brain with slogans like 'Use it or lose it'. Your brain will get better as you get older and, if you exploit your brain's maturing powers, it will get better still. Think about it!

Suggested further reading

Austad, S. (1997) *Why We Age*, Wiley.

Brown, G. (2007) *The Living End: The New Sciences of Death, Aging and Immortality*, www.macmillanscience.com.

De Grey, A. (2002) 'Time to talk SENS', *Science*, 959, p451.

Dementia UK (2007) *Prevalence and Cost*, LSE/Alzheimer Society.

Deppen, J. (2002) 'Broken limits to life expectancy', *Science*, 296, p1028.

Hall, S. (2005) *Human Life Extension*, Mariners.

Hayflick, L. (1996) *How We Age*, Ballantine.

Hayflick, L. (2000) 'The Future of Aging', *Nature*, 408, p266.

Hughes, J. (2001) 'Future of Death', *Journal of Evolution and Technology*, 6, p1.

Olshansky, S. (2005) *Science of the Frontier of Ageing*, Norton.

Robine, J. (1998) *Healthy Active Aging*, REVES/Insert.

Thane, P. (2005) *History of Old Age*, Thames.

Vaupel, J. (1998) 'Trajectories of longevity', *Science*, 280, p854.

Yesavage, J. (2002) 'Incidence of Alzheimer's and cognitive impairment', *Journal of Psychiatric Research*, 36, p280.

first thoughts

Neuroscience and the developing power of the 50+ brain

Terrorism, wars and motorbikes have cracked many skulls, enabling brain science to make rapid progress! The effects of these head injuries have been studied by biologists, mathematicians, physicists, chemists, psychologists, pharmacologists, sociologists and philosophers. Their collective studies have given birth to what we now call cognitive science.

As cognitive science grew, so did ideas about the way the brain could enable you to think reflectively and to think creatively as well as critically. Your brain will give you the ability to respond differently, at different ages and stages for the rest of your life. Your brain is the basis of your freedom to choose.

'I think, therefore I am.'

becomes...

'I can think differently, therefore I can change.'

You are not entirely a prisoner of your genes or your age. From the 1960s onwards, cognitive scientists were able to provide scientific support for important human values, like personal freedom, personal choice, personal responsibility and personal development, at a time when such ideas were under attack from postmodernist thinkers. Cognitive science helps you to challenge the idea that your life is determined by your economic or social circumstances, or your date of birth!

The electrical brain

One idea, popular in the 1970s and 1980s, was that it was useful to view the brain as computer hardware, and the mind as the computer software.

The idea is beguiling. There are many useful parallels. For example, when you turn off a computer, the software cannot work. Your brain needs a reliable supply of energy or it will suffer rather like your computer suffers. Also, a computer needs background software, for example, the software that periodically clears 'garbage' and consolidates memory files. Your brain is the same – it has autonomic activities that operate when you are asleep. Likewise, just because a computer is turned on, doesn't mean that all the software programs are running. Some programs need to be requested explicitly. In the brain, this 'requesting' is called metacognitive thinking. It involves the part of the brain called the frontal cerebral cortex. Many of the exercises in this book will help you to exploit the frontal cortex of your brain, so that you can learn to direct your own thinking. This part of the brain is very underdeveloped in young adults but matures with age.

So beguiling is the computer metaphor that it still holds sway, despite being seriously challenged by Professor Susan Greenfield's book on the human brain, which was published in 1997. She described how traditionally viewed products of the mind, like ideas or images, could cause chemical changes in the brain. Importantly for this book, cognitive science has demonstrated that mental and physical exercises can develop the chemical structures that underpin your memory and your intelligence.

Brain research and brain scanning: the lessons and limitations

Recently, ideas on brain training have benefited greatly from our ability to watch images of brains while their owners are thinking about different types of decisions, problems and plans. CAT scanners use computers to combine X-ray slices of the brain and can be used to establish the structures of the brain, whereas PET scanners, which follow traces of radioactive isotopes introduced into the brain fluid, are better for monitoring brain activity. The uses of these two types of scanners are limited, because overdoses of X-rays or radioactivity would be harmful. Much safer is the use of MRI scanners which can be used to monitor blood flows in the brain, in real time.

Health warning!

The new technologies and tools of the cognitive scientist are impressive, but you should not suspend the healthy scepticism which brain training in critical thinking will encourage. Brain scans, for example, show what is happening when people think. This is a correlation. But a correlation is not necessarily a cause, or a consequence. Remember also that the person under the scanner is not you. Throughout this book, we offer you suggested plans of action that are clearly implied by the reasonable conclusions we have inferred from normally reliable sources. However, these tests were not carried out on you. As an individual you are unique. The action plans we offer may have been tried by our students, but it is for you to decide for yourself how well they work for you.

The chemical brain

From the 1970s onwards, we have been trying to imagine what happens inside your brain when you try to think. We and others have been trying to help students, teachers, managers, therapists, social workers and public sector workers to learn to think more effectively about the kinds of decisions they need to take, the kinds of problems they need to solve, and the kinds of plans they need to make.

At first, we were helped by the then prevailing model of 'brain-as-computer'. But we kept finding aspects of the ways our students were thinking that the computer model failed to explain. In 1997, Susan Greenfield's model of the brain as a chemical factory liberated us from the straightjacket of our computer model. Suddenly we could better understand the successes and the difficulties we were having with our students. Her neurochemical approach gave us ways to understand what we already knew.

At last, we could understand why, for many students, learning almost anything seemed to increase their capacity to learn, irrespective of the subject matter. For other students, lots of repetitions of relatively simple thinking tasks seemed to produce marked improvements in their capacity to think. This supported our emerging view that thinking was a combination of ten or so contributory skills (Figure 1.1).

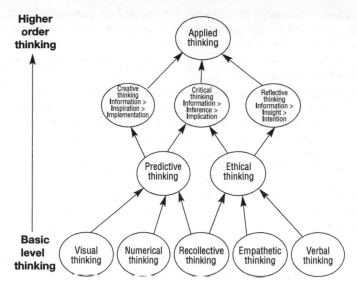

Figure 1.1: The hierarchy of thinking skills (Horne and Wootton, 2007)

Although logic (deductive and inductive) remains the backbone of clear thinking, it is a necessary, but not sufficient, condition for thinking at its best. Parts of the brain other than the frontal cerebral cortex, have a role to play if thinking is to be first class.

The parts of your brain that control visual images, and the parts of your brain that empathize with the likely thoughts and feelings of other people, can work in concert with the parts of your brain that hold different facets of your memory. All these different parts of your brain can help the frontal lobe of your cortex to take a more logical decision or to make a more rational plan. Susan Greenfield's work gave us confidence to extend our ideas on combination thinking and to devise brain training exercises that involve the simultaneous use of different parts of the brain.

The structure and composition of the brain

If you want to train your brain, it can be helpful to find out something about the structure and composition of the brain you are seeking to train.

Inside your skull, your brain has the consistency of a sloppy undercooked egg. It has no moving parts. It is surrounded by a colourless fluid (CSF), which is circulating constantly. CSF contains mainly salt and sugar.

The brain itself is wrinkled and creamy in colour. Although it would fit into the palm of your hand, it is as heavy as three bags of sugar. The brain has two halves and looks rather like a small cauliflower whose stalk tapers to become the top of your spinal cord. The back of the cauliflower overhangs the stalk slightly. The overhang is called the cerebellum. The main part is called the cerebrum.

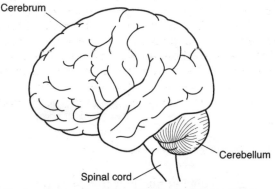

Figure 1.2: The human brain (taken from Wootton and Horne, 2007)

If you turn the brain over, you will see distinct regions that occur in pairs, so that the underside of the brain appears to be symmetrical about a central line running from the front to the back of the brain.

Different jobs for different bits of the brain

Your cerebral cortex is divided into about 50 different bits, many of which have a definite specialized function. In some parts of the cortex, towards the back for instance (the posterior parietal cortex), the distinction between the areas is more blurred. The posterior parietal cortex handles many sensations – sound, sight, touch and movement.

The frontal lobes of a mature brain become active when they are asked to empathize, make predictions, or tackle problems that involve planning, complex decisions or creative thinking. Teenagers, or young adults under 25, often struggle with these kinds of thinking tasks. Often, the development of this frontal area of their cerebral cortex lags behind the bushing of the dendrites in the back of their brain, which is preoccupied with sensation and stimulation. Until the development of their frontal lobes catches up, young people are usually reluctant to volunteer verbal information, and they can appear to be anti-social and to have 'heads like sieves' when it comes to remembering things.

Neurons – the building blocks of the brain

Neurons have a squat, blob-like body called a soma, about 0.04 mm across. The soma sprouts tiny branches called dendrites. Commonly, neurons appear elongated, with dendrites at either end, sometimes on the end of a long, thin fibre called an axon. The axon is commonly two to three times longer than the body of the neuron, though spinal neurons can trail axons a metre long. So, squat somas, with stubby dendrite branches and long thin tails – these are your neurons. Neurons are the building blocks of your constantly developing intelligence.

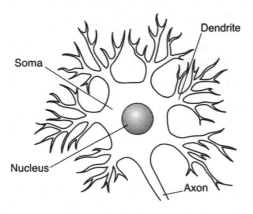

Figure 1.3: The nerve cell and branches (taken from Wootton and Horne, 2007)

Dendrites and axons – what do they do?

The dendrites are receiving stations for chemical messages sent out by neighbouring neurons. The chemical messages converge down the dendrites into the neuron body. If the signals are strong enough, the neuron will generate an electrical charge, which will be conducted along the axon towards the dendrites of neighbouring neurons.

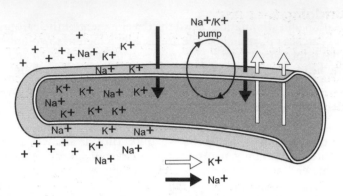

Figure 1.4: The dendrite (taken from Wootton and Horne, 2007)

The charges are carried either by positively charged sodium, potassium or calcium cations, or by negatively charged chloride anions. The charged anions and cations cannot normally pass through the fatty inter-layers of the neuron wall. However, an accumulation of negatively charged ions on the inside of the neuron wall will attract, rather like a magnet, ions and proteins of opposite charge to the outside of the neuron wall, thereby generating a difference in potential across the cell wall. This potential difference can be measured in millivolts. When the potential difference reaches about 80 millivolts, channels open through the neuron walls, to allow positively charged ions (usually sodium) to enter the neuron to neutralize the negative charges on the inside of the neuron. When the charge inside the neuron becomes about 20 millivolts positive, then potassium ions, positively charged, are allowed out through the wall of the neuron, until a negatively charged state is restored inside the neuron. All this happens in a thousandth of a second.

The direction of transmission of the electrical charges, and the speeds of the transmission, are determined by the directions and condition of the axons. If the axon is already connected to a dendrite of another neuron, then that pre-determines the direction taken by the charge. If the axon is surrounded by a thick sheath of healthy myelin insulation, the transmission will be fast and accurate. Because you often wish to minimize the delay between one thought and the next, or between thought and action, chemical charges will hustle down your axons at about 400 km/hour, as long as the myelin insulation on your axons are in good enough condition. What happens when the electrically charged chemicals hit the synaptic gap between the end of the axon and the dendrite of a neighbouring neuron?

Bridging that gap

With the advent of electron microscopes, which have magnification factors of over 10,000, chemicals can be detected in the synaptic gap. Among the chemicals detected in the synaptic gap are many differently shaped acetylcholine derivatives. These acetylcholine molecules belong to a general class of brain chemicals known as neurotransmitters.

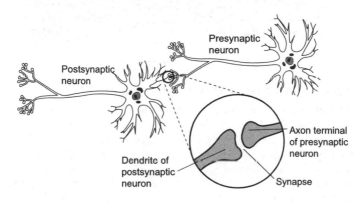

Figure 1.5: The synapse (taken from Wootton and Horne, 2007)

The more frequently electrically charged chemicals were seen arriving at the end of the axon, the more frequently acetylcholine neurotransmitters were seen to be launching themselves into the water in the synaptic gap. The small size of the neurotransmitters enabled them to diffuse very quickly across the salty water that surrounded the axons and dendrites. They crossed the gap in less than a millisecond, but how did they know which dendrite to choose?

Each neurotransmitter swimming across the gap is like a jigsaw piece, looking for a dendrite with a receptor molecule of exactly the right shape to make a perfect fit. Once the neurotransmitter finds and locks onto a right-fitting receptor, this signals to the channel in the wall of the second neuron to admit a charged chemical. An accumulation of charged chemicals moves down the dendrites of the second neuron into the cell body and out along the axon of the second neuron to the edge of the next synaptic gap, where it stares across the water at a third neuron. This is going on inside your amazing chemical brain a million times a second!

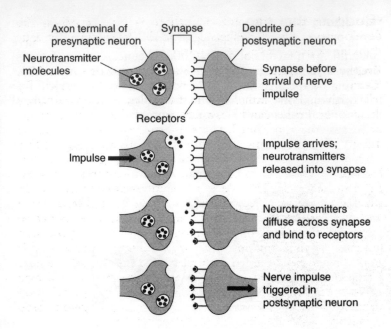

Figure 1.6: Synaptic transmissions (taken from Wootton and Horne, 2007)

While neurotransmitters like serotonin, dopamine and even acetylcholine frequently get a mention in popular accounts of brain chemistry, there is another neurotransmitter that rarely gets a mention but which is important to understanding why the 50+ brain is so powerful. It is called glutamate. It is important for memory. It can also cause neuron death. Too much glutamate appears to over-excite receiving neurons (by causing too much calcium to flood in), causing death by excitotoxicity. Excitotoxicity is one of the main causes of death in strokes, head injuries and Alzheimer's disease.

Your amazing brain

It is the quantity (and quality) of your neuron connections, not the number or weight of your neurons, that appears to determine your cognitive capacity and your mental performance. This has changed our view on the way the adult brain continues to develop. Work by Siegler, at Carnegie in the late 1990s, on embryos, babies, pre-school infants, teenagers, adults and seniors, indicates that brain development is ongoing throughout your life and that there is no cut off in the development of your intelligence or in the development of your thinking skills (look back at Figure 1.1).

Every year, the young adult brain shrinks and loses weight. This loss is now thought to be due more to a loss of weight by individual neurons, rather than to the loss of individual neurons themselves. Losses can be compensated for by learning things, almost anything, because learning almost anything increases the density of your synaptic connections. Also, by applying, reciting or repeating what you have learned, or thought about, you increase the thickness of the myelin insulation around the axons of your neurons. This thicker myelin insulation results in quicker and clearer electrical transmission through your brain and more secure storage of information. Thicker myelination improves the recall of your memories and the speed and accuracy of your thinking. The brain training activities in this book have been designed to increase the number of synaptic connections in your brain and to thicken the myelin insulation of your axons. This process, whereby the act of thinking chemically modifies the route along which the thought has been chemically transmitted, is called neuromodulation.

The young adult brain

The brain growth spurt that began when you were a teenager started at the back of your brain, heightening your awareness and sensitivity to sounds, lights, tastes and touch. Because development in the middle of the brain comes later, young adults often do not feel in control of their emotional reactions and impulses. Young adults often feel awkward or clumsy. But the lag in the development of their frontal cortex is the biggest disability for young adults. This frontal cortex is involved in reasoning, planning, predicting and decision making. Small wonder the behaviour of many young adults often seems to you to be unreasonable and lacking in direction and to have little regard for risk and consequence. According to Giedd, reporting in 2004, this is because many young adults lack the ability of the 50+ brain to reason, to decide and to assess risk and consequence.

The mature brain

Your brain can start to show a net loss of neurons if you drink alcohol or use certain other drugs (Chapter 01). Don't panic!

You can still preserve and improve your IQ and the intelligence of your behaviour. This is because many of the thinking skills that contribute to intelligent behaviour (Figure 1.1 again) improve as you get older, as long as you learn to apply them explicitly when you need them. This kind of thinking – called 'applied thinking' – produces more intelligent behaviour (Chapter 05). It is a mistaken belief that memory necessarily deteriorates with age. In fact, your ability to recall early knowledge and experiences gets better. This is because recall benefits from repetition and you are more likely to have repeated a particular recall the older you get. On the other hand, what is likely to deteriorate from 50 plus years is the speed at which you can form new memories. New information processing often does slow down. There are brain training exercises in Part Two that mitigate this. In Chapter 04 there are also exercises and activities that can help you to reverse any decline in processing speed and new memory formation that may have taken place already. You can also learn to use predictive thinking skills so that you can make an earlier start on thinking tasks that might otherwise be impaired by slower processing (see Chapter 08 in *Teach Yourself Training Your Brain*, Horne and Wootton, 2007).

Risks of damage to the 50+ brain

It is fortunate that brain training can repair brain damage, because all of our brains are at risk from, for example:

- extended grief, depression, low mood or pessimism (Chapter 01)
- alcohol (Chapter 04)
- oxygen depletion and toxins, due to lack of exercise (Chapter 04)
- poor diet and the additives in processed food (Chapter 04)
- all manner of environmental threats (Chapter 04)
- raised blood pressure, often alcohol or stress related (Chapter 04)
- lack of stimulation or lack of conversational relationships (Chapter 06).

Mental performance does not inevitably decline with age, if you stay healthy. While it is true that certain diseases can lower mental performance, if you build up sufficient reserves of spare cognitive capacity such diseases will have less or no effect. This book is full of exercises, problems and games that can help you to create reserves of spare cognitive capacity. It also contains scientific advice on minimizing the chances that you will develop those diseases in the first place. People who do not use their brains productively tend to drag down the average scores for older adults, and so obscure the high and increasing scores of those older people who use their brains productively.

Edward Coffey, of the Henry Ford Foundation, reported that adults aged 65 to 90 who used their brains actively, continued to perform well with no signs of loss of memory or reason, despite their MRI scans showing shrinkage in the size of their brains. In 2002, Quartz reported on a famous study of 4,000 nuns. This study was commenced by David Snowdon in Kentucky in 1986. The study is particularly interesting because all the nuns have very similar lifestyles, but some continue to teach and to be mentally active, and some don't. The nuns who continue to be mentally active are currently living, on average, four years longer, and their brain autopsies show, on average, 40 per cent more synapses and thicker myelin insulation on their axons. So, thinking helps you to live longer and thinking helps your brain to keep getting better and better. Thinking adds years to your life as well as life to your years.

The advantages of a chemical brain

Because chemicals react to different extents, and at different speeds, depending on the chemical environment in which the chemical reaction takes place, and because you have the ability to change the chemical environment in which your brain is trying to do its chemical work, you can affect the extent and speed of the chemical reactions in your brain and so improve its performance. You can change the chemical environment in your brain through diet, sleep, ergonomics, stress reduction, and by doing mental and physical exercises.

A chemical model of the brain can help you to understand how the frequent practice of the skills shown in the thinking skills model (Figure 1.1), even at a relatively undemanding level, can progressively improve the speed and accuracy of your thinking. As a result of the process known as neuromodulation, each repetitive pass through a neuron increases the thickness of its myelin insulation (for a systematic workout of all ten contributory skills, consult *Teach Yourself Training Your Brain*, Horne and Wootton, 2007).

Excitingly, a chemical model of the thinking process leaves open the creative possibility that you won't come up with exactly the same response, or solution, even if a problem replicates itself. Because the first occurrence exercised neurons which were changed by that process, the chances are increased of a novel response, should the same problem or input be presented a second time. Not only do we think and learn, but the way we think and learn improves in the process. In a chemical brain, there is no need to threaten:

'Use it or lose it.'

The chemical model of the 50+ brain says:

'Use it as much as you can, it can get even better.'

However, it does seem to matter how you use it and for what purpose. More chemical connections are generated by activities such as drama, coaching, dancing or rock climbing, which involve memory, calculation, problem solving, decision making, prediction and oral presentation than by physical activities alone.

A chemical brain predicts an improvement in mental functioning, rather than decline as you get older.

Neurodegenerative diseases

Alzheimer's and Parkinson's are diseases. Diseases may cause premature ageing, but diseases are not a necessary consequence of getting older. The likelihood of disease can be lowered dramatically (Chapters 03 and 04). That is not to say that your neurons will not change as you get older. They will. Consequently, you may perform less well on time-constrained problem solving and on tasks that require rapid memorization of new information. However, these disadvantages can be more than compensated for by exploiting the many aspects of mental functioning that improve with age, like verbal reasoning, reflective learning, predictive thinking and creativity (see also Chapters 08, 09 and 10 in *Teach Yourself Training Your Brain*, Horne and Wootton, 2007). In the end, what matters most is the extent and quality of your brain's interconnectedness and this is helped by working for yourself or for others (Chapter 05) or through social learning, thoughtful conversation and meaningful relationships (Chapter 06).

This book will encourage you to exploit the advantage which your 50+ brain already has over brains of younger colleagues.

You can build on these advantages. All other things being equal, your younger colleagues will find it hard to close the gap before you reach the age of about 100. By age 120, you will hit genetically imposed limitations. Beyond 120 is off our radar, and may depend on genetic re-engineering, which is beyond the scope of this book. We do not need to promise miracles – your 50+ brain is already miraculous enough.

The vista from the viewing point of neuroscience is awesome. It is expanding so fast that this book already updates its mother ship book on *Teach Yourself Training Your Brain*, which was published in 2007. We are so excited by what we have discovered about the 50+ brain that we need constantly to remind ourselves to balance our excitement with prudence, especially in relation to the most recent discoveries. Much as we try, throughout this book, to distinguish between well-replicated scientific findings, educated guesswork and hopeful speculation, you should not suspend the sceptical disbelief which we urge upon you in Chapter 05. As you have seen already, the state of your brain between now and your one hundredth birthday will largely be down to your own choice of lifestyle. It is wise to discuss major changes of lifestyle with people close to you or with a doctor, and then make up a mind of your own.

The 50+ brain – making up your mind

Your 50+ brain, as we have seen from Susan Greenfield's work, is a 1.5 kg chemical factory whose neurons fire a million times a second inside your skull. Your mind, on the other hand, is harder to define. According to Dr Jeff Victoroff, the very different words for the mind – the Greek ('nous'), as compared with the Roman ('mens'), or the more modern French ('esprit') – epitomize its scarlet pimpernel nature ('they seek him here, they seek him there'). Your mind does seem to be located in your brain. When you think, your brain changes. When your brain changes, you change. So when you think, you change. That's how you make up your mind. You can use your 50+ brain to change your mind. As you continue to mature beyond 50+, your mind set of different ways of thinking will continue to get better and better. While learning languages is easiest done by your brain at age three, and learning mathematics is easiest done by your brain at around 17, your brain's powers of prediction, critical evaluation, reflective wisdom and creativity are just getting into their stride as you reach 50, and some areas of social science, art, philosophy and law are dominated by the minds of the 70+. But while a child can quickly memorize new information (and should be encouraged to develop its brain capacity by doing so as often as possible), the 70+ judges will likely need to take copious notes.

Living to a ripe old age

Your mind can continue to ripen till the day you die. Maybe that is what is meant by living to a ripe old age. The ripening of the mind does not, however, take place automatically with age. The ripening of the mind takes place through experience. That is why you can sometimes find 'old heads on young shoulders'. Clearly, the longer you live, the more opportunities there are for formative experiences. But you have to take the opportunities. To extract maximum value from your experiences, practise reflective thinking (see Chapter 08 in *Teach Yourself Training Your Brain*, Horne and Wootton, 2007). By continuing to pack in new experiences you can either play 'catch up' or you can ensure that you 'stay ahead'. A ripe old age is everyone's potential. How ripe is within your gift. How ripe depends, among other things, on the extent to which you choose to implement the ideas in Part One of this book, or to have fun solving problems like the 300 we have collected in Part Two.

The reason we say 'among other things', is because it is self-evident that this book alone cannot support an advance in the mental power of millions of people – for you are each individuals. Each individual brain will blossom, in part, according to its own biological plan – but you can help shape the extent and direction of this blossoming. Your neurons will continue to respond to whatever life experiences you continue to put in their way, and the new neural pathways forged by those experiences will increase your spare cognitive capacity, so that you will have sufficient reserves to support increasing mental performance. As your body becomes frailer, it does not follow that your eyes will grow dim. Humans are not as other mammals are. Humans have brains that are self-repairing and resilient, and which can constantly adapt, improve and learn new things. At 50+, you can deploy thinking skills that younger minds cannot yet muster, let alone master.

All is not roses

But it's not all roses. While younger bodies struggle with the threat of facial acne, at 50+, you may need to fend off threats that bring fatigue (Chapter 04) or reduced optimism (Chapter 01). You may come into a room and forget why you came. You may become more hesitant to speak your thoughts, because your brain has more words to search through before it finds the exact one you want – the one that is on the tip of your tongue (Chapter 03). You may waste some time – not much in the scheme of things, but very irritating none the less – looking for keys or glasses.

Such things are worth learning to live with, in return for your increased ability to predict, to evaluate, to judge, to discern, to learn, to invent and to plan strategically. None of our 50+ students, feeling the power of their 50+ brains, have ever said that they would choose to be young again, despite having hairs in their ears, a near miss in the car, and the daily shock of seeing their parents in the bathroom mirror!

Living longer – living well

In the Western world, neurological diseases are rapidly overtaking heart disease, cancer and strokes as the most frequent reasons why we fail to live to our full, genetically determined 120 years. According to the World Health Organization, mental illnesses have recently overtaken traditional killers, like bacterial, or insect or water-borne diseases, as the world's most common cause of premature death and disability (Chapter 01). In the West we have learned to live longer, and now we must learn to live well.

Your 50+ increase in cognitive capacity is like boring out the cylinders in an engine under the bonnet of a car, or even adding an extra cylinder or two. To get the best from your bigger 50+ engine, you might now need to develop some more advanced driving skills. You might need a more advanced engine management system. The part of your brain that manages your thinking is called the metacognitive system and it appears to be controlled mainly by the frontal lobe of your cerebral cortex. You can strengthen and train this part of your brain by doing the exercises and solving the kinds of problems that you will find in Part Two of this book.

Hedonistic baby boomers

If you are a hedonistic baby boomer, you may be looking forward to retiring between five and 20 years from now. You may think that brain training sounds too much like hard work. Perhaps you just want to relax and enjoy the prosperity that you have earned through years of sacrifice, saving and working long hours for some less-than-grateful organization.

All the more tragic, then, if the enjoyment of your well-earned prosperity is snatched away at the last moment by premature loss of your ability to enjoy stimulation, plan trips, choose a new car, feel pleasure or find love in an intimate, thoughtful relationship. The 50+ brain is ready to shift up a gear, not retire. There are alternative strategies (Chapter 05) that will help you to preserve and expand your 50+ brain, so that you can enjoy the things you have earned.

Do not retire to find yourself reading books on 'the problems of aging'! As far as the brain is concerned, there are no problems – except those of physical health, or those of your own choosing. Baby boomers can continue to develop their brains and live the life they have worked so hard to fulfil.

The economic consequences of crumbling minds

The economic and social consequences of an epidemic of crumbling minds are so dire that governments might usefully promote brain fitness with the same urgency and resource allocation that they are now belatedly bringing to physical fitness, through the encouragement of sport, physical activity and accident prevention. Brain training at 50+ will bring benefits quite commensurate with costly campaigns for health, hearts and cancer cures. Brains can be defended from disease-borne decline. Disease-borne decline could rapidly consume more economic resources than the present younger generation generate. It is time to rank brain fitness alongside body fitness.

We can turn this potential problem into an opportunity: advances in neuroscience and in brain scanning have shown that we can exploit the advantages and powers of the 50+ brain to generate great economic gain. The thinking skill set of the 50+ brain is well suited to entrepreneurialism. Last year, 50+ entrepreneurs added new business worth more than £24 billion a year to the UK economy (research undertaken for Yellow

Pages). Companies set up within the past five years by people over 50 now account for 16 per cent of all new businesses in the UK. Professor Mark Hart, at Kingston University, says that because older entrepreneurs can draw upon years of personal experience, this helps to account for their high success rate and their growing importance to the UK economy.

Feet on the ground

To make a large leap forward, you need to start with your feet on solid ground. That is why we have started with Information about the brain – its construction and the science of how it works as a marvellous, 24-hour chemical factory. In Chapters 01–06, we will look at what we may reasonably Infer from this Information, in which we have justifiable belief. For each Inference we will examine the Implications for affordable, feasible and practical steps which you can take, the games you can play, and the types of problems on which to best train your brains. We have designed about 300 such problems and collected them together in Part Two. This pattern of moving from justifiably believable Information, via reasonably believable Inferences, to practical and feasible Implications for action, characterizes the rest of the book. It is the basis of effective applied thinking, which is taken up again in Chapter 05.

Glossary

Axons – long, slender projections from a neuron. They conduct electrical impulses away from the neuron's soma, the bulbous end of a neuron.

Cerebral cortex – so-called 'grey matter' of the brain. The thinking cap, responsible for functions such as language, logic and information processing.

CT or CAT scanner – a machine that uses X-rays to take pictures of slices of your body and your brain.

Dendrites – the antennae of the neurons.

MEG scanner – a scanner that allows brain activity to be viewed while a particular task is performed. It measures the tiny magnetic fields generated by brain activity.

MRI scanner – a machine that uses a magnetic field and radio waves to show what is happening inside the body and the brain.

Neurons – electrically excitable cells in the nervous system that process and transmit information. Neurons are the core components of the brain.

PET scanner – a machine that detects radioactive material that is injected or inhaled to produce an image of the brain.

Serotonin – a neurotransmitter.

Synapse – a small gap separating neurons. The gap is between the axon of one neuron and the dendrite of the next. The gap contains neurotransmitters such as acetylcholine derivatives.

Suggested further reading

Duorty, S. (2007) *Liars, Lovers and Heroes: what new brain science reveals*, Harper Collins.

Giedd, J. (May 2004) *Time Magazine*, p63

Greenfield, S. A. (1997) *The Human Brain: a guided tour*, Basic.

Howard, P. J. (3rd edn) (2006) *The Owner's Manual for the Brain: everyday applications from mind and brain research*, Bard Press.

Kendel, E. et al (eds) (2000) *Neural Science*, McGraw Hill.

Meseelam, M. (2000) *Behavioural and Cognitive Neurology*, OUP.

Robertson, I. (2007) *Stay Sharp*, Random.

Schaie, K. (1996) *Intellectual Development in Adults: the Seattle study*, OUP.

Victoroff, J. (2003) *Saving Brains*, Boulan.

Wootton, S. and Horne, T. (2007) *Teach Yourself Training Your Brain*, Hodder Education.

part one

one

making love and

making money at 50+

01

the pursuit of happiness

In this chapter you will learn:

- that chemical reactions in your brain determine whether you feel high or low, optimistic or pessimistic, and that they affect how well you think
- that you can control chemical reactions in your brain by what you do and what you think, and by what you eat and what you drink
- that the pursuit of happiness is largely fruitless and that you can more easily achieve a state of BLISS, through Body-based pleasures, Laughter, Involvement, Satisfaction and Sex.

There is nothing either good or bad, 'tis thinking makes it so. (after Shakespeare)

Introduction

In this chapter, you will discover that chemical conditions in your brain change when you experience emotion, and when you think about the emotions which others may be feeling. Thinking thoughts and feeling feelings are chemical processes. Each affects the other.

The need for you to consider what you are feeling, as well as what you are thinking, arises in a number of thinking tasks, for example:

- An important part of **thinking critically** is the evaluation of an action's potential consequences for others. At 50+ you are much better at predicting likely consequences than a younger person. We call this empathetic thinking.
- When you need to **think creatively**, your emotions are an important source of the mental energy needed to generate a long list of novel possibilities. At 50+ you have many more possibilities at your disposal than a younger person. Your emotional response to emerging ideas feeds both your intuition and your capacity and courage to make novel associations and creative connections between the many memories and images in your 50+ head.
- When recalling what was felt, as well as what was seen and said and done, you need to **think reflectively**. At 50+, you have so much more experience from which to learn.
- In general, optimistic expectations correlate with the strength of your immune system – the probability that you will recover from serious diseases, like cancer, correlates to the likelihood that you will achieve successful outcomes on thinking tasks, like problem solving and strategy formulation.

Emotional intelligence

The capacity to link emotions to thinking was described by Goleman as 'emotional intelligence' in 1996, and as 'social intelligence' in 2006. Goleman's and Damasio's work shows that you need to involve your emotions, particularly when thinking about problems and plans.

Emotional information is processed in a part of the brain called the amygdala. The amygdala is constantly sending messages to the prefrontal lobes of the brain. This means that there is a constant flow of emotional information to the parts of the brain involved in calculation and argument. McGaugh points out that the effect is not always helpful. For example, when fear or anxiety rises beyond a certain level, your ability to think and remember is impaired. On the other hand, when you feel positive or amused, the messages sent by the amygdala appear to improve your ability to think. Feeling positive or amused seems to increase the likelihood that you will come up with original solutions.

To discover for yourself how closely connected are your thoughts and feelings, try the following activity.

A thinking and feeling experiment

Try the following experiment, either with a partner, or a pen and paper. Look around and write 'I am noticing…' (write down what you are looking at or listening to) and 'I am thinking…' (write down what you are thinking at that moment) and 'I am feeling…' (write down a single word describing that emotion). Keep this up for about 15 minutes. Review the results. Notice how many times you can change what you are feeling, even in 15 minutes. Notice what kinds of observations and thoughts are followed by what kinds of feelings.

Repeat, trying to increase the number of positive feelings you can experience in 15 minutes. Notice that you can choose what you notice – what you look at, what you listen to. This increases the chance that you can find something positive to think about and that this in turn means that you can feel better.

Try to complete the following sentences in succession. When you have completed number three, go back to number one. Keep going round the loop for as much time as you can spare. When you can do it easily, do it as often as you can. Keep it up to maintain mental fitness:

1 Right now I am noticing… (a person, a colour, a sound, a smell, a taste, a texture).

2 And right now I am thinking… (e.g. an opinion or a judgement).

3 And right now I am feeling… (e.g. an emotion – a simple word).

For increased mental suppleness, just keep going round the loop. For increased concentration span, increase the number of repetitions you do at one time. For increased mental agility and thinking speed, try to go round as quickly as you can without hesitation. You may notice that how you feel is changed by what you think, and what you think is related to what you notice. Because you can control what you notice by where you choose to focus, you can exert increasing control over your thoughts and your emotions.

Emotional and verbal thinking

The use of verbal thinking (Chapter 06) to identify and label the feelings you are experiencing, is more productive than just expressing the feelings impulsively. This is because, when you shout or otherwise give vent to your anger, for example, you leave a neural pathway between the amygdala and the brain's frontal lobes. This increases the ease with which subsequent stray feelings can disable your ability to think, especially under pressure.

> *Make me thoughtful not moody,*
> *Let me see good things in unexpected places,*
> *Let me see unexpected talents in unexpected people,*
> *And, oh, let me have the grace to tell them so.*
> (from a seventeenth-century nun's prayer)

The limitations of the young adult brain

In young adults, a hormone-driven dendrite explosion reaches the back of the brain, which deals with stimulation and emotion, well before it reaches the front of the brain, which deals with verbal reasoning. This leaves young adults vulnerable to confusing feelings, which they are not able to label, let alone challenge. Because their amygdala are connected to the pre-frontal lobes of their brains, the emotions of young adults take up short-term memory space which they need to make judgements, comparisons, calculations, decisions and logical arguments. Gottman realized that the thinking space of many young people, young men in particular, is quickly overwhelmed and disabled by their emotions. This is especially true following criticism. For example, for a typical male–female relationship between two young adults to survive, she has to make at least five positive comments about him for every one negative comment she makes about him.

Are you feeling anxious or are you feeling just worried?

At 50+, people can experience increased anxiety – often unattached to anything in particular and for no obvious reason. Anxiety can obsess your mind to the point where you no longer have enough free working space in your brain.

When people at 50+ are worried, it is right to take note. The 50+ have experience of the kind of things that can go wrong. Often a 50+ worry is a sensible preparation and rehearsal for things that may indeed go wrong. Worrying enables the 50+ to prepare contingency plans and these are often reassuring to others, as well as themselves. Contingency plans can be a good defence against chronic anxiety, which lowers performance on thinking tasks. One hundred and twenty-six studies of more than 36,000 students have shown that anxiety, and difficulty in managing emotions, is highly correlated with under-performance.

The biochemistry of emotion

I feel it in my fingers, I feel it in my toes.

According to Candace Pert, Professor at Georgetown University, the brain signals the release of different chemicals, each of a different molecular structure, each time your feelings change. These molecules enter your blood and flow around your body until they find a receptor site which exactly fits their shape. These receptor sites thus pick up the messages from your body's hormones, like oestrogen and testosterone, and from your neurotransmitters, like serotonin and dopamine, and from other biochemicals called peptides. Your body's receptor sites also pick up messages from endorphins. Endorphins make you feel good. You can cause your 50+ brain to release endorphins into your bloodstream through exercise, or through sex, or by eating dark chocolate.

Emotional thinking and learning

When you feel anxious, resentful, angry or bitter, or when you feel helpless, or very sad, this has an adverse effect on your ability to learn. Unmanaged emotion disables learning because it disables some of the thinking skills involved in learning. When you are emotionally distracted, it is hard to take interest in new information, or to persist with trying to make sense of information that is confusing or incomplete, or to recall accurately what you read earlier. You may find it hard to take decisions or think critically.

When young people are finding it difficult to take decisions there is brain-scan evidence of traffic between the amygdala, processing emotion, and the frontal lobes of the brain.

Unmanaged emotions, like fear and anxiety, can lead to mental paralysis. This can happen during examinations, or when trying to work to someone else's deadlines or schedules.

Positive mental energy and motivation

As long ago as the 1980s, Horne found that adults needed to apply themselves over a long period in order to develop certain intellectual skills, like numeracy. The self-motivation to do exercises, to tackle questions and to practise presentations, comes from your emotions – like your fear of failure, or your desire to perform well in front of an audience. Emotions give you the mental motivation to deploy your full repertoire of thinking skills. The repetition involved in learning or rehearsing something new not only contributes to your present success, it also thickens the myelin insulation around your neural axons, enabling your 50+ brain to think more quickly and more accurately about future tasks. Repetition is often tedious or boring, so the motivation to study and practise needs to be based on strong overriding emotions.

Emotions can sometimes cause younger people to act impulsively. Often younger people close down thinking prematurely. In order to achieve a more thoughtful response, emotions like anger and anxiety need to be managed. By 50+, you will have had experience and practice at doing this. By 50+, you are more likely to have learned when to bite your tongue! Feelings, as well as facts, need to be thought about.

Getting to a 'yes'

If you are trying to get someone to make a decision, act on the assumption that they will need an emotional gain from the decision. Ask them to imagine a good feeling they will feel when they have decided in your favour. Then ask them what convincing reasons they could give to other people for having made the decision in your favour. People often feel the need to rehearse good reasons to give to others, even when their decisions are intuitive, emotional or irrational. The world often expects decisions to appear rational, even when we know they're not.

Those old familiar feelings

To understand some habitual but undesirable behaviour on the part of your 50+ friend or colleague, you could test the hypothesis that people will keep repeating behaviours that result in them feeling 'old familiar feelings'. 'Old familiar feelings' are feelings which they have become very used to feeling, possibly since they were children. One person's 'old familiar feelings' will probably differ from another person's 'old familiar feelings'. They may not be feelings that you would consider to be pleasant.

This can help you to understand why some undesirable behaviour gets worse when you punish a young offender. The culprit's familiar feelings may be feelings that result from punishment. In which case, repeated punishment my lead to repeated offending. Study the pattern of the undesirable behaviour. Ask yourself, 'How does this person end up feeling?' Can you change how the person reacts to these behaviours, thereby thwarting the emotional pay-off which you suspect the person is getting?

Is optimism that important?

When the messages we receive, via television soaps and radio news or via the daily press and the internet, are so predominantly pessimistic, it can be difficult to feel optimistic. Does this really matter? How important is it to think positively?

True, the world is full of unhappiness and disease. But there is also love, compassion and joy. Research on selective perception has shown that you can observe things with a preconceived notion of how you think they should appear and that your perception can be so selective that you may find it difficult to change your mind, even when you see, or hear, contradictory evidence. Instead of reality, you selectively perceive what you expect to see. The older you are, the more likely you are to have had opportunities to reconfirm your preconceived views. To guard against this, you will need to be more deliberately 'open minded', lest you draw false Inferences from mistaken Information, or draw false Implications from a false Inference.

Sports psychologists Bull and Rushall have tried to reverse 'negative' thinking in football teams and tennis players. They have discovered that optimistic self-confident moods increase a player's chance of winning. They have shown that optimism improves speed of thought and performance in sports like snooker, tennis and Grand Prix motor racing, and when taking penalties in soccer.

Memory, too, has been found to be very sensitive to optimistic suggestion. If you tell yourself, 'I'll never remember that', then the chances are you won't. Feeling pessimistic, for example about your prospects in a job interview, impairs your thinking skills during the interview, especially your memory. The main benefit of planning, or revising or preparing or rehearsing, is that not only are you likely to feel less anxious, but the condition of your brain will be enhanced by the repetition (as long as you don't cancel this out by staying up all night to do it! See Chapter 04). Consequently, you remember better and think better, even when answering questions on things which you haven't prepared. Written tests best suit people who are optimistic. People who are less confident do better when they are assessed through assessment centres, or through continuous assessment.

Positive thinking – the effect on mind and body

The effect of mood on your chances of recovery from serious illness, or from major surgery and cancers, has been the object of much study. According to Fosbury, the management of diabetes has been shown to benefit more from mood management by cognitive therapists, than from information provided by nurse educators. According to Cohen, negative emotions, such as anxiety, increase the frequency with which people suffer from common colds. Colds impair breathing, lower energy, cause headaches and impair clear thinking. Cohen had found that swimmers could improve their performance by concentrating on optimistic thoughts.

Seven types of negative thinking

Seven 'sick making' types of thinking develop the kind of pessimism that has been found to impair health and mental performance:

1 **Black and white** – things are good or bad; pendulous, either/or thinking.
2 **Perfectionist** – less than perfect equals failure; nit picking, blemishing.
3 **Comparative** – performance is judged only by comparison with other people.
4 **Generalized** – this sees a single event as part of a never-ending and inevitable pattern; characterized by use of 'always' and 'never'.

5 **Telepathic** – believing you can tell when others think negatively about you.

6 **Basket** – you give yourself one bad label and then assume any similar, or related, labels also apply to you.

7 **Guilty** – characterized by frequent use of the words 'should' and 'ought'.

Down on the farm

Many people regularly watch popular dramas or 'soaps', like *Emmerdale*, *Coronation Street* and *Eastenders*. These are frequently tragic. Hyams found that negative preoccupations undermine your thinking performance.

Seven steps to overcoming your negative emotions

1 Do an audit of your strengths (not your weaknesses). At 50+ you have skills and resources. At 50+, you have knowledge. At 50+, you have experience.

2 Forgive someone, if only in your head. Rehearse an imaginary conversation in which you forgive them. Let go of the negative memories that steal your headspace. You need your headspace for more positive thoughts. At 50+, you have nothing to lose by forgiving.

3 Visualize how things will look when you are succeeding. Hear the applause it is bringing and notice from whom (this is important). Feel how you feel when you are receiving applause and recognition for your success.

4 Applaud yourself. Discover that you do not need the constant approval of others, even though you are enjoying this as it is becoming more frequent.

5 Try things that are difficult and give them your best shot. When you are doing your best at difficult tasks, your best is good enough. Be the best that you can be.

6 At 50+, you can admit that you are not superwoman or superman (i.e. you can't be the cause of all that is bad, or the cause of the bad feelings of others). Others are responsible for how they feel.

7 Stop nagging and nit picking and complaining. It lowers the mood of people around you. This in turn might lower your mood, because moods are contagious. Your good mood will lift the mood of others. Their good mood will then lift yours. When you see something you like, comment on it.

The black dog of depression

Depression is the black dog that barks in the night and in the daytime. In 1999, mental disorders, like depression and manic depression, became the world's commonest cause of premature death and disability (World Health Organization). Seek professional or medical help if you think you might be suffering from depression. You would not try to cure yourself of pneumonia. Tell a counsellor or doctor if you have five or more of the following symptoms:

- fatigue
- loss of mental energy
- insomnia
- early waking
- over-eating
- no appetite
- loss of sex drive
- increased drinking
- increased smoking
- aches and pains
- piercing own body
- hurting yourself

- recklessness
- accident prone
- loss of confidence
- loss of enjoyment
- feeling hopeless
- feeling helpless
- feeling guilty
- feeling worthless
- feeling agitated
- unable to work
- unable to concentrate
- thoughts of death.

Studies show that levels of work-related stress are a significant precursor to depression (for further details see Chapter 05 in *Teach Yourself Training Your Brain*, Horne and Wootton, 2007). Building closer relationships with other people at work and learning to participate in problem solving and decision making can reduce stress and can improve your mental health.

The brain chemistry of depression

Adverse social and economic events are associated with biochemical changes in your 50+ brain. There is a strong correlation between the amount of serotonin and norepinephrine in your brain, and your mood. If your levels of serotonin (and norepinephrine) get too low, you will experience lowered mental energy, diminished pleasure from normally pleasurable activities and reduced sex drive.

The practical pursuit of BLISS

There are many books that offer you happiness in a few steps. Howard asserts that unless you are one of the 10 per cent who seem genetically programmed to be happy, searching for happiness will be futile. The difficulties experienced by seekers of happiness are compounded by living in a world that advertises and exploits this futile expectation of happiness. In America, happiness is a constitutional right. Americans have the right to life, liberty and the pursuit of happiness. Such expectations lead to much expenditure for some, and inevitable disappointment for others. In the end, everyone's mood is lowered by our failure to be happy. You are less likely to be disappointed if, instead of pursuing happiness, you pursue BLISS:

Body-based pleasure
Laughter
Involvement
Satisfaction
Sex

(Horne and Wootton, 2007)

The components of BLISS are not expected to persist. If they persist too long, or are repeated too frequently, your chemical receptors become desensitized. Imagine receiving non-stop applause and cheers, a standing ovation... for 3 hours. You would be desperate to get off the stage and sit down!

Body-based pleasure

This first component of BLISS can be considered in relation to the five senses: taste, smell, sight, hearing and touch.

---

50 sensations to try before you die...

Eat: herbs and wild honey, creams and curries... and dark chocolate.

Taste: lips, skin, liquorice, aniseed... and dark chocolate.

Smell: cut grass, wood shavings, honeysuckle, pine resin... and dark chocolate.

Savour: a barbeque, a baby's neck, seaweed smells... and dark chocolate.

Gaze: at sunsets, distant hills, modern paintings and the faces of models.

Admire: cathedrals, temples, modern architecture, pottery and gardens.

Hear: babies babbling, Mozart's clarinet concerto (2nd movement).

Listen: to running water, wind in trees, choir boys and bird song.

Enjoy: Mendelssohn's violin concerto, Status Quo, Harold in Italy, Pavarotti.

Stroke: clean hair, petals, warm sand, smooth skin, soft skin.

Feel: velvet, silk, fine cotton, linen, and dark chocolate melting in your mouth.

The laughter (and the tears)

There is now much neuroimmunological evidence of the benefits of laughter. But the benefits of a 'good cry' have been less well publicized. There are many sorts of tears – tears of joy, tears of anger, tears of frustration, tears of relief, tears of hysteria or just awe at the sight of a DB5 Aston Martin Volante! Witchalls found that emotional tears contain emotional brain chemicals, like leucine (associated with pain) and prolactin (associated with stress).

So cry me a river...

- Animal tears do not contain emotional chemicals. Is crying a hallmark of humanity?
- People suffering from depression, ulcers and colitis cry less than healthy people.

Is laughter the best medicine?

Laughter may not be the best medicine, but immunology studies confirm that it does augment other medicines that you take. The levels of immunoglobin in people's saliva are predictably:

- lower than average in people under stress
- higher than average in people who feel loved by others
- higher in people whose prevailing mood is optimistic or elevated
- higher in people who laugh, and in people who make other people laugh.

We counsel against abandoning conventional treatments to rely solely on positive emotions to cure disease (although there are 15 years of studies confirming the beneficial effects of laughter, positive mood and optimism in enhancing your immune system!). In research on heart surgery, men basing no optimism on religious beliefs were three times more likely to die, and men basing no optimism on the supportive optimism of friends and/or family were four times more likely to die. Clearly the impact of optimism is great and the supportive optimism of friends or family is particularly beneficial (Chapter 06). The impact of laughter is immediate. Cousins found that levels of life-threatening toxins were reduced after only a few moments of laughter. Laughter also appears to intercept emotional messages from the hypothalamus to the frontal cortex, thereby leaving the frontal cortex freer to be logical in its planning and decision making.

Ten things to do to raise your optimism

  1 Collect qualifications and certificates.
  2 Read anything from the 'Further suggested reading' sections of this book that catch your eye.
  3 Commit a random act of gratuitous kindness every day.
  4 Reduce the number of stressors in your life.
  5 Spend time with people who share your sense of humour.
  6 Dispose of some assets to release cash for shopping sprees.
  7 Make a contact list of close family and old friends and keep in touch.
  8 Improve your appearance, through exercise and self-tanning moisturizers.
  9 Collect funny cards to send when people are ill, to say thank you, or for no reason.
  10 Keep a file of funny stories or jokes, preferably at your own expense. Share one a day.

Get involved

The next thing you need to do is get Involved.

Involved in what? And exactly what does it mean to be Involved?

The object of Involvement is not sensory pleasure or emotional lift. The object is to become totally engrossed and totally absorbed in an activity, such as a game, a sport, a hobby or a conversation. You need to become so Involved that you lose track of time and, maybe, even lose track of where you are or cease to notice any physical discomfort that you may be suffering. When you really get Involved, little else will intrude into your awareness.

The seven elements of Involvement

1 Your goal is clear – you know what you are trying to achieve.
2 You feel you have a very good chance of achieving your goal.
3 You are able to concentrate and to push aside conflicting cares.
4 You feel up to it – you have sufficient energy, resources and skills.
5 You feel in control of the outcome.
6 Your sense of achievement is immediate.
7 Your sense of time is altered – how time flies when you are enjoying yourself!

(Wootton and Horne, 2004)

Your chances of getting Involved are greatest when the difficulty of the task and the level of skill needed are evenly matched. Too much skill and you will be frustrated. Too little skill and you will be bored. The beneficial effects of Involvement are more enduring than Body-based pleasure, or even Laughter, because they involve you in activity. Activity helps to fix things in your memory (Chapter 03). This is because it is you who is playing the game – you are not just a spectator. You are acting on the stage – you are not just sitting in the audience.

'I just want some satisfaction...'

You 'just want some satisfaction' of your needs. Horne and Doherty (2003) found it useful to classify human needs as:

• the need for **Warmth**
• the need for **Applause**
• the need for **Possession**.

The relative importance, to you, of each of these areas of need is unique to you, and their relative importance will have changed now that you are 50+ compared with when you were younger.

Your 'warmth' need is your need for persistent affection, acceptance, belonging, friendship, support and unconditional positive regard. This tends to grow, relative to your need for possession as you pass 50+. 'Warmth' needs have traditionally been easier to meet outside of work, but there is no real reason for this to continue to be the case (Chapter 06).

Improving the quality of working life is a preferable route to arguing for a better work–life balance. The nature of your work should not leave you needing to balance or compensate for it. Get the work sorted (Chapter 05).

Your 'applause' need is your need for some ephemeral things that will need constant reaffirmation, such as approval, admiration, congratulation, gratitude, recognition and success. The scale of your need for 'applause' should determine your choice of partner. Your need for applause will probably increase past 50+, so be prepared to discuss this with your partner (Chapter 06).

'Possession' need is your need to be able to say 'this is mine' (as in... this is my space, this is my child, this is my home, my garden, my hobby, my invention, my poem, my painting, my kind of music, my opinion, my idea). Normally, this need for possession is stronger when you are 30–35. Often, as you get well past 50+, you can take it or leave it. You can meet your needs for warmth, applause and possession at home, or at work, or in the community.

The 50+ can often meet their 'possession' needs just by thinking. For example, this is my idea, my poem, my thought, my memory, my experience, my opinion. The 50+ need not be dependent on money or on other people to meet their needs for 'possession'.

And so to bed... (or wherever)

The final S in our state of BLISS is for Sex. It is easy to see why sex is such an important source of well being. Sex combines... Body-based pleasure (ideally from all five senses), enhanced mood (elevated by endorphin release), very focused Involvement (for both the male and the female brain – see Chapter 06), with the Satisfaction of all three needs, i.e. for 'warmth', 'applause' and 'possession'.

The effect of sex on your thinking depends on whether or not your pre-sex stress levels are excessive, whether or not you have an orgasm, and what type of thinking you are concerned about.

Look at 'The seven steps in the sex life of your brain' on page 151 of Chapter 04.

Combating the obstacles to BLISS

While being 50+ can't guarantee happiness, you can minimize unhappiness. Five major obstacles to feeling good are anger, disappointment, fear, sadness and boredom. The table below suggests what you can do to minimize each.

The obstacle	What to do
Anger	• Have a pillow fight. • Run, or walk briskly. • Do something physical. • Join a martial arts club. • Dance, sway or shout to loud music. • Talk to yourself, a pet, a tree or a hillside.
Disappointment	• Watch a heart-warming movie. • Read *Chicken Soup for the Soul*. • Perform an act of unsolicited kindness. • Write a list of your lifetime achievements.
Fear	• Keep a diary. • Write to someone. • Call and old friend or cousin. • Weed someone's garden (can be yours!). • Rent an action movie (not a suspense thriller and not a mystery movie).
Sadness	• Exercise (Chapter 04). • Watch *When Harry Met Sally*. • Listen to *La Traviata* or *Madame Butterfly*. • Arrange flowers or photographs or plant a shrub. • Visit, mourn, discuss or commemorate the cause.
Boredom	• Join a club. • Work with young people. • Enrol for a class or a course. • Volunteer to visit a hospital, a hospice, a prison or a school. • Become a representative, e.g. councillor or school governor.

So, manage the five negative obstacles, i.e. anger, disappointment, fear, sadness and boredom, and pursue the five positive components, i.e. Body-based pleasure, Laughter, Involvement, Satisfaction and Sex and you may not achieve happiness, but you can reasonably aspire to a state of BLISS and your 50+ thinking will benefit. Here are some further tips.

Tip 1 – Read a poem

'No longer gazing'

As I gaze upon the sky
Vague
Unattributable
Unattached
There descends
A drowsy unimpassioned sadness,
Having no relief in word, or thought, or tear.
In this mood, heartless,
Without thought, thoughtless,

I must gaze no longer on the sky.
For hoping from outward forms to win
The passion and the life whose fountains are within,
I might gaze forever.

We win but what we give
And through our lives
Alone
We live
And learn
And might hope to gaze forever.

(Terry Horne, 1982)

Tip 2 – Walk tall

Step 1.   Slump in your chair and hang your head and your chin on your chest.

Step 2.   Now try to remember a time when you had a good time and felt good. Hard, eh!

Step 3.   Now try again, but this time, stand with your feet as wide apart as your shoulders, feet gripping the ground. Relax your knees. Breathe deeply, suck your belly button back toward your lower spine. Raise your head, pulling your chin back as far as comfortable. Look straight ahead into the distance and open your arms and chest as though to embrace someone. Notice how much easier it is now to remember a 'good time', and notice how the memory is raising your spirits now.

Step 4. Repeat and keep looking ahead. This time, without moving your eyes, see how far to the side and behind you can see with your peripheral vision. Use your imagination to complete the 360° around you. Relax your eyes and notice how much calmer you feel, less angry, less anxious.

Tip 3 – Maintaining morale

Keep tanned – even if it's only fake.

Live somewhere grand – even if only in one room.

Eat in a good restaurant – even if only one dish (e.g. a starter).

(based on a conversation with Aristotle Onassis)

Tip 4 – Keep up the talk

Some indication that bad feelings reside in the right (visual) rather than the left (verbal) side of the brain came in 1999 when psychologist Fred Schiffer used an EEG to find out why blanking the left eye on a pair of safety goggles lifted his patients' depression more dramatically than anti-depressant drugs. The exposed right eye had to work harder, thereby stimulating the opposite left side of the brain – the side usually used for talking. Maybe that's why talking about things helps to lift mood (Chapter 06).

The effect of jealousy at 50+

Jealous feelings can completely overwhelm the short-term memory and working space in your brain, leaving the pre-frontal lobes of your cerebral cortex – normally your logical mediators – very vulnerable to distracting emotional chemicals which will come from your amygdala. Clear thinking (and sometimes any thinking) will be nearly impossible. How prone are you to jealous feelings? How upset would you be in the following hypothetical situations?

	Score: 1 = indifferent, 2 = quite upset, 3 = very upset, 4 = extremely upset	Score
1	Your best friend preferred to do things with others, not including you	
2	You kept finding yourself 'out of the loop' at work, or in a club, church or family	
3	You discovered a partner was having an affair	
4	A brother or sister seemed to be or had been favoured by your parents	
5	A partner flirted	
6	A partner who generally did not talk a lot to you or to your family was very animated and chatty with other people	
7	Your partner commented on a how attractive other people were	
8	Your partner had sexual relationships with other people	
9	At a party your partner repeatedly kissed someone else	
10	Someone flirted with your partner	
11	Your boss gave full credit for your hard work to a co-worker	
12	Your partner danced with someone else	
13	Your partner went out several nights a month without you	
14	Your long-standing boss supports the promotion of a new worker ahead of you	
15	Your partner is slowly developing more and more interests that exclude you	
16	Your partner constantly talks about someone else	
17	Your partner readily hugs others but no longer hugs you	
18	Your partner wants to meet up with an ex-partner	
19	Your partner shared a long and involved project with an attractive co-worker	
20	Your partner suggested that you were both free to develop other relationships	

How did you do?

20–45   85% of adults scored more than this.
46–53   70% of adults scored more than this.
54–57   Half of all adults scored more than this.
58–62   30% of all adults scored more than this.
63–67   Only 15% of adults scored more than this.

(Cautionary note: although the normed respondents were cross cultural, they were not representatively so, and although many respondents were 50+, they were not controlled for age.)

The percentiles above are largely based on data collected in the 1980s. Are 50+ baby boomers less prone to jealousy? Are you more mellow and relaxed?

Only you know how jealousy affects you as an individual. Few emotions are more frightening, or more dangerous, or less amenable to clear thinking. Each day, husbands murder wives, wives murder husbands, mistresses or both. If your jealousy score is high, go back to your high-scoring situations and think about them now, rather than act impulsively in the middle of one of these situations. If any of these situations do occur, a well-rehearsed thought may be able to intercept messages from your amygdala before you say or do something you may regret. Your behaviour under provocation will depend on what you believe at the time – but belief is a combination of an emotion plus a thought. When you are jealous, your emotions are likely to be so strong that unless you have a very strong counteractive thought well rehearsed, and readily available, you are likely to be overwhelmed by your emotions and may act precipitately.

Jealousy is more than just insecurity. Insecurity provokes natural anxiety or fear of loss. Jealousy, on the other hand, provokes anger and aggression, betrayal, revenge and retribution. Jealousy feeds generalized pessimism, despair and low self-esteem – all of which lower performance on thinking tasks. Once feeling jealous, people can become obsessively hyper-vigilant, compulsively suspicious and even paranoid. All this takes up working space which the brain needs to think clearly about taking decisions, solving problems, making plans, learning from experience, or creating new ideas or developing greater intimacy in close relationships. The corrosive effect of jealousy extends beyond the person who is its object, and adversely affects wider family, social and working life.

Even if your jealousy score is in the highest band – 70+ – all is not lost. At 50+, you will find it easier to change than a younger person. You will need verbal thinking (Chapter 06) either as an internal dialogue or, preferably, with a thinking companion. If the jealous object is a partner, you will need to hug and welcome back your partner, even when your partner returns late. Even if your suspicions are well founded, anger will not make your relationship closer, which is what is needed (Chapter 06). Tell your partner how much you care. At another time soon, open a more general review of your relationship, of other problems that either of you may be experiencing.

Likewise, even if your score is very low – below 40, say – this is no reason to let someone take advantage of your unusually placid nature. You are entitled to respect and consideration. Say clearly that 'it makes me uncomfortable... embarrassed... anxious... etc. when you do X or Y'. Be clear, not judgemental. Stick to explaining, as clearly as you can, how you feel. If the transgression is serious, lay out your partner's options as clearly as you can. Share your feelings about the past and your thoughts on possible options for the future. By sharing your feelings, as well as your thoughts, you have a chance of getting things the way they need to be for you. If you are impulsively hostile and abusive, you may lose your relationship in the long run.

On being irritated – grumpiness at 50+

It is best not to blow grumpiness out of proportion or, in fact, to take any offence at it at all. Grumpy 50+ people generally know that they are grumpy and whether they like the fact that they are grumpy, or do not like the fact that they are grumpy, they are generally unable to stop themselves. In either case, they will not find it helpful to be reminded of the fact that they are grumpy. Being reminded of it is likely to make them grumpy! The scale of your irritation and the size of its cause will often be inversely related. It is the withdrawal of love that can make them irritating.

Irritation and grumpiness are useful (see Chapter 06) – if not endearing – in the 50+. They are emotions that do not lead to hatred. For example, say to yourself, 'I really like Neil, he is so irritating!' And you can, of course, and frequently do, feel grumpy with yourself, for example when you catch yourself repeating what you have said many times before.

Moods too good to be true

Low moods can lower your performance on thinking by reducing the energy you have available for thinking and also by reducing your optimistic expectation that you will succeed in thinking well. But very high moods also impair performance in thinking tasks by making it difficult for you to concentrate, or to pay adequate attention to relevant detailed information. Have a go at filling in tables 1, 2 and 3 below.

1 Mood level		
Was there ever a time when…?	Yes	No
You were so hyped that other people thought you were not normal?		
You were so irritable that you shouted at people or started a fight?		
You felt supremely confident in your self or your ability?		
You slept much less than usual but didn't feel tired as a result?		
Your thoughts raced and you couldn't slow them down?		
You were so easily distracted you had trouble thinking straight?		
You had enormously more energy than usual?		
You attempted many more jobs than usual?		
You rang people late at night or were very much more social or chatty?		
You did things that others might have thought were risky?		
You were much more interested in sex than you normally are?		
Your spending/shopping got you (or your family) into trouble?		
People complained that you were talking too fast?		
Total 'Yes' ticks		

2 Mood frequency	Yes	No
Were there more than three of the things to which your answer was 'yes' in 1 happening at the same time?		

3 Mood consequence	Yes	No
Thinking about such things as work, family, money, the law, arguments, were the consequences of your actions in 1 ever moderately serious?		

How did you get on?

If your number of 'yes' scores for section 1 was greater than seven, plus your answers in sections 2 and 3 were 'yes', you should seek professional help.

The 50+ feel insecure about...

Nuclear war no more – and terrorism neither. The 50+ feel insecure about identity theft, uncontrolled immigration and benefit fraud, insecure supplies of water and electricity, and unpredictable storms and weather. They are more anxious about corrupt public servants and organized crime, violence on the streets and rudeness in shops, and avian flu and superbugs in hospitals, than about Muslim fundamentalists. The insecurities of the 50+ electorate have not been reflected in the responses of their government. Since 1997, the UK government has spent £1,000 billion on 'national security'. Should more of it have been spent on things the 50+ actually feels insecure about?

Affluenza – a virus to which the 50+ are especially vulnerable?

Still haunted by postwar hardship? The 50+ generation often resort to buying what they want, not what they need, according to marketing educator, Jeanne Hill, at the UK University of Central Lancashire. Her favourite examples are big-screen televisions, luxury cars, face lifts, breast implants and new partners. Jeanne is concerned that we medicate our consequent unhappiness by using alcohol or anti-depressants. Do you have the 50+ affluenza virus?

Do the following statements apply to you? Please answer 'Yes' or 'No'.

Do these apply to you?	Yes	No
I like to have luxuries in my life.		
I admire nice homes, cars and clothes.		
I spend a lot of time and research on purchases.		
I like to know what is fashionable.		
The things I own show how well I have succeeded.		
What I am paid matters as much as what I do.		
I compare myself with others.		
I like other people to say I am attractive.		

How did you get on?

The more 'Yes' answers, the greater your infection!

Feeding your feelings – diet, dieting and depression

During 2008, Chef Anthony Worrall Thompson provided recipes to the Mental Health Foundation, which helps to combat depression, anxiety and poor concentration.

His recipes contain fish, pulses and nuts to provide protein to keep your brain cells healthy, and fruit, salads and vegetables to provide vitamins and minerals needed by your brain's chemical factory. Rising levels of depression and anxiety are thought to be linked to the 50+ being the first generation for whom consumption of fresh food has fallen (down to 13 per cent in men and down to 15 per cent in women) at a time when the use of chemicals and additives in processed food has risen.

To perform well and stay sharp, your brain needs a balanced supply of water, complex carbohydrates, vitamins and the Omega 3, 6 and 9 fats, found in fish, pulses, nuts and seeds and in unsaturated oils like olive oil, soya oil and oils from pressed nuts or seeds. Deficiencies in your diet can limit the capacity of your brain's chemical factory to produce amino acids, the neurotransmitters that transmit your thinking messages from one brain cell to the next. Serotonin, a key neurotransmitter, helps to regulate your feelings of contentment, anxiety and depression. Your level of serotonin is in turn regulated by tryptophan, which is why you should snack on nuts and seeds, not sweets and biscuits. Yoyo dieting is bad for prevailing mood, as well as producing chemicals in your brain that impair thinking (Chapter 04).

A chip off the old block (of dark chocolate)

Since the 1960s, Helsinki and Oula universities have been studying the progress of 1,367 businessmen born between 1919 and 1934. They are now well 50+!

In 2007, in the European Journal of Clinical Nutrition, they reported that people who ate dark chocolate were healthier, slimmer and happier, better qualified and felt less lonely and more optimistic. Their predictive thinking was better and they were more likely still to be making complex plans for themselves and others. Eating the dark chocolate released endorphins into their brains creating feelings of pleasure, while reducing sensitivity to the aches and pains of old age. So why not take a chip off the old block... of dark chocolate?

50+ hearts rule 50+ heads

In 2007, the journal *Nature* reported on the work of Professors Antonio Damasio of UCL and Marc Hausser of Harvard, who showed that emotion and intuition worked in tandem with logic (Chapter 05) to take decisions, especially when there was an element of moral reasoning or ethical thinking required. Damasio and Hausser's piece of brainwork looked at what happened in the ventromedial cortex (VMPC) when 30 volunteers were separately asked to take decisions which could involve killing another person. For the first time, this work gave us some brain-based insight into how and why humans are humane, and not just robotically rational, in the way we decide things.

The group included six patients with brain damage in the VMPC. Unlike the rest of us, these six patients were capable of taking utilitarian decisions to kill individuals – 'for the greater good' – without compassion or compunction. For the rest of us, our emotions come into play *during* our decision making, not just *afterwards* as a reaction to the consequences of our decisions. Our humane human 'hearts' send lots of traffic to our frontal cortex, to contribute to the actual taking of the decision. Our 'hearts' really do try to rule our 'heads', thankfully!

Happiness at 50+

Research reported in the *British Medical Journal* by Professor Gow at Edinburgh University, UK, looked at people who took IQ tests at ages 11 and 79. Professor Gow found that self-assessed 'happiness' depended not on how bright you were as a child aged 11, or even on your lifetime gain in IQ, which was often substantial (Chapter 02), but on your ability to defend yourself against the loss of cognitive function. It was loss, or fear of loss, of cognitive functioning that caused unhappiness. The best defence against unhappiness caused by the loss of cognitive function is to make lifestyle choices to protect against disease (see Chapters 04, 05 and 06) and to train your brain to create spare cognitive capacity (see Part Two).

Summary

- You need to explore what you are feeling, before you can think rationally.
- Emotions can motivate, de-motivate or disable thinking tasks.
- High hopes enhance mental performance. Anxiety and fear diminish it.
- Persistent low mood not only impairs thinking and health, it can have other serious consequences.
- The pursuit of Body-based pleasure, Laughter, Involvement, Satisfaction, and Sex will benefit the speed and accuracy of your thinking.
- The pursuit of happiness may be fruitless, but unhappiness caused by fear or loss of cognitive function can be reduced through lifestyle choice and brain training.

Suggested further reading

Berns, G. (2005) *Satisfaction*, Owl Books, NY.

Browning, G. (2005) *Pull*, Atlantic.

Browning, G. (2005) *Small Rules for Little Problems*, Guardian Books.

Fredrickson, B. (2003) *The Value of Positive Emotions*, American Scientist, 91, p329–36.

Howard, P. (3rd edn) (2006) *The Brain*, Barol Press.

James, O. (2007) *The Affluenza Virus*, Vermillion.
http://www.psy.ed.ac.uk (accessed 15 July 2005)

Layard, R. (2005) *Happiness: The New Science*, Penguin, NY.

Schwartz, B. (2004) *Paradox of Choice – Hope is Less*,
Collins, NY.

Seligman, M. (2002) *Authentic Happiness*, Free, NY.

Witchells, C. (2007) 'Join the blub', *The Independent*,
10/04/07, p8.

Wootton, S. and Horne, T. (2000) *Strategic Thinking,*
Kogan Page.

http://www.psy.ed.ac.uk (accessed 15/07/05).

02

exploiting the superior thinking skills of the 50+ brain

In this chapter you will learn:
- how to exploit superior intelligence at 50+
- how to improve scores in employment IQ tests
- how to preserve your superior ability to think at 50+ by creating spare cognitive capacity as a buffer against disease.

The young sow wild oats, the old grow sage.
(Winston Churchill)

Introduction

A study made in 1947 of the IQs of 70,000 11-year-old children in Scotland, has recently been re-discovered 60 years later by Professor Ian Deary of Edinburgh University. Professor Deary's study shows that smoking, bad food, lack of exercise and disease correlate with declining IQ scores, but age, in itself, does not. Quite the reverse!

So far, 1,500 of the people who took the IQ tests in 1947 have been traced and persuaded to re-take their original IQ tests, to complete lifestyle questionnaires and to undergo MRI brain scans. In the absence of disease, or adverse lifestyle choices, average IQ improved by 10 per cent – a huge upward shift according to John Starr, consultant at Royal Victoria Hospital Edinburgh, when compared with a current assumption that IQs decline steadily from age 17 onwards. Staying physically fit, and eating Omega 3-rich fatty foods, were among the positive contributors to the gain in IQ with age. When adversely affected subjects were removed, the average gains in IQ with age were even more dramatic and were still increasing at age 70+.

The largest gains in IQ with age were associated with freedom from major illness and with persistent physical and mental activity. Chapter 04 shows how you can protect your brain from disease through simple physical exercises and by ditching diets and favouring the low oxytoxic foods that are listed in the appendices.

Part Two of this book contains 14 brain workout 'circuits', comprising the kind of brain training activities that favour continuing gains in IQ after 50+. The brain training circuits are designed to maintain and thicken the myelin insulation on the neural connections between the different parts of your brain. As you age, your improving IQ seems to be a measure of the extent to which the different parts of your brain continue to connect to each other. Continuing to learn and create close relationships (Chapter 06), adds new connections. Training maintains and thickens the myelin insulation around the new connections, even as you get older.

Beyond a certain point, increased connectedness does not seem to go on adding to your tested IQ indefinitely, but what it does seem to do is to create spare cognitive capacity which you can hold in reserve, just in case you contract a disease that damages some of your existing connections. The important realization is that such damage is disease related – not age related. And the risk of damaging disease is lifestyle related. According to Professor Carol Brayne, at Cambridge University, UK, you can control your own exposure to damage and reverse earlier damage.

Ironically, one of the pupils tested in the original 1947 study was Richard Wilson, who played the character Victor Meldrew, the elderly character in the BBC drama *One Foot in the Grave*. In some ways, the 50+ generation is guilty of helping to perpetuate ageism by colluding with prejudicial stereotypes of older people like Victor Meldrew (see the 'Final thoughts' section). Richard Wilson has agreed to help Professor Deary publicize his project and its important finding that IQ does not necessarily decline with age, and that it can, and does, improve with age. And if you train your brain, your IQ at 50+ can continue to get better and better.

The use of IQ tests for job selection

When you go for a job with an employer who uses psychometric selection tests, the battery of tests will almost certainly include some traditional IQ tests. These may be pen and paper tests or, more likely, they will be screen-based tests. You must attempt as many questions as you can within a time limit, which will be strictly enforced. There are always more questions than you can complete within the time. The questions will usually get harder as you work through the test, so relax, it is not you that lacks mental stamina – all the evidence points to the 50+ generation having more, not less, mental stamina than younger applicants. Since incorrect guesses do not count against you, you should make a quick, once over attempt at all the questions, before going back to the start to work systematically through all the questions you skipped over.

If you were allowed even a little more time, at 50+ you would likely have such an advantage over younger applicants that you could easily come out ten points ahead. This is a very significant difference – equating, for example, to senior executive and top civil service administration jobs, as opposed to senior clerical or executive grades. This argues for plenty of advanced practice, preparation and time efficiency on the day of the test. An employer using psychometric tests will almost certainly also have open-ended, less time-constrained, tasks in their test battery. These tasks will require creative thinking, reflective learning, general knowledge and judgement based on experience. This will give you, as a 50+ candidate, a tremendous advantage over younger applicants – just as long as you relax and enjoy it.

Modern tests of multiple intelligence

There is a trend, especially in American organizations, towards tests that assess multiple intelligences (see Table 2.1 on page 63). This trend gives 50+ candidates a clear advantage over younger applicants, because many of the additional intelligences measured in modern tests of multiple intelligences benefit from general knowledge and experience. Obviously, the older you are, the more general knowledge and experience you are bound to have. At 50+, you also have greater skills in prediction and in the streetwise evaluation of what is likely to work in practice, as opposed to in theory.

Modern tests of multiple intelligence require applicants to use a lifetime of acquired information to infer the most likely answers (Chapter 05). Older people tend to score higher than younger people on numerical, predictive and reflective thinking. The capacity for predictive thinking and reflective thinking, and the ability to estimate and quantify consequences, are key components of 'streetwise' intelligence. This confers further advantages on the 50+ candidate.

A more modern IQ test

Answer as many questions as you can.

1 Woman is to X, as Criterion is to Criteria.	Is X: Child, Father, Gender or Women?
2 Past is to X, as Spun is to Spinning.	Is X: Present, Participle, Predictive or Rotation?
3 Planes is to X, as Lines is to Cross.	Is X: Arc, Eclipse, Intersect or Chord?
4 Breakfast is to X, as Meal is to Hearty.	Is X: Continental, Full English, Light or Eat?
5 Plane is to X, as Polish is to Stone.	Is X: Flight, Hydrofoil, Timber or Wheat?
6 Buddhism is to X, as Median to Average.	Is X: Séance, Monk, Meditation or Religion?
7 Submarine is to X, as Helicopter is to Air.	Is X: Yacht, Fish, Lake or Water?
8 Meaning is to X, as Category is to Homogenous.	Is X: Acronym, Anonymous, Synchronous or Synonymous?

How did you get on?

The answers are at the base of this page. Our students range from 2–3 correct answers; 4+ is a good score.

The disadvantages of youth and the 'streetwise' 50+

Older people have the advantage of having been young, whereas younger people have the disadvantage of never having been old.

(Simon Wootton, 2007)

Young people who have high verbal IQ scores can sometimes think and talk so quickly that they can defend the intellectually indefensible. They can argue for an unreasonable inference, or gloss over an impractical implication, especially when they are

(Answers: 1. Women 2. Present 3. Intersect 4. Full English 5. Timber 6. Religion 7. Water 8. Synonymous)

more quickly rewarded for doing a clever demolition job on a 50+ idea than they would if they took time to examine their own.

Intelligent young people are used to getting things right, from school onwards. Getting something wrong is unfamiliar. Intelligent people generally do not like the unfamiliar feeling of getting things wrong. Delusions of infallibility are often intact in younger people and the preservation of these delusions is sometimes more important to them than entertaining the possibility that they may be wrong.

Awareness of other possibilities and other possible consequences increases as you get older. According to Sternberg, this leads the 50+ to have 'streetwise' intelligence, which shows its wisdom through having 'good' or 'bad' feelings about people and situations. The 'streetwise' intelligence of the 50+ depends on broad general knowledge linked to experience. Both increase as you grow older.

Eminence

To be eminent, the 50+ need to exhibit only one type of intelligence. Eight possible types of intelligence have been identified.

Intelligence type	The capacity...
Environmental	to observe and see patterns
Interpersonal	to empathize and respond
Intrapersonal	to know one's motives, goals and feelings
Kinaesthetic	to manipulate concepts, to use the body
Linguistic	to use language (oral or written)
Musical	to use tone, accent, rhythm, pitch
Logical	to think logically, to calculate scientifically
Visual	to use graphics, to think spatially

Table 2.1: Eight types of intelligence (after Gardner 2004)

Wordsworth, Beethoven, Einstein, Turner, Picasso, Freud, Winston Churchill, Ghandi and Darwin had some intelligences which lay dormant until they displayed them well after they turned 50 years of age.

Which intelligences could you display later in your life? Study Table 2.2 and then check out the 'Steps to eminence'.

Masters	Know all there is to know in a particular field. Masters are people with whom others feel privileged to work, or to whom others seek to be apprenticed, or under whom others seek to serve. One thinks of master painters, like Turner.
Makers	Know enough about the rules of a particular discipline to be able to break them. Like writing sentences without verbs! Makers bring new ways of thinking. People like Darwin and Freud.
Influencers	Work through others, often behind the scenes. They are the power behind thrones, like the 'silent accountant' behind Richard Branson. Philosophers like John Locke influenced Thomas Jefferson, who wrote the American Constitution. Karl Marx, Martin Luther King and Mahatma Ghandi illustrate how powerful an idea can be. Sometimes written. Sometimes quietly spoken in small circles.
Introspectors	Keep detailed diaries, write long letters or make extensive notes and leave them for posterity. Novelists, poets and politicians sometimes do this. People like Virginia Wolf, Wordsworth and Tony Benn.

Table 2.2: Types of genius often displayed in later life (after Gardner 1995)

Steps to eminence

Step 1 – First, decide which of the following interest you most. Ring the letter below your choice.

If...	Groups Management	Individuals Psychology	Nature Biology	Engineering Maths
Ring	A	B	C	D

If...	Bodies Sport	Words Teaching	Sounds Music	Appearance Art
Ring	E	F	G	H

Step 2 – Next, decide which of the following you think describes you best. Put a ring around the number below it.

If...	Planning Organizing Controlling	Articulate Numerate Logical	Good at learning Reflective	Curious Experimental Risk taking	Adaptable Easy going Streetwise
Ring	1	2	3	4	5

Step 3 – You now have a number/letter combination, e.g. A2. If you find the position of your number/letter combination on the matrix below, it will be at the epicentre of words that enable you to explore the opportunities open to you in later life.

	1	2	3	4	5
A	Production control	Manufacturing Management	Quality control	Research Development	Sales Services
B	Planning administrator	Counselling Therapy	Academic research	Writing Editing	Social work Youth work
C	Middle management	Editor Publisher	Academic research	Inventor Designer	Environment Ecology
D	Project management	Systems analysis	Purchasing Logistics	Design Engineer	Team leader
E	Own business	Commentator Sports writer	Dance Performance	Outdoor Active	Trainer Journalist
F	Literary PR/ agent	Actor/Editor Teacher	Critic Professor	Poet Writer	Journalist PR/Media
G	Agent, Arts management	Lyrics Advertising	Music Critic	Composer Musician	Teacher Accompanist
H	Arts admin., Museum	Designer Trainer	Exhibitor Development	Artist Creative	Director Innovation

Can you increase your intelligence and your IQ score?

Yes, you can. Reviews of more than 200 studies, including studies of adopted siblings and twins, have shown that less than 50 per cent of your IQ is determined by your genes – though good genes clearly get you off to a good start! In the longer term, you can improve your IQ score by 4 points just by what you choose to eat and drink (Chapter 04). You can add another 6–7 points by regular thoughtful conversations (Chapter 06). You can avoid short-term deficits of up to 15 points by following regular patterns of sleep (Chapter 04). According to Ostranger, you can add up to 14 points to your test score by preparation and stress reduction. That's a very significant increase when related to a 'normal' IQ score of 100.

Preparing for IQ tests – a six-point plan

1 If your diet has been haywire recently, then take the stipulated daily doses of vitamins B1, B5 and Vitamin C, plus mineral supplements of boron, zinc and selenium. Take with plenty of water (Chapter 04).

2 Practise mixing yourself booster drinks to find the mix and concentration that suits you. You may need a boost on the day, especially if the tests are held in the afternoon. Booster drinks can be made from hot water and a spoon of honey mixed together in a mug. Add the juice of a lemon. Drink it with a capsule of vitamin E. Experiment the week before with one to four capsules but do not exceed the daily dose. Take the drink and the vitamin E capsules about one hour before the test. Sip sage tea during it (Chapter 04).

3 Make sure your prior sleep pattern is stable and sufficient (Chapter 04).

4 Raise or reduce your stress level so that you enjoy a sense of well-being. Use lavender oil if you need to calm yourself. On the day, put peppermint, basil, sage or rosemary oil on a tissue, so that you can control your level of mental alertness.

5 If you think you may be overtired and low in energy on the day, practise making 3G cocktails. A 3G cocktail comprises the herbs ginger, ginkgo and ginseng. It is important not to exceed the stated dose.

6 Career advice services, or job centres, will often let you practise taking tests under 'test' conditions. This is a good way to desensitize yourself to test trauma.

Does lifelong learning help?

In the first part of this chapter, we introduced Professor Ian Deary's discovery of 70,000 test papers which were taken when the candidates were 11 years of age. The results of his subsequent study did not surprise those of us with experience of working with mature learners. Mature learners commonly improve their IQ scores by about 10 per cent during two years of part-time study. A 10 per cent shift, e.g. from 100 to 110, or 110 to 121, or 120 to 132, is a very significant gain. Professor Deary discovered that other IQ gains, especially among the physically fit candidates who had remained mentally active, were very high indeed. This 'elite' group are still being studied. It is already clear that on-going learning and on-going mental activity correlate strongly with these larger gains in IQ. The only vitamin supplements that appeared to have any long-term correlation with IQ gain were B12 and folic acid. The implication for those of you who wish to improve your IQ as you get older is to carry on learning, formally or informally, no matter what your age, and to train your brain much as you would train your body.

First of all, what you learn will likely add to the breadth of your general knowledge and this will support many of the thinking skills which contribute to your intelligent behaviour – like your capacity for critical, creative and reflective thinking. Secondly, how you learn can promote the formation of new neuron pathways, newly connecting different parts of your brain. For this reason, you should consider the following advice on learning methods:

• Check out *how* you will be learning as well as *what* you will be learning.
• Avoid programmes that rely heavily on a traditional lecture/seminar format, especially if seminar numbers are too high to support the kind of 1:1 conversations that foster cognitive development (Chapter 06).
• Be wary of academic courses that rely heavily on information transfer via IT, or distance learning packs, or handouts.
• Ask how much 1:1 face-to-face contact you will have.
• Ask whether paired learning will be used (Chapter 06).

The neurochemical basis of intelligence

So far, we have only considered ways to improve traditional IQ scores, but a multi-faceted model of intelligence leaves open the possibility of activities that can further enhance your intelligent behaviour. The work of Haier and Miller suggests that the better connected the different areas of your brain, the more intelligent you are.

Exercises like the ones in Part Two of this book may work, in part, by stimulating the growth, thickening and replacement rate of the myelin, the insulation that surrounds the nerves in the brain. This is like replacing the poor-quality leads that come with a boxed set hi-fi or home cinema system with a more expensive set of leads. The more expensive leads enhance the definition of your television picture and the quality of the sound from your speakers.

The density of the neuron connections in your brain can be increased by learning new things and by tackling tasks and exercises that require you to use different parts of your brain in combination. As you will see in Chapter 03, activities that involve your memory will activate an extensive neural network, radiating out from your hippocampus.

Here are two sample combination thinking tasks for you to try.

Combining visual and emotional thinking

- A young child has returned home from school to find seven pebbles, a carrot, and a wet scarf on the grass outside the house. Why is the child crying?

Combining visual, numerical and creative thinking

- Because this is a dark chocolate cake, made to Sally's recipe, all eight people at the party want an equal slice of the cake. You are allowed up to three cuts.

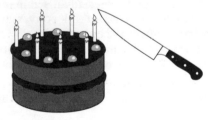

How did you get on?

Answer 1 = the snowman melted

Answer 2 = use two vertical cuts to cut into four and then one horizontal cut parallel to the base gives eight pieces in three cuts

Students doing combination exercises as part of their brain training circuits, often complain that such exercises make their 'heads hurt', a bit like muscle fatigue after working out in a gym. Part Two helps you to create your own mental gymnasium. By working through the 14 'brain circuits', of matched difficulty, you can gauge your progress as you proceed from Circuit 1 to Circuit 14.

After the initial burn...

Haier's work, using brain scanners, has shown that when the more intelligent 50+ people think about a problem, initially many different areas of their 50+ brain light up and link up. Initially, your 50+ brain burns a lot of energy, while feeling its way around the problem area. Quickly, the frontal lobes of your cerebral cortex appear to delegate the brain work to an appropriate selection of areas in the brain, that support the kinds of thinking needed to address the problem. This local area neural network then takes over, allowing the rest of your 50+ brain to relax.

50+ geniuses are created not born

Ellen Winner of Harvard has been studying prodigiously high IQ children. These high IQ children often do not even shine as adults (and certainly don't necessarily become geniuses). Twin research by Professor Michael Howe has shown that the role of inherited IQ in genius is overplayed and that motivation and intention, planning and persistence, and capacity for hard work are all big factors in genius. These are all factors that are in short supply in younger adults and in better supply as you reach 50+. Although this research is recent, the knowledge is not:

> *In life, it is the training, not the brain, that counts.*
>
> (Ihara Siakaku 1642–93)

The Volvo effect

In discovering what he termed the Volvo effect, Professor Yaakov Stern studied the blood flow in the brain, using a zenon scanner. He discovered that people who did more learning in their lives had more reserve capacity and more resistance to Alzheimer-related intrusions, causing impairment of mental functioning. ('A tough car can keep rolling despite a bump or two.') The idea of cognitive reserve capacity had been earlier advanced by neurologist Robert Katzman and neuropathologist Robert Kerry. They had found extensive Alzheimer's plaques and tangles in the brains of their control groups – the ones with normal thinking abilities! The results have been replicated by Professor Caffey, using a PET scanner on the brains of 320 people with normal mental functioning.

Growing old gracefully and intelligently

As you grow older...

- You have the advantage of information and experience that can only be acquired through living long enough.
- You can use this information to feed your predictive thinking.
- You can use predictive thinking to remind you to make an earlier start on things that take longer.
- You can keep learning and trying new things.
- You can use the thinking skills in Appendix A to exploit your 50+ IQ.
- You can do brain training like that supplied in the brain circuits in Part Two, in order to open up new neuron pathways and add to the processing power of your brain. As you progressively complete more and more chapters, you will be able to combine the processing power of different parts of your brain. You will become more intelligent.

'For I am 50+!'

Those people want it all.
But what these people do not know,
Is that the world is very complex, imperfect and oppressed.
What those people need is prophets, wise and not too stressed.
I am waiting for their call.
I'll have their problems soon finessed;
I'll rejuvenate the railways,
I will nationalize a mine,
I'll manipulate the mailways,
I'll use my intellect to shine.
I can illuminate their problems,
I can make them crystal clear,

But I saw your eyes go cloudy,
As you saw me lean to hear.
Yet, I had felt so confident
And I still feel very strong
Yes, I know that I am fallible,
Yes, I know I can be wrong,
Yes, I know my voice is nasal,
It has been boring all along.
You're right,
They did stop coming,
To stop and make a fuss,
I know that I am unstoppable,
Yes, that's me at 50+.

(Terry Horne, 2008 – indebted to Pam Ayres, *Surgically Enhanced*, Hodder & Stoughton)

Summary

- At 50+, you can keep learning about intelligent things to do.
- IQ tests can measure some important thinking skills that do contribute to your intelligent behaviour.
- In addition to the thinking skills measured in IQ tests, creative thinking, reflective thinking and predictive thinking are major contributors to your intelligent behaviour and all these improve as you grow older.
- Your scores on IQ tests can readily be improved by up to 14 points – a very significant improvement.
- A high IQ test score is no guarantee of intelligent behaviour. For example, some fast-thinking people are more adept at defending poor thinking than they are at thinking well.
- Genius requires intellectual values that only come with age.
- Speed and accuracy of thinking are correlated with the quality of the myelin insulation surrounding the axons of the neurons in your brain, and this can be improved through brain training exercises.
- Intelligence is linked to the number of neuron connections in your brain and this number can be increased by the way you use it.

Suggested further reading

Ayres, P. (2006) *Surgically Enhanced*, Hodder & Stoughton

Cobb, J. (1995) 'Learning and dementia: the Framingham study,' *Neurology*, 45, pp1706–13.

Fixx, J. (1972) *Games for the Super Intelligent*, Muller.

Gardener, H. (2004) *Changing Minds*, Harvard.

Gould, E. (1998) 'Learning and neurogenesis in nature', *Neuroscience*, 2, pp259–66.

Howard, P. (2007) Centre for Applied Cognitive Studies, Carolina, US.

Janski, R. (2005) *Wrinklies' Wisdom*, Carlton.

Leventhal, A. www.neuroscience.med.utah.html, accessed 02/10/07.

Miller, E. M. (1994) 'Intelligence and brain myelination', *Personality and Individual Differences*, 17, pp803–33.

O'Keefe, J. (1994) *Mind Opening for Managers*, Thorsons.

Rosenzweig, M. (1996) 'The effect of training and experience in the brain', *Behaviour Brain Research*, 78, pp56–66.

Snowden, D. (1996) 'Linguistic ability and cognitive function: the nun's study', *Journal of the American Medical Association*, 275, pp527–33.

Stern, Y. (1999) 'Education, occupation and the rate of memory decline in AD: the cognitive reserve', *Neurology*, 53, pp1941–46.

Stern, Y. (1994) 'Learning, occupation and Alzheimer's', *Journal of the American Medical Association*, 271, pp1003–11.

Sternberg, R. (1997) *Successful Intelligence*, Plume.

www.brainwaves.com. Conditioning exercises for six intelligences.

03

the superior memory of the 50+ brain

In this chapter you will learn:

- that your long-term memory at 50+ is better than when you were younger and should continue to get better
- that the speed at which you can form new short-term memories will decline slowly from age 50+, but that this can be worked around
- that tips, tricks, tools and training can speed up new memory formation
- that as a bonus, memory training expands the already enhanced cognitive capacities of the 50+ brain
- how and why training your age-enhanced 50+ brain will help protect its increased intelligence and thinking skills against erosion by disease.

I am growing older and will someday be old. I do not
ask for improving memory but for lessening cocksureness,
For greater humility when my memory clashes with
that of others. Teach me the glorious lesson that
occasionally I may be wrong.

(Nun's prayer, circa 1600)

Introduction

Millions of people around the world are worrying about their 50+ 'senior moments'. Names, keys, glasses, 'where's the car' or 'what was it I wanted in the first place!' At 50+, it is normal to sense a dip in your ability to retain new information. None of this means that you are losing your mind or your marbles. Just the opposite – each of the ten thinking skills (see Appendix A) that contribute to your thinking power become more powerful as you get older. This chapter is about dealing with one, admittedly very irritating, aspect of only one of those skills: the speed at which you can form new short-term memory. If you don't learn to work around this (or just take more time over it), it can seem like you have lost the ability to do it all together, and because it is the gatekeeper to many of your other thinking skills, it can undermine your confidence in your ability to think generally. This can be very disconcerting – alarming even – but your alarm is misplaced.

Recollection of long-term memory, on the other hand, actually improves with age – because, as you've grown older, you have had many more opportunities to recollect things, and each recollection thickens the myelin insulation around the neural pathways used to collect together the fragments of that particular memory. The earlier the original memory, the more likely you are to have had occasion to recall it. More recalls equals better retention.

It is perfectly possible to remain very sharp until you are very old – way beyond 50+. People like Winston Churchill and Golde Meir remained very sharp until they were much nearer 100 than 50.

For the sake of your body, over the last 15 years you may have become resigned to the need to adopt better eating and drinking habits, to perhaps stop smoking, and even to exert yourself more physically. You can now do exactly the same for your brain. You can, if you wish to, make lifestyle choices that will improve or maintain the fitness of your brain. Chapter 04 will detail some the choices you can make. Part Two gives you 14 brain training circuits that illustrate the kinds of mental exercises that help your brain to get fitter. Each circuit contains exercises aimed at thinking speed, suppleness, stamina and strength. Because each circuit is graded you can monitor your progress. This chapter will concentrate on your memory.

Is it wise to eat sage?

Apparently, if you rip sage leaves into small pieces and add a teaspoon of the ripped leaves to a cup of boiling water and sip your infusion during a test, or an interview or a presentation, you will improve your performance. Sage inhibits the breakdown of acetylcholine which the brain uses when it thinks.

Age is not a problem – but disease can be

Up until recently, we thought that certain diseases, like arthritis, erectile dysfunction, or Alzheimer's, came with age. We now know that this is not the case. These diseases often make people look older, but they are not themselves caused by age.

If you have already reached 50+, and you are still physically healthy, you should start planning what you are going to do for your one hundredth birthday! Sure, by then you will probably have become a lot slower at processing new information into short-term memory – but you can limit this, you can learn to work around it. Some other mental changes will be detectable, through specialist psychological testing, but they will not necessarily turn up as problems in your everyday living. You can add life to your living, not just years to your life. There are some tests in this chapter that will enable you to detect some changes, but there are also tips, steps, diet changes etc., that can help you to reverse, ward off or work around any changes you do detect.

From the age of 50+, you can sometimes start to lose up to 1 per cent of your brain cells each year, but that does not necessarily need to lead to loss of mental performance as long as your brain stays fit. You can tip the odds of enhancement and preservation decisively in your favour. You can add new brain cells. On tests, many 70+ brains out-perform 20+ brains.

By 2003, Dr Jeff Victoroff had already pointed out that brain scientists were already 'swimming in an ocean tide of promising discoveries'. By 2008, that tide had turned decisively. It is time to harness brain science into a movement for brain fitness that will rival the movement for body fitness.

Is there a 50+ memory pill just around the corner?

Not at the moment, but ask your doctor about:

- **Amparines** – it is a cognitive booster, even if you don't have Alzheimer's.
- **Donepezil** – it boosts concentration, even if you don't have dementia.
- **Modafinil** – it improves thinking, even if you don't have narcolepsy.
- **Ritalin** – it improves concentration and visual thinking, even if you don't have ADHD (look up Vitamin R, on the internet).
- **Propranol** – it suppresses distracting or distressing memories, even if you don't have a heart problem.
- **MEM compounds** – currently under test in the US.
- **Gene therapy** – neurological professor Mathew During reported on successful gene treatment of Parkinson's disease in the *Lancet* (June 2007) and one of the research team, Dr Kaplitt, believes it may be effective for other neurological conditions

Memory and surgery at 60+

People aged over 60 are twice as likely to suffer a memory loss and mental sharpness after surgery, report doctors at Duke University in North Carolina, USA (*Anaesthesiology*, January 2008). Those who lose mental ability after surgery are also significantly more likely to die within a year of having the operation. Hence keeping both your mind and your body fit are equally important.

Memory test

Test your long-term memory

1 What did you eat at your last meal?	
2 Where were you last Saturday?	
3 What did you do on the Thursday before that?	
4 Where were you at midnight on New Year's Eve?	
5 What was the title of the last film you watched?	
6 Where were you when you heard that President Kennedy had been shot?	
7 How did you last celebrate something?	
8 What was the last book you read?	
9 Where were you when you first remember being kissed?	
10 Who kissed you?	

To score: 0–6 is poor. 7–8 is average. 9–10 is good

Test your short-term memory

Read one of the horizontal lines of numbers and look away.

How many numbers can you remember?

8						
13						
46	12					
7	10	35				
18	98	84	6			
4	69	25	38	13		
20	22	68	85	16	17	
78	56	88	91	24	46	80

If you can remember three or fewer, then your short-term memory is poor.

4–7 then your short-term memory is average.

8–10, then your short-term memory is good.

Sudoku is good, Scrabble is better, cryptic crosswords are brilliant!

Sudoku requires several parts of your brain to work together to support numerical, visual, emotional and critical thinking. As patterns emerge and fragments are remembered, many neural links are activated in over 30 different areas of your cerebral cortex. Many of these neural linkages involve your hippocampus, which plays a central role in your memory. When you play Sudoku or Scrabble or do cryptic crosswords, these neural links are run over and over again, thickening the myelin insulation around the axons of your brain cells and thereby improving the speed and the accuracy of your thinking. Emotional thinking is involved in managing your impatience, frustration, and the disappointment you feel as you compete with yourself or with others.

Your memory switchboard (the bit that looks like a seahorse)

Your hippocampus, the bit that looks like a seahorse, seems to act like a central switchboard. Your hippocampus links fragmentary components of your memory that may be stored in many different parts of your brain.

The hippocampus has been the focus of much of the research that has been done on memory and recollective thinking. Why? Is it just because it is distinctive in its appearance and therefore easy to see and isolate? In *Stem Cells and the Labyrinth of Memory*, Elizabeth Finkel jokes about the preoccupation of brain researchers with the hippocampus:

'A brain researcher is like a man who has lost his keys in the street. The brain researcher is found crawling about, on his hands and knees, near a street lamp. When asked if he has dropped his keys near to the street lamp, he replies, 'No, but it is too dark to search for them anywhere else.'

(E. Finkel, *Stem Cells and the Labyrinth of Memory*, Cosmos, 2007)

The rules of Sudoku

A Sudoku puzzle is usually a 9 × 9 grid sub-divided into 9 squares – like noughts and crosses.

6					1			
		9	7	5		2		8
	5	7		4		9	6	
5	6	2			3		8	
	4						1	
	8		6			5	7	3
	3	5		1		8	9	
1		4		6	8	3		
		2						7

The puzzle starts with some given numbers – called clue numbers – already inserted. The object of the game is to fill all the empty boxes such that each row, each column and each 3 × 3 large square, contains the numbers 1 to 9 – without repeating any number.

Tips on solving Sudoku puzzles

- Use an HB pencil with an eraser in the end, or a ballpoint that has more than one colour.
- Start by picking the 3 × 3 grid that has most number clues already given. Look at the rows and columns going through the square you have picked. Pick a row or column that has several clue numbers already in place. Pick a 'vacant' square in the grid you have chosen to work on.

- In pencil or in green ink, enter in a small font the 'missing' numbers, i.e. missing from the square, and from the row and the column in which the vacant square is sitting. If there is only one such number, you have found your first answer number. Enter the answer number in the vacant square by over striking your missing numbers in black. Write the answer number as big as the clue numbers.

- Repeat for all the vacant squares in the row, the column and the 3 × 3 grid. By elimination, each time you enter a big black answer number, you can erase or strike out the small missing numbers that you have entered in other places in the row, column or 3 × 3 square. As soon as you have only one missing number left in a small square – that is, an answer number – over-write it large and black.

- This will get you started and enable you to use basic Sudoku puzzles for brain training. Your brain will get most benefit from doing easier puzzles as quickly as you can. Note your times and note how much quicker you are getting.

The answer to the Sudoku above can be found at the end of this chapter. There are more puzzles in Part Two of this book.

A myth about memory

'You are born with all the brain cells you will ever have.'

Not true. Memory researchers have discovered that your chemical brain is a complex organ which develops and changes with every thought that you have. This means that old, diseased or deteriorating brains can change and repair themselves with the right diet, exercise and brain training. This explains why it is that the brains of many older people show no deterioration in thinking performance (*Teach Yourself Training Your Brain*, Horne and Wooton, 2007).

The myth of dementia

When pathologists dissect the brains of people who have remained mentally sharp and active up to the time they died, they sometimes find that the brains of the people who have remained mentally active are riddled with Alzheimer plaques! Yet those mentally active people had shown no signs of impaired memory when they were alive.

Michael Valenzuola's analysis, covering 66,000 people, published in 2006, showed that people who kept their brains active, for example through work, leisure activities, or brain training, had half the risk of suffering dementia. The pathologists' reports in David Snowden's nun study are particularly useful because the nuns with Alzheimer's who had impaired mental functioning had a virtually identical lifestyle/environment/diet etc., as the nuns with Alzheimer's who showed no sign of mental impairment. The only difference between the 'impaired' and 'non-impaired' groups was the level of on-going learning and mental exercise. In a convent, other lifestyle variables are largely controlled and comparable.

Memory, diet and dieting

Don't do it! Don't do it! Don't go on a fat-free diet.
Fats are the building blocks of your brain. If your fat-free
diet is very successful, you may become slim and beautiful,
but the only thing you will be fit for is reality TV.
(Terry Horne, 2006, after George Burns)

Your body fuels your brain by burning food. Brain activity can require your body to 'burn' more than 25 per cent of the food you eat – depending on how mentally active you are. Burning food (or calories) is more scientifically described as 'oxidizing' the glucose in your food, thereby releasing energy – physical and mental energies. Unfortunately, one bi-product of the oxidation of glucose in our food is sometimes an 'oxygen free radical'. An oxygen free radical can attack a human cell and precipitate diseases like cancer or Alzheimer's. Alzheimer's disease may, in turn, impair your memory.

Normally, this chain of events would be interrupted because our bodies also produce antioxidants which can mop up oxygen free radicals before they can do any harm. If, however, you eat foods that are very rich in glucose, your body's normal production of antioxidants may not be sufficient to mop up all the free radicals that will be produced when your body oxidizes all the glucose in those foods. In this book, we have called foods that are too rich in glucose 'oxytoxic' foods. There are low oxytoxic versions of most of the foods you eat. Appendix H lists the oxytoxic values of many common foods you are likely eat, so that you can make an informed choice to eat foods that are less likely to result in surplus free radicals and, thereby, more or less risk of precipitating neurodegenerative diseases. As an added precaution, you can increase your consumption of foods that contain antioxidants. Fresh fruit, vegetables and dark chocolate all contain flavenols. Flavenols are the naturally occurring antioxidants found in food. You can compare the flavenol contents of foods by consulting the US CRIC index tables in Chapter 04, page 131 – dark chocolate comes out very high!

Of mice and men

Eating less definitely increases the lifespan of mice and monkeys – by up to 50 per cent. The lifespan of humans also increases if you eat less. But it matters what it is that you eat less of. There is no point in living much longer if you are brain dead for the last 10–20 years of your life. So, do not completely cut out unsaturated fats, for example. Your brain needs them or the walls of your brain cells may become brittle and the brain cells may die. The amount of acetylcholine in your brain is related to the quantity of Omega 3, 6 and 9 fats that you eat, and if you have insufficient acetylcholine in your brain, it could mean that fewer messages will be passed between your neurons.

If you want to live longer by eating less, then eat less salty or sugary or refined or processed foods. Eat less of foods that need little chewing, or that are eaten quickly. Such foods have side effects like diabetes and heart disease. Also such foods don't satisfy your hunger for very long, whereas prolonged chewing sends messages to your brain that you are becoming full and satisfied and that you will not be requiring any more food at the moment. Refined sugary foods provoke excessive insulin production, and this in turn produces strong, hunger-like pangs in your stomach, which disturbs your mental concentration and also causes you to eat more.

Incidentally, the mice not only lived longer, their brains were more resistant to neurodegenerative diseases. In the case of people – as opposed to mice – the incidence of memory problems caused by Alzheimer's disease in China and Japan, where the average calorie intake is lower but unsaturated fat intake is proportionally higher, is about half of the incidence of Alzheimer's in the United Sates and Western Europe. A longitudinal study of 980 older volunteers in New York has reproduced the connection between Alzheimer's disease and higher daily food intake. The same study also found that the incidence of other brain diseases, such as Parkinson's disease and damage from strokes, also reduce when you eat less.

If you do decide to eat less, don't go on a weight-loss diet. Yoyo dieting has deleterious effects on your mood and on thinking performance.

Does starving your brain feed your mind?

It's not as simple as that!

It's fitness that counts – not fatness. And it's what you eat less of that matters. For example, John might be a high-metabolic-rate consumer of junk food, might not be overweight and might have a body mass index (BMI) in the normal range – yet John may still be at risk of memory loss from Alzheimer's, because the total quantity of food eaten by him is not producing sufficient antioxidants to mop up all of the free radicals which are produced when his body oxidizes all the junk food he is eating. John will not have any antioxidants coming to his rescue from his junk food. The fat in John's junk food will have been converted to transfats – a form that his brain cannot utilize. All the salt in John's junk food will increase his blood pressure, risking further damage to his brain. Yet if John jumps on and off his bathroom scales every day and calculates his body mass index, he may think he's on a healthy diet.

The fact that John is not overweight will help, of course. Because he is not overweight, he will find it easier to exercise and that will help his brain. Exercise will increase the supply of blood to his brain and this will speed up his thinking. The exercise will also stimulate the production of new and replacement brain cells – particularly near his hippocampus, which is central to the working of his memory. Because John is not overweight, he is also less likely to develop diabetes or high blood pressure and so his brain is less at risk from stroke damage. While we do not advocate leaping from the frying pan of excessive eating into the fire of calorie counting diets, moving from a daily average of 2,700–3,000 calories per day of oxytoxic food, to around 1500–1800 calories per day of less oxytoxic foods will at least halve your chances of getting Alzheimer's disease.

This does seem well worth considering. If you don't do physical work, and if you don't work in cold or wet conditions, an average of 1,500–1,800 calories per day is more than sufficient for your needs. If you live or work in a country with a knowledge-based economy, most physical work will be carried out by machines, and most of the machines will be minded by computers. However, an average is just that – an average. Each individual 50+ person has to work out whereabouts in relation to that average they need to be. Whether you need to be a bit higher or a bit lower, will depend on your genes.

Is there something fishy going on?

Your brain is at least 70 per cent fat. Fats and cholesterol are the building blocks of your brain. Brain fats are not the same kinds of fat that you store in your buttocks. Brain fats perform vital functions and your brain needs a constant supply of them to maintain and repair itself. Your brain also needs to be able to clear away any excess fat very quickly.

This tricky balancing act has been studied in around 700 people living in Rotterdam in the Netherlands. The study showed that your brain prefers the kinds of polyunsaturated fatty acids found in coldwater fish, such as tuna, trout, salmon and mackerel, but your brain is damaged by saturated or transfats, because any excess saturated or transfats are very hard to clear away. Saturated or transfats are found in meat, pastries and dairy products. You can easily recognize saturated fats as they are solid at room temperature. Transfats are produced when food is cooked at very high temperatures for long periods, for example by deep frying. In deep frying, the fat is often reheated repeatedly. The industrialized production of food often increases the content of saturated or transfats. Specifically, the Dutch researchers found that a diet which is high in saturated fats increased the risk to your memory from dementia, whereas only half an ounce of fish (20 g) a day was sufficient to lower the risk to your brain. This finding was replicated in 2003, when 800 people were studied in Chicago. Even eating fish only once a week was sufficient to reduce the risk of Alzheimer's by 60 per cent.

Neither of these studies proved that it was beneficial to take fish oil supplements instead of eating the fish. Dr Tan's Framingham study, in 2003, reported that blood cholesterol levels that are high enough to damage your heart do not necessarily increase the risk to your brain from Alzehimer's. The jury is still out on cholesterol. The cholesterol story is confused because someone with a low blood cholesterol level is more likely to be the kind of person who eats fewer calories, exercises more, enjoys learning, does Sudoku and cryptic crosswords and reads books on brain training – all of which are good for your brain. When it comes to a general link between fat consumption and the brain, the jury's verdict is definitely in on four counts:

1 The less you eat, the better for your brain (down to about 1,500 calories a day if you are a sedentary brainworker).

2 The 1,500 calories you eat must include some fats.

3 The fats you eat should be unsaturated. Saturated fats are definitely bad for your heart and may be bad for your brain too.
4 Eating coldwater fish, rather than eating fish oil capsules, may be the best way to get the unsaturated fats your brain needs. (The studies showed that you only needed to eat a small quantity of fish: 20 g a day or 150 g a week.)

Memory, alcohol and other myths

It is widely believed that moderate alcohol consumption is good for your health. If we are talking about the health of your brain, this is not borne out by the brain science.

True, there is strong evidence that very light alcohol consumption, for example a 40 g measure of 11 per cent red wine per day, does benefit your heart. In so far as this reduces your risk of having a stroke, this also benefits your brain, because a stroke can cause extensive brain damage. Although brain training can greatly accelerate brain repair and recovery in stroke victims, it can be a lengthy process – taking up to 2–4 years – and it may be incomplete. It is better to reduce the risk of having the stroke in the first place.

However, drinking even only one small 40 g measure of alcohol is sufficient to delude drinkers into thinking that their mental judgement is improving, when it is, in fact, deteriorating. The immediate effect of alcohol is to depress many of your brain's functions. The longer-term effect is nutritional deficiency leading to permanent mental impairment and physical damage to your brain. Repeated exposure to alcohol damages tissue in many of your body's organs and your brain is not exempted. The more alcohol you drink, the more extensive will be the brain cell damage and the more memory problems you will have.

On the other hand, a study of 1,800 Swedish volunteers is reported to show a lowered risk of Alzheimer's in a group that drank alcohol compared with a control group that did not. The problem is that a control group of total abstainers in Sweden would likely have other stress-related lifestyle correlates that would increase their risk – so we might not be measuring the benefit of alcohol, just a risk associated with having an abstinent lifestyle. Also, the tradition in Sweden is to eat herring when drinking alcohol, so we may be measuring the benefit of eating the herring!

A study tracking 3,000 Japanese men, over a period of 18 years, showed that performance on memory tests worsened in line with increased alcohol intake. There could be a long-term beneficial effect on the brain of very light alcohol consumption, but that is not clear, whereas the short-term impairment in mental judgement, and in the speed and accuracy of calculation and thought, is very evident. Non-drinkers should not start drinking in the hope of protecting their memories in the long term. Existing drinkers might usefully cut their intake to seven units, or less, of alcohol per week, on the basis of first do no harm!

The role of physical exercise

Where possible, talking about life should supplement, not replace the muscular activity of living it.

(Simon Wootton, 2004)

It is about 2,000 years since the Roman poet Juvenal guessed that there was a connection between having a sound mind and having a sound body. By 2005, research by Dr Zaldy Tan was revealing why it is that having a fit body can help you have a fit brain.

Many benefits of having a fit body are already known – enhanced attractiveness, a more optimistic disposition and a heightened sense of well-being. Physical fitness is already known to help prevent heart disease, strokes, diabetes and osteoporosis. Connection between physical fitness and the prevention of Alzheimer's and the preservation of memory, is relatively recent. In 2003, the *American Journal of Gerontology* reported on Dr Barre's six-year study of 345 people, aged 50+, living in Sonoma. Dr Barre's study showed that increasing your physical fitness did indeed increase your mental fitness and improve your thinking skills. This confirmed a five-year study of 9,000 people, aged 50+, in 36 urban and rural communities in different provinces of Canada. This Canadian study also showed that physical exercise reduced the risk of Alzheimer's. In Japan, a seven year study of 800 people aged 50+ also showed that physical exercise not only deferred dementia but that it could improve the mental performance of people who already had dementia.

In 2005, Kramer used an MRI scanner to show that the normal rate at which the brain loses weight with age can be reduced, or even reversed, as a result of physical exercise. William Greenough at Illinois, and researchers at Pisa, studied the effects of physical training and of brain training, and discovered that each encouraged the growth of new capillaries – the tiny blood vessels that deliver blood to the cells of your brain. The blood vessels of people aged 50+ who did physical and mental exercises worked as well as those of athletes who were half their age! The brain chemical nitrous oxide – yes, the one produced during sex (see Chapters 04, 05 and 06) – scours the blood vessels, and helps protect them against clogging and keeps them dilated. The nitrous oxide scouring system was found to work as well in 63-year-olds who did the exercises as in 27-year-olds. Of course, it might be that it is the continued sexual attractiveness, not the results from being physically fit and mentally alert, that result in more sex, that result in more nitrous oxide, that result in cleaner capillaries, that result in healthier brain cells, that result in fewer diseases, that result in the better memory – but hey, take the sex – the memory of it will be a bonus!

Myers divided 65-year-olds into three otherwise matched groups that had either retired, or retired and exercised, or had continued to work. Within four years, Myers found that cerebral blood flows – a measure of the rate of supply of oxygen to the brain, and therefore of the rate at which the brain can work – had declined in the people who had retired, but had remained high in the groups that had either carried on working or who had started exercising on retirement. Why not do both? In other words, don't retire and start exercising!

Which kind of exercise is best?

Dustman divided 50+ men into three groups. For four months, one did aerobic exercise, the other did muscle body building, and a control group made no changes. Cognitive abilities were tested before and after. The scores of both the exercise groups improved over the control group – but the gain was greater for the aerobic exercisers.

Groups of 50+ women were studied for 12 months by a medical research institute in Australia. The 50+ exercisers did better on both memory tests and on tests of rapid problem solving. According to Dr Victoroff, these findings have been replicated at least five times. Arthur Smith's case study of people who did a sport showed they were 3.5 times less likely to develop Alzheimer's, and that they had less beta amyloid in their brains. Beta amyloid is very debilitating to neuron activity. In 2001, Canadian researchers who had been tracking nearly 5,000 50+ people, found a 50 per cent reduction in the incidence of Alzheimer's among the 50+ people who took exercise three times a week (or more).

This does not mean that it is impossible for a 48-year-old marathon runner to get a degenerative brain disease – of course it is possible. You can only play the percentages and improve your chances of saving your brain for longer. The longer you live, the longer you need your brain to stay fit – or your longer life will only mean a slower death.

If possible, combine physical activity with social and mental activity. If you don't fancy a swingers' weekend with members of MENSA, try joining a Ramblers group or an amateur dramatic group, or a ballroom dancing class. It is never to late to learn rock climbing.

What counts as 'vigorous' exercise?

Technically, subtract your 50+ age (whatever it is), from 220, and then take 85 per cent of your answer. Exercise till your heart rate/pulse rate, reaches that number. Ideally, do that five times a week, however briefly, but at least three times a week. This moderate regime – reaching 85 per cent, briefly, three to five times a week – seems to produce the same brain benefits as anything more 'vigorous'. Bodily fitness may be more demanding, of course. Anyone for a walk (briskly, of course)?

New tricks

When sluggish old rats are given exercise wheels, they develop more new mitochondria. Mitochondria provide power to brain cells. So you can teach old rats new tricks! Importantly for the memory, exercise seemed to regulate and reduce the production of inflammatory cytokines. Cytokines are believed to be involved in the production of Alzheimer's plaque deposits. So exercise seems both to offer increased protection of your memory and brain against degenerative disease, and, in the meantime, to increase the efficiency with which you can think and tackle mental tasks.

At the University of Irvine, scientists further divided the groups of rats into those who has an exercise wheel once a week, and other groups who had them two, three, four and seven times a week. The more the rats ran, the greater the level in their brains of BDNF, which is the protein involved in growing new neurons, especially around the hippocampus. The hippocampus plays a key role in memory creation and retrieval. Diets that are high in saturated fats lower BDNF levels, but older rats who had been fed a lifetime diet with excessive saturated fat, were able to reverse their decline in BDNF by doing exercise.

> **A tip from Dr Victoroff – get a TV treadmill!**
> If you are under the tyranny of a television, put a treadmill in front of it. Whoever is on the treadmill gets the best view of the screen!

Out-performing younger minds

Does all this reduction in brain disease, do all those billions more oxygen-rich blood cells, rushing through cleaner and more dilated blood vessels, reducing inflammation and increasing growth of new brain cells, does all this translate into brains that can actually perform any better on mental and thinking tasks? Yes, it does. Studies at universities in Ohio, Texas, Maastricht and Australia have shown that the 50+ brain becomes healthier and fitter following exercise and brain training. Average results on all cognitive tests improve. Because these are averages, there will always be exceptional sedentary cats who are still mentally brilliant, and fit butcher's dogs who are not so bright.

Exercise alone is not sufficient to determine your absolute level of cognitive capacity, because it does not improve scores on all of the necessary components of effective thinking. But one of the components that does benefit is memory. Memory does play an important role in many thinking tasks, especially those involving creative and reflective thinking, both of which get better and better as you get older, so long as you stay fit. Staying fit does not necessarily mean staying slim. Importantly and luckily, exercise and increasing physical fitness act to improve thinking components that might otherwise decline with age, i.e. the speed of new information processing, and hence of new memory formation. So there is only one age-related area of mental decline and you can reverse it if you want to – through physical and mental exercise. Alternatively, you can work around it, by using your improving predictive thinking to make an earlier start on thinking tasks. Why not do both?

How to speed up your brain

The speed of new information processing is determined by the frontal lobes of your brain – the area that you use for planning and decision making – and this is one of the areas that responds most positively when you train your body and your brain. This explains why 50+ people who do not have a regime of physical exercise, or brain training, may struggle with navigation and driving a car in complex, fast-moving traffic, in a new town, in an unfamiliar hire car. But then, so do many younger drivers. The ability to perform such tasks is measured by using CRT tests – tests of complex reaction time. Following physical and mental training, 50+ people had much better CRT scores than 24-, 25-, 26- and 27-year-old comparators.

Among nearly 7,000 UK men and women, aged 18–94, those who just occasionally walked, rather than drove/rode, had higher CRT scores than those who always preferred to ride. But a correlation is not necessarily a cause – perhaps an inclination to walk is a genetic, or socioeconomic, or lifestyle marker for other things that are the real determinants of high CRT scores. That is why a study of 222 Swedish twins, reported by Dr Victoroff, is important. Despite having identical genes, the twins that did mental or physical exercise scored higher in cognitive tests! In your 50+ years, fitness regimes greatly increase the probability that you will retain your age-related advantages for longer.

Flexible shoes – flexible brain

Check your footwear. Could you run to rescue a child from a road if you had to? Could you run for a train or a bus? Can you go quickly and safely up and down a flight of stairs? If not, next time you buy new shoes, buy something more flexible and make them your normal wear – just in case you ever fancy a walk at lunchtime, or a walk in the park with your thoughtful companion (Chapter 06).

Is 50+ IQ being enhanced, or merely restored to former levels?

It is not certain that 50+ IQ is necessarily being boosted. It is possible that lifestyle choices may have degraded mental performance of the 50+, from the teenage years onwards, and that all we are doing here is reversing degradation in performance to a genetically determined capacity that was already there. Professor Ian Deary's comparison of IQ scores at 11 and 70+ (Chapter 02), suggests that there is definite enhancement in IQ just through getting older, and that exercise and brain training can add to that, or prevent that advantage from being eroded through lifestyle behaviour or other changes in your environment.

How to make connections

- Create as many links or associations as possible, so as to increase the number of future possible access cues, thereby increasing the chances of future retrieval. Since we can only hold up to 5 ± 2 new items of information in our short-term memory, making notes and associations, and linking and mapping things together, are essential steps in memorizing more than, say, three things.

- Associations can be simple – the 'g' in stalagmite reminds you that it grows up from the ground, while the 'c' in stalactite reminds you that it comes down from the ceiling.

- Sometimes whole sentences (acrostics) can be used to recall the initial letters of a list of words needing to be remembered. The acrostic 'every good boy deserves friends' gives you the musical notes, E, G, B, D, F, while the acronym FACE gives you the musical notes F, A, C, E for the spaces. The more bizarre the association, the more memorable it will be. Adding in emotion, texture, sex and smell are particularly evocative.

- 'I can't quite place it' is another way of saying, 'I can't remember it'. Over 2,500 years ago, the Greeks propounded the idea of finding a place for things in order to aid recollection. You can use a room in your own house in which you know from memory the relative positions of all the major items of furniture. You can then imagine a giant hammer on the chest, a teddy bear burning in the fireplace, the steam iron completely filling the sofa, a football bouncing along the piano keys, a hairdryer scattering the chess pieces. As you go round your room in your mind's eye, you can recreate your shopping list of hammer, teddy bear, steam iron, football and hairdryer!

How to grow new brain cells

Physical exercise not only results in a stronger flow of blood, glucose and oxygen to the brain, it also stimulates the growth of new brain cells, especially in and around your hippocampus, which plays a key role in your memory.

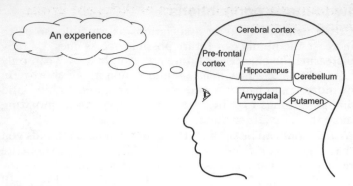

Figure 3.1

Yes, you do have a photographic memory

It is so good that you can't turn it off – even after two and a half mind-numbing days of looking at over 10,000 boring photographs, many of them similar to each other.

In May 2007, Professor Richard Wiseman took over the ground floor of Waterstones in London to expose people to up to 10,000 photographs and slides and then show them that they had remembered them (even though they denied it!). Recall rates ranged from 15 out of 16, after looking at 800 photographs for about 1 second each, to recognizing 86 out of 130 photographs after viewing over 9,200 photographs up to 3 days earlier. (The results replicated a similar study 30 years ago in Canada, when subjects also scored 98 per cent and 70 per cent, in equivalent tests of their photographic memories.)

MRI scans showing benefits of different brain training activities

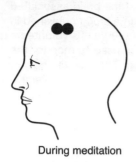

During meditation

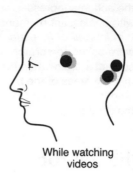

While watching videos

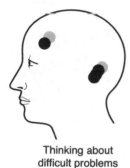

Thinking about difficult problems

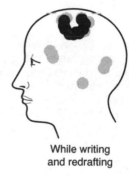

While writing and redrafting

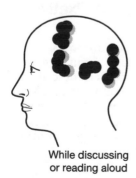

While discussing or reading aloud

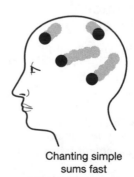

Chanting simple sums fast

Figure 3.2 Based on research by Professor Kawashima (2007); his electronic exercises are available from Nintendo

Scratching the elephant in the room!

Images of the brain's response to scratching have revealed that the action suppresses activity in regions of the brain associated with unpleasant memories and emotions. In a study published in the *Journal of Investigative Dermatology* (2008), 13 volunteers were asked to scratch their legs. MRI was used to monitor the subject's brain while they were scratching. The results showed that the areas of the brain associated with unpleasant or aversive emotions and memories became significantly less active during the scratching.

The neurochemistry of memory

Pass the parcel – a relay race down memory lane

The memory messages from your hippocampus travel through your brain's neural network rather like a baton travels in a relay race.

In 2000, Eric Kandel was awarded a Nobel Prize for his work on the Californian sea slug. Kandel's work on the sea slug helped to explain how the baton is passed down your neural memory lane. His work confirmed the central role played by sodium ions, which we encountered in Susan Greenfield's work (see 'First thoughts'). The sodium ions help to transfer the charge along the length of each of your neurons. At the end of the neuron's axon, the baton is picked up by neurotransmitter chemicals which then swim across a synaptic gap to the dendrites on your next neuron.

Emotional molecules – the 'chemical fixatives' of memory

Your hippocampus receives messages from all areas of your brain, in particular from your amygdala. Your amygdala controls the production of what Candice Pert described as 'molecules of emotion' (Chapter 01). These emotional molecules seem to play an important role as 'chemical fixatives' of memory. These chemical fixatives help you to 'burn' learning into your memory. Hence the importance of emotional engagement when you are learning new things.

Flashbacks, emotional trauma and 'chemical fixatives'

When strong emotions, like joy, horror or disgust are associated with a memory, this causes a cocktail of chemicals, such as norepinephrine, adrenaline, enkephalin and vasopressin, to be released into your brain. Hooper and Teresi suggested that this cocktail of chemicals has the same effect as spraying varnish onto a chalk pastel painting. It stabilizes the picture, or the pattern, and reduces the risk of it getting smudged or distorted. The stronger the emotion, the easier it is for you to remember the incident later. Both Thayer and Maguire identified that each emotional state had its own library of memories. When experiencing pride in a success, for example, you may well recall a previous success. When expressing anger or resentment, you are more likely to dredge up earlier resentments which may not have been expressed at the time. It's a bit like collecting trading stamps of similar emotions you have saved up over your 50+ years and then cashing in 50+ years' worth of emotional trading stamps all at once.

Does cell loss necessarily mean memory loss?

No. This is because information is stored in the brain in many fragments, widely distributed around different areas of the brain. (This is why exercises involving your memory are so good for brain development). Even if there happens to be the odd cell missing on the neural route to a particular fragment, a diversionary route can usually be found. Even if one of the fragments cannot be located, the brain can generally join up the dots and recover the original memory.

Also, your brain does not shed cells dramatically as you age. The greatest loss of brain cells occurs in childhood. After that, even though your brain shrinks by up to 10 per cent by the time you die, this has recently been found to be largely because your individual cells shrink, not because your brain cells are lost. Cells can be lost through illness, or through drinking alcohol, which can kill up to 60,000 brain cells a day.

Even then it is not all bad news. Firstly, it is the number of connections in your brain, not the number of neurons in your brain, that determines your cognitive capacity. You can add daily to the number of connections you have in your brain through learning and brain training. Secondly, it has recently been discovered that your brain can continue to produce new neurons up until you die. Your hippocampus routinely produces new neurons. This has led to speculation that the new neurons might be needed for new memories. This adds to the importance of physical and mental exercise, because exercise has been shown to accelerate the production of new neurons near to the hippocampus. The carbon dating of brain cells in people who have died, shows that there are many cells that must have been added after their date of birth. As long as you avoid illness and keep your brain fit and well connected, senile decay is not inevitable.

Long-term v. short-term memory

In Australia, Clarke Raymond stuck electrodes into either end of slices of a hippocampus, and recorded the residual voltages in the receiving neurons. When he gave the hippocampus neurons a single charge, the residual voltages in receiving neurons rose slightly. But the effect did not last. The receiving neuron 'forgot' its recent experience. If Raymond repeated the stimulation – another ten times, say – a higher residual voltage was found in the receiving neurons. This time the effect lasted for weeks. In August 2005, the journal *Science* reported that Jonathan Whitlock had replicated Clarke Raymond's findings using the hippocampus of a living brain.

In the case of the short-term memory effect, the molecules of the receptor chemicals were modified by the stimulus. The memory faded because modified molecules were slowly replaced with unmodified molecules. In the case of the long-term memory effect, the repeated stimulus not only modified the molecules of the receptor chemicals, it also increased the number of receptor sites, and so made new synapses available to support further learning and extra cognitive capacity.

Alzheimer's disease

What is Alzheimer's disease?

Alzheimer's disease is the most common cause of memory loss and generalized dementia. Dementia is the term used to describe loss of cognitive capacity in the brain. Alzheimer's progressively impairs memory, and then the ability to concentrate, and then the ability to reason. Eventually, Alzheimer's affects verbal thinking and speech, and then emotional thinking and finally physical mobility. But fortunately, or unfortunately, you may not die quickly. Even with such severe Alzheimer's symptoms, it could take years of debility and disability before death does finally bring, perhaps, some kind of relief. It may be it is unwise of governments and individuals to prioritize body shape and body weight or even body fitness, over the fitness of your brain!

Who gets Alzheimer's?

Currently, in the UK, one in six people over 80 years of age have Alzheimer's disease, but if you are 50+ that does not mean that you have a one in six chance of getting it in the next 30 years. You can greatly reduce those odds by following the advice in Part One of this book. Also, by doing the kinds of sequences of brain training exercises that we have designed and collected together in the brain circuits in Part Two of the book, you can greatly increase the spare cognitive capacity of your brain, so that, like David Snowden's nuns, even if you do contract Alzheimer's disease, you may still have enough residual cognitive capacity to support your memory and your mind at the enhanced levels to which you will already have become accustomed at 50+.

The causes of Alzheimer's disease

Some people's genetic make up can give them a pre-disposition to develop Alzheimer's, but lifestyle choices play a big part in whether or not this predisposition is ever manifested. Smoking, high blood pressure, head injuries, for example, can each raise the risk of manifestation. So does dieting, so ditch the diet and favour foods with a low oxytoxic index (Chapter 04 and Appendix H).

Fitness matters more that fatness, as far as the brain is concerned. That is *not* to say that fatness is harmless. It isn't. Fatness competes for the oxygen supply that your brain needs. It's just that the effect of serial dieting in lowering thinking performance and increasing cortisol levels and the risk of neurodegenerative disease is far worse, especially as 90 per cent of people who diet regain the weight they lose within two years anyway. By contrast, 70 per cent of people who protect their brains by eating the low oxytoxic foods which we have tabled in Appendix H, report losing weight and the weight stays off. People eating low oxytoxic foods tend to have a BMI which is very stable and at the bottom end of the 'normal' BMI range in Western countries.

The symptoms of Alzheimer's disease

The symptoms of Alzheimer's include: putting things in strange places; failing to recognize people or places; cooking the same meal twice over; difficulty finding the right words; using a wrong or inappropriate word; dressing inappropriately for an occasion or time of year; feeling agitated or irritable; and also repeating the same conversation with the same person, just a few minutes later.

Alzheimer's disease – six ways to stave it off

1 **There's a word for it!** A 2007 US study showed that doing cryptic crosswords (Part Two) or playing games like Scrabble, Adverbs, Password or the Association Game (Chapter 06), slowed down production of the protein found in Alzheimer's plaques.

2 **Chill out:** Research done in California in 2006 showed that excessive stress increases Alzheimer's risk.

3 **De-saturate your fats:** According to Dutch research in 2007, saturated fats in biscuits, cakes, pastries, hard cheese and butter, increase the risk of Alzheimer's.

4 **Move it!** A Seattle study in 2008 reported that just three 15-minute exercise sessions a week reduce your Alzheimer's risk by 40 per cent.

5 **Lose the booze:** Limiting alcohol to seven glasses (40 g) of wine or seven measures of spirits per week, greatly reduces Alzheimer's risk.

6 **Stub it out:** The London Institute of Psychiatry says that smoking increases your risk of Alzheimer's by four times.

The treatment of Alzheimer's disease

The rate of Alzheimer's advance, or of corresponding cognitive decline, can be slowed. Some of the effects can be treated. For example, the depression often associated with Alzheimer's can be treated with anti-depressants, and irritable behaviour and violence can be sedated.

Alzheimer's disease – seven natural ways to sharpen up

1 **Omega 3:** In January 2008, the UK edition of *Health* pointed to the *Journal of Neuroscience* finding that Omega 3 fats helped to break up plaques.

2 **Glutamine:** Patrick Halford has found that L-Glutamine boosts memory and learning

3 **Sex and dark chocolate:** These raise dopamine and norepinephrine in the brain. This raises mood and performance.

4 **Vitamin B:** Vitamin B complex reduces the level of homocysteine in your blood. High homocysteine levels are associated with lower performance on thinking tasks.

5 **Acetylcarnitine:** This replaces missing acetylcholine. Your brain needs acetylcholine to transmitt the neural messages that are used to collect up and piece together the fragments of your memories.

6 **Ginkgo biloba:** Ginko biloba boosts blood flow and this, according to the Brain Research Institute, slows the spread of Alzheimer's disease.

7 **Gotu kola:** This relieves memory problems and mental fatigue when these are caused by or exacerbated by stress.

At 50+, things that only you might remember

1 The first Dansette multi-change record players

2 Half-timbered cars, like the Morris Minor Traveller

3 Bubble cars like the Reliant or the Fiat 500

4 Toys that you wound up with a key (no batteries)

5 Televisions… with wooden doors that hid the screens

6 Meccano sets and Box Brownie cameras

7 When a joint was something you ate for Sunday lunch

Memory – ten top tips

Tip 01: Picture it

Take exactly two minutes to memorize as many as possible of the 30 words in the table. Then cover the words and write as many of them as you can remember in two minutes in the box labelled 'before visualization'. Note your score.

Story	Midday	Slice	Tube	Corner	Fruit
Tiger	Folder	Ceramic	Extract	Thought	Music
Dew	Office	Point	Shop	Watch	Life
Sister	Cardboard	Relax	Honey	Colour	Braces
Brain	Rain	Hole	Puzzle	Magic	Secure

Before visualization

Score

Re-read the original list and create an image in your head associated with each word – an image as large, as colourful, as weird as possible. Connect that image with an equally colourful image of another word, until all the words are interlinked into a story, or a grand collage or picture. Imagine it hanging on a wall near where you are. Again cover the words, and this time, fill in the box below, again taking two minutes.

After visualization

Score

Note how much better your score is.

Tip 02: Count on your memory

- Count aloud to 99 in threes as fast as you can. Note the time you take. Note how you get faster every successive day you do it. When your time stabilizes, start the exercise again, only this time count backwards from 99 to zero.
- Count in fives as quickly as you can while cleaning your teeth with your wrong hand. Notice how much further you can get in successive days.
- Repeat while moving your eyes back and forth from extreme left to extreme right.
- Once a week, count aloud from 1–130, as fast as you can. Notice how much faster you get each week. This uses both sides of your pre-frontal cortex.

Tip 03: Put a name to it

'I can remember your face, but I just can't place...'

People are irrationally offended, or delighted, by whether or not you forget or remember their names. The names – the words, especially if foreign – are hard to remember, because they are only letters, devoid of meaning, or of any associations that could be placed in your brain to be picked up later as cues. You must repeat the name out loud. Check the spelling. If it is a foreign name ask what it means, and if appropriate, ask why their parents chose it, etc. The more you talk about it and repeat it, the more likely you are to find a way to associate it with a feature in their face.

If you have forgotten a name, you've forgotten a name. It's not surprising and you just need to admit it. You will probably find they have forgotten yours and you will both be grateful for a second chance to swap names. Because you will associate their name with the embarrassment of forgetting it and having to ask a second time, you will be less likely to forget it a second time.

Tip 04: PIN it down

'The number of times I have forgotten...'

Numbers are hard to PIN down because they are even more devoid of meaning than letters and words.

You have to create a meaning, a strong visual meaning.

For example, one (1) might be a mast or a tower near your home or work; two (2) a pair of white swans on black, still water; three (3), her moist pink lips; four (4), a white sailing yacht on blue water against the green edge of a seaweed-smelling coastline, and so on. Whatever works for you. You can then connect these images in a daft story to make a sequence, or place them with the objects on your memory walk (look at 'A walk down memory lane' below).

If numbers have more than three digits, they may exceed your cognitive limits, i.e. 5 ± 2. The first task is to 'chunk' them – to break them up into groups. Get into the habit of reading numbers like 9922196833369 as, say, 99, 22, 1968, 333 and 69. Read them aloud to add sound and rhythm to what you are trying to remember. The next task is to make each chunk personally meaningful. For example, 99 might be a parent's age – picture the parent as you say 99 aloud; 22 might be the number of a house – visualize the door with the number on it as you say 22, etc. Now imagine your 99-year-old parent going into the doorway of the house numbered 22. Perhaps 1968 was the year of a famous sporting event – picture it taking place on the television inside the house numbered 22, and already you can remember 99221968. Continue the process, by associating 333 and then 69 with people, addresses, historic dates, birthdays etc. and then connect all these images together in a story or sequence, adding movement, colour, sound, smells and tastes wherever possible.

Tip 05: Learn the lingo

Joining a language conversation class ticks many brain training boxes. Learning second languages involves social and emotional intelligence (Chapter 06), as well as recollective thinking, speaking aloud and much useful repetition. Learning a second language also involves a different part of your brain from the part that you use to speak your first language. It develops some of the parts you also need for mathematics and for music. This results in a lot of 'neural' traffic back and forth between the amygdala region and the pre-frontal cortex. This is very good for synaptic growth generally and for myelination.

Tip 06: Spell it out

Obtain a list of the 100 most commonly misspelt words in your language. At 50+, you can probably spell a lot of them already. If so, generate your own list. Stick it up in the toilet and learn one a day. Cumulatively recite the spellings of the ones you have already learned. After 100 days, make a new list, for example 100 words that describe emotions. Important as it is to spell accurately, it is the practice of memorizing – even a word a day – that is as important as what you memorize.

Your verbal thinking (Chapter 06) is limited by your vocabulary, so it is a good idea to expand it. A word a day = 1,000 new words after 3 years. To put the value of that extra 1,000 words into perspective, some daily newspapers can be read with a vocabulary of 100 words (Chapter 06)!

Tip 07: Get a whiff of that

Get a book and find a paragraph you would like to remember. Then:

1 Inhale a favourite scent (e.g. sage, lavender, basil).
2 Underline the key words.
3 Give the paragraph a subtitle, like you would see in a newspaper.
4 Read the paragraph aloud, as if you were a newsreader – stand up and give it the same drama and emphasis.
5 Write out all you can remember, sounding out the words as you go.
6 Next day, inhale the same smell and write out the paragraph again.

Tip 08: Map it out

When constructing a shopping list, group like things together, for example vegetables/fruit, tins, chilled, dairy, sweet, frozen, hardware. Put the groups in the order in which they appear in the store.

Tip 09: Dont forget it

Remember that to forget is normal and healthy. It is your healthy default to forget, unless you deliberately decide to remember. To give yourself a fighting chance to not forget, put your car keys, or door keys, on top of what you must remember to take with you. Put your watch on the other hand to remind you.

N.B. Make a note of it

> 'The horror of the moment', the king went on, 'I shall never, never forget'.

> 'You will,' the Queen said, 'if you don't make a memorandum of it.'

> (Carroll, 1865)

Always make notes. Take a pad, or ask for a page from someone else when you need one. Map what is being said. Three chunks of three. Most people can remember three new things.

Tip 10: Take a walk

Go for a walk that you can reliably reproduce in your head. As you go round your walk, identify, say, 27 distinctive objects on your way from A to B. Be sure that you can see, or imagine, each object clearly as you retrace the walk in your head. Then associate each object with something you want to remember, for example a point in a presentation, speech, exam question, sales pitch or job application. The crazier, more bizarre, more emotional, or sexier the association you make between the object on your walk and the point you are remembering from your walk, the better. You will then be able to recall your points in any order or even amaze your audience by telling them what points you are skipping over, so as to finish on time. You can, of course, remind them in reverse order of the 27 points (3 groups of 3 groups of 3 points = 27 points) you have just covered. (What a speaker, and without notes!)

Winston's rule of three

*If you have a point to make don't try to be subtle –
  use a pile driver:
Hit the point once;
Then come back and hit it again;
Then hit it a third time – this time with a
  tremendous whack.'*

(Winston Churchill aged 80)

Eight steps to a better memory

1. Novelty

Every year, pick a novel topic, skill, craft or country, as foreign to your previous life or experience as possible. Research the possibilities. Select one and aim to get to the bottom of it, within the year.

2. Imagine

Go for a mental walk every day – somewhere familiar. Report, in detail on everything that you can see in your mind's eye. Count things as you go, for example 'tree number'. Describe the details out loud as you take your mental walk. Preferably, describe what you see to a partner. Do mental arithmetic by visualizing yourself doing it on paper or on a whiteboard. Learn lists of words by imagining a vivid image which you can associate with each word. Imagine odd connections between one image and the next.

3. Make a slide show

Practise trying to turn what you read in a book or magazine or on the internet into a slide show – a sequence of images that are interconnected in your mind. Hear yourself giving a talk to accompany the slide show. Afterwards, recall what you have read as best you can. Your visual memory will back up your verbal memory and will eventually become a faster, more comprehensive way for you to remember things.

4. Be a poet and know it!

When words rhyme, they are easier to learn, for example: one is a John, a con, etc. (whatever is easiest for you), two is a shoe, three is a tree, four is a door, five is a hive, six is sticks, seven is heaven, eight is a gate, nine is a mine, ten is a hen.

Make sure you learn your rhyme off by heart. Then whenever you want to remember ten names, ten items, ten points for a speech, you can link an image for each of your points to the image of your number. The more absurd the images and their juxtaposition, the easier they will be to recall – especially if they evoke a strong emotion like disgust, or argument, or laughter, or sex. Neurons that fire together – wire together.

5. Add sensation

In addition to visual images, smells, sounds, emotions, touches and tastes can also be used as effective associations with the thing you want to remember. Try adding a sound, or smell, or feeling to your visual images and so double your chances of locating a retrieval clue when you are next searching for the item you have remembered. Most 50+ people find visual or auditory clues the easiest to think of and use. It is more difficult to associate smells with items to be remembered, but if you can, smells can be deeply evocative.

Examples of sounds might be imagining the grunts of a sweaty weightlifter lifting a ton for item one; the sound of heels clicking, echoing down a hallway for a shoe (smelly?) for two; trees for threes, rustle or creek; four is a door – hear it once more; the buzz or a drone goes live with the hive for five; sticks for six can crackle and hiss and spit on a fire (can you smell the smoke?); seven is heaven (can you hear the choir singing?); eight is a gate so creaky it needs oil (the smell of WD40?); nine is a mine so hear the explosion, or the noise of drills; ten is hen, a fat clucking hen, or a crowing cock. The more neurons that are firing, in more places in your brain, at the time you remember, the easier your subsequent recall will be. Remember, neurons that fire together – wire together.

6. Question, list and link

When trying to remember something you have read, for a subsequent meeting or presentation:

- Decide on the **questions** it is trying to answer. (A handy checklist of possible questions is 'who?' (has done, needs to do), 'what?', 'when?', 'how?' and 'why?').
- **List** the answers to the questions as bullet points. Group the bullet points, three to a group.
- Number the bullet points and **link** your image of the number to an image you can associate with the bullet point.

7. Mix it to max it

What does not quite kill us makes us stronger – or so Nietzche tried to reassure us. Multi-layered, multi-faceted, multi-topic, multi-recall memorization does not quite kill us, but it does take longer, and therefore it does stick stronger. The more arduous the process of memorization, the stronger the memory. A quick cram the night before an exam is gone the day after. What a waste. A waste not only of the value there might have been in the topics that you revised, but what a wasted opportunity to extend and strengthen the neural structure of your brain.

At 50+, if you can enrol for a few night classes, or weekend courses, do not choose closely complementary or mutually supportive modules. Instead, go for chalk and cheese contrast, for example chemistry, computing and conversational French. Have several books on the go at once. Progress will be slower and more torturous, but much more beneficial in the long run. The more of your neurons that are active at the time you are trying to memorize something, the better. As Professor Ian Robertson says, 'neurons that fire together, wire together'. That is why you are more likely to remember something if there is a lot else going on – for example, if you are moving, smelling and listening or having strong feelings about what is happening. That is why some memories are so vivid that they can be a problem – vivid flashbacks of emotionally exhilarating or devastating events can play havoc with your attempts to concentrate on the thinking task in hand.

8. The churning is the learning

The important thing about memory games is the taking part. Even if at first you don't succeed, eventually you will make 'head' way! It is the very act of trying that produces the development. All your attempts to run and re-run your neuron pathways – trying to find your memory fragments – that's what thickens the myelin insulation around the axons of your neurons. That is what is going to make your subsequent storage and retrieval of memories quicker and less prone to interference and error. The more mistakes you make – the more false starts – the more restarts and re-runs, the stronger your memory will become.

N.B. Because each of the eight steps above are multi-faceted and intentionally complex, just pick one technique and practise it until you have mastered it – or have become bored with it. Then pick another, until you have mastered all eight.

The effect of stress chemicals on memory

In 1994, the *Journal of Neuroscience* reported that 19 adult volunteers had been given a stress chemical, glucocorticoid, or a placebo, for four consecutive days. The volunteers listened to a tape and were asked to recollect what they had heard. The placebo group found this easier and easier on successive days, consistent with the idea of neuromodulation (see 'First thoughts'), whereas the recollections of the group receiving the stress chemical deteriorated significantly. Worryingly, none of the stressed group seemed aware of the deterioration in their mental performance, even though observers had very quickly noticed considerable and rapid deterioration in their memories, even under low levels of stress! If you think your memory may sometimes be made worse by excessive stress, read Chapter 05 in *Teach Yourself Training Your Brain*, Horne and Wootton (2007).

Protecting your brain from disease

1. Learning

It is never too late to learn. It does not seem to matter so much what as how. Learning in pairs is especially good for your brain.

2. Brain training

Brain training exercises have been shown to be effective, however late they are started. Some of the exercises in the 14 brain circuits in Part Two of this book specifically target memory. There are more specific memory workouts in the recommended readings (Dr Tan and Professor Robertson). Nintendo DS by Dr Kawashima works if you keep doing it.

3. Physically activity

You literally need to win hearts to win minds! The health of your memory will be limited by the health of your heart. If it doesn't pump hard enough, your brain will be short of oxygen and mental energy. If it pumps at too high a blood pressure, you risk damaging your brain. By warding off depression and raising self-esteem, self-confidence and optimism, physical activity improves thinking and promotes growth of brain cells

4. Ditch the diet – eat less oxytoxic food

Ditch diets that deprive your brain of the unsaturated fats it needs. Select foods with a low oxytoxic index (Appendix H) and choose foods that mop up random free radicals that you might still produce (Appendix I).

5. Pop some pills?

Check with your doctor, pharmacist or health worker, the advisability of supplementary Vitamin E, Vitamin D, Vitamins B6 and B12, folic acid and the minerals zinc and selenium. If you have significant memory loss symptoms already, or if you have a family history of severe forgetfulness in old age, ask about statins, ibuprofen and homocysteine **now**.

6. Improve to protect

Many of the memory improvement techniques also have a role in protecting the brain. They encourage myelination and create reserves of cognitive capacity that act as a buffer.

7. Kill the stress, before it kills you

The impact of stress becomes more detrimental as you get older. Your brain reacts to perceived threats, or stress, by inducing your adrenal glands, next to your kidneys, to release cortisol, which in turn increases blood sugar, breaks down proteins and releases fat. This is great for an immediate fight or flight situation, but if it is persistent, it destroys your brain. Stress is manageable, but unmanaged can lead to depression. Depression greatly impairs thinking and is much harder to treat. Depression is not the same as psychological sadness, or grief, or feeling a bit down. It is a brain chemical imbalance and you may need to see your doctor for a treatment to restore that balance. Not only can depression make it hard for you to concentrate on thinking tasks, it can shrink your hippocampus and affect your memory. At 50+, it can precipitate dementia. Selective Serotonin Reuptake Inhibitors (SSRI) treatments often stimulate the production of new brain cells, though their effectiveness in lifting depression may be a placebo effect. Talking helps.

8. Seek treatment

If you, or more usually someone else, suspects that you are already showing symptoms of Alzheimer's, you can get the symptoms treated. There are treatments that slow, or temporarily arrest, the spread of the disease. There is no present certain cure – but many possible cures are on the horizon, so it is well worth trying to hold your situation in the meantime. You could consider volunteering to take part in a current medical trial.

Ask about Aricept™, Exelon™ and Reminyl™ , which are acetylcholinesterase inhibitors. These can improve memory and performance on other thinking tasks, even if you don't already have Alzheimer's. In general, they can restore your level of performance to what is was about a year before you commenced treatment. That is why it is so important to act quickly, before your performance drops significantly. In 2004, the Food and Drug Administration in the US approved Memantine for treatment of Alzheimer's that is already well advanced. Memantine has been in widespread use in Europe for at least 13 years. Memantine works by blocking the dendrite receptors that would otherwise over-stimulate the movement of calcium ions in your neurons. Excess calcium kills neurons. Ask also about Cerebrolysin, which is widely used in China, and also about the trial result for Ginkgo biloba, if you would prefer herbal treatment.

In short...

We have evidence from the nun's study, from studies of occupation and mental activity, and from the neurochemistry of the brain, that brain training not only improves your memory, but that training your brain improves your brain's capacity to resist and reverse the effects of disease, and increases the power of your brain to support more effective applied thinking and more intelligent behaviour. Time to train your brain, so... turn to one of the brain circuits in Part Two. Why not start with Circuit 01?

Here is the answer to the Sudoku puzzle from earlier in this chapter (page 79):

6	2	8	3	9	1	7	5	4
4	1	9	7	5	6	2	3	8
3	5	7	8	4	2	9	6	1
5	6	2	1	7	3	4	8	9
7	4	3	5	8	9	6	1	2
9	8	1	6	2	4	5	7	3
2	3	5	4	1	7	8	9	6
1	7	4	9	6	8	3	2	5
8	9	6	2	3	5	1	4	7

Summary

- Forgetting is normal and necessary. When you need to remember, take deliberate steps to counter your normal mechanisms, which are designed to make you forget things.
- Effective strategies for countering forgetfulness exist and can be learned.
- Loss of long-term memory is not an inevitable consequence of getting older. Long-term memory normally improves with age.
- Memory loss can be caused by diseases, like Alzheimer's.
- Your risk of contracting Alzheimer's can be drastically reduced.
- Even if you do contract Alzheimer's, there are strategies and treatments for slowing down the effects or for avoiding them altogether.

- Memorizing new things stimulates new neuron growth and forges new synaptic connections. Memorizing things involves repetition, which strengthens myelination. Memorizing things develops spare cognitive capacity. Having spare cognitive capacity helps you to protect your ability to think, as well as to remember, should you contract a disease like Alzheimer's.

Glossary

Alzheimer's disease – is commonly characterized by progressive loss of cognitive functions, often termed dementia.

Dementia – is a decline in cognitive function due to disease, not ageing.

Amygdala – are almond-shaped groups of neurons located deep within the medial temporal lobes of the brain. They perform a primary role in the processing and memory of emotional reactions.

Suggested further reading

Barnes, D. (2003) 'Fitness and cognitive function in older adults', *American Gerontology*, 51, pp458–66.

Cotman, W. (2002) 'Exercise, brain health and plasticity', *Trends in Neuroscience*, 25, pp294–302.

Dumas, S. (2000) 'Neuron plasticity during mood disorders', *Biological Psychiatry*, 48, p731–40.

Evans, D. A. (2003) 'Fish consumption and Alzheimer's disease', *Archives of Neurology*, 60, p939–47.

Finkel, E. (2007) *Stem Cells and the Labyrinth of Memory*, Cosmos.

Fratoglioni, L. (2002) 'Alcohol and dementia', *Clinical Epidemiology*, 55, pp958–65.

Gedo, M. (1999) 'Depression not age shrinks the hippocampus', *Journal of Neuroscience*, 19, pp5033–44.

Hultch, D. (1998) *Memory Change with Age*, CUP.

Joseph, C. (2002) 'Drinking and cognitive performance', *American Journal of Public Health*, 90, pp1253–60.

Kalmijn, S. (1997) 'Dietary fats and dementia', *Neurology*, 42, p775–83.

Kawashima, R. (2007) *Train Your Brain*, Penguin.

113
the superior memory
of the 50+ brain

03

Logan, A. (2006) *Nutrition, Mental Health and Intelligence*, Camberland.

Mattson, M. (2002) *Diet–Brain Connections – impacts on memory, mood and disease*, Kluwer.

McKay, R. and Cameron, H. A. (1999) 'Restoring the production of hippocampal neurons in old age', *Nature Neuroscience*, 2, pp894–97.

More, A. (1999) 'Stress, age and oxidative damage', *Neurochemical Research*, 14, pp11478–98.

Otten, L. (2006) 'Brain activity predicting recollection', *Nature Neuro Science*, 90, pp488–92.

Robertson, I. (2005) *Mind Doctor*, Vermilion.

Rupp, R. (1998) *Committed to Memory*, Aurum Press Limited.

Tan, Z. S. (2006) *Preventing Memory Loss*, Warner.

Victoroff, J. (2003) *Protect Yourself Against Alzheimer's*, Bantham.

Wiseman, J. (2007) *Quirkology*, Macmillan.

Yosipovitch, G. and Carstens, E. (2008) 'Report from the 4th International Workshop for the Study of Itch', *Investigative Dermatology*, 128, pp256–57.

Zaldy, T. (2005) *Delay and Prevent Memory Loss*, Warner.

04

oxytoxic food and mental fitness

In this chapter you will learn:

- to eat food your brain needs, when it needs it
- to convert food into nutrients that your brain needs in order to think clearly, quickly and creatively
- to minimize damage caused by alcohol, tea, coffee, cannabis, cola, ticks and dieting and to avoid 'oxytoxic' foods that increase the risk of brain diseases like Alzheimer's
- to use sleep, exercise, smart drugs, dark chocolate and sex to rejuvenate your brain.

The state of your brain is as much a lifestyle choice, as a genetic inheritance. (Horne, 2003)

Introduction

Thinking is a chemical process. How well your 50+ brain thinks, depends on how well those chemical processes work. The chemical processes in your 50+ brain are affected by the presence in your brain of water, acids and other trace chemicals. You can affect the chemical conditions in your brain by the things that you do, the things that you eat and the way that you feel. Chapter 01 looked at what you can do about the way that you feel. This chapter will look at the effect on the brain chemistry of the 50+ brain of the things you choose to do, and the things you choose to eat. The chemical conditions in your brain are largely down to lifestyle choices that you can make. You can choose to create conditions in your 50+ brain that favour high-performance thinking and intelligent action, or you can do and eat things that greatly increase the risk of brain diseases and dementia.

Your brain can change in response to the way you exercise and the way you breathe. It can also change in response to what you eat and drink and smoke. It is changed by what you do, and by what you don't do, in and out of the bedroom. Your brain can change in response to your lifestyle. Your brain is able to adapt because, according to Colin Blakemore (CEO, UK Medical Research Council), your brain is not only a chemical factory, it is an extremely busy chemical factory. Your brain needs energy for more than one million chemical reactions every second!

The chemistry of your brain can be changed by what you do with it – hence, in Part Two of this book, there are exercises for you to do and problems for you to solve.

Sharper synapses at 60 – a six-point summary

1. Nutrition

Omega 3 fatty acids, found in oily fish such as smoked mackerel, sardines, salmon and tuna, will improve your cognitive ability, as long as you maintain a balance between Omega 3, 6 and 9. B vitamins are important and they can be found in Marmite.

Complex carbohydrates can be found in fruit, vegetable, salad and wholemeal grains. Complex carbohydrates not only fuel mental energy, they release mood-enhancing chemicals, like serotonin, that raise mood, optimism and hence performance on mental tasks (Chapter 01). Fat-free diets destroy memory and kill your brain cells, and serial dieting does your head in. We suggest you 'ditch the diet', and eat as much as you need of low oxytoxic food (see Appendix H). Saturated fats, such as those found in crisps and biscuits, will increase your risk of dementia. Blueberries, strawberries and spinach are rich in flavenoids which will help protect your brain from attack by free radicals – but dark chocolate (must be dark) has ten times more flavenoids than all of them put together (Appendix I)! Your brain is 80 per cent water – so things that dehydrate it, like alcohol, salt, strong tea, cola and coffee are bad news. Drink two to four pints a day of preferably plain water, or weak tea – preferably fruit or herbal.

2. Exercise

Walking, jogging or cycling improve the supply to your brain of the oxygen that it needs to oxidize your food, thereby fuelling the chemical reactions that need to take place when you think. Exercise also stimulates the production of new or replacement brain cells, especially round the hippocampus – an area crucial to memory, especially in the brains of the 50+ (Chapter 03). Exercise also helps to protect the brain against the cortisol derivatives produced by excessive stress. Don't yoyo exercise, i.e. don't join a gym unless you intend to use it for life. Paul Williams studied 23,000 exercisers. His report, in *Science of Exercise*, (Feb. 2008), showed that if you stop working out your metabolic rate will fall to lower than before you started. Your thinking will slow and your waist will grow bigger than before you started.

3. Relaxation

Breathe in counting five; hold your breath counting five; breathe out counting five. You feel better already! That's because you have just relaxed your body and boosted your brain. Yoga, meditation and breathing exercises rejuvenate your brain by reversing the effects of stress-induced cortisol which can cause neuron damage, cell death, depression and memory loss, especially in the 50+ brain. Lowered mood and lowered optimism reduce performance in mental tasks (Chapter 01).

A study at Boston University has identified breathing exercises that can restore and even increase the levels of Gamma Amino Butyric Acid (GABA) in your 50+ brain, thereby restoring or elevating its performance. A 2005 study in Massachusetts found that meditation exercises will thicken the pre-frontal lobes of your cerebral cortex. Cortical thinning, which has contributed historically to a slowing down in the speeds of new memory formation in the 50+ brain, can now be reversed (see later for details of the exercises).

4. Sleep

People who claim to sleep like babies have never had one.
(Les Burke)

Find out how much you need. At 50+, you need less sleep than when you were younger – but maybe not as little as you think. Shortage of sleep, or disturbed patterns of sleep, produces a dramatic deterioration in performance on thinking tasks. The time it takes you to restore your performance to normal levels also increases from 50+ onwards. Power naps do help but you need deep sleep to rest your 50+ brain and to aid long-term memory (Chapter 03). You also need shallow dream time sleep (REM sleep) to help you make sense of new information.

5. Sex

During four of the seven stages of sex, from arousal to afterglow, the chemicals released in your brain favour better thinking. In women who have orgasms, sex may boost the number of neurons in their brains.

6. Thinking skills

Appendices A–F at the back of this book show that the three pillars of effective applied thinking are critical thinking, creative thinking and reflective thinking, and that these are supported, in turn, by skills in predictive, ethical, verbal, emotional, recollective, visual and numerical thinking.

All these thinking skills, like any skill, profit from repetitive practice. One way to practise them is to keep learning new things – what you learn does not seem to matter as long as the learning involves using new combinations of thinking skills. If the learning involves lots of repetition, like juggling, ballroom dancing, skiing, mountaineering, playing a musical instrument or speaking a foreign language, so much the better. In 2004, older people in Toronto were found to have faster mental reflexes and longer concentration spans after they learned another language.

Another way to practise your thinking skills is to do (much as you would in a gymnasium) brain training exercises that work each area of your brain. Such brain 'circuits' need to be graded and systematic and to be based on the most up-to-date models of what happens chemically in your brain when it thinks. Part Two of this book contains 14 different brain circuits, each graded so that you can experience the gain in your brain as you work your way through them, at your own pace.

Food for thought

Under normal circumstances, the brain uses mainly glucose for energy. The glucose is oxidized to produce water, carbon dioxide and energy – enough to fuel a million chemical reactions a second! Neurons, and the sheaths surrounding their axons, need to be kept in good condition, and phosphatidyl choline is essential for that maintenance. However, in order to work, Maguire discovered that phosphatidyl choline needs certain B vitamins. Folic acid and selenium boost cognitive functioning. Folic acid is found in dark, leafy green vegetables. Selenium is found in seafood, wholegrain breads and nuts.

Folic acid sets back aging

In 2007, *The Lancet* reported that 818 participants aged 50–70 had been given 800 micrograms of folic acid per day and had then out-performed younger subjects on tests of memory and thinking speed – the only area in which the 50+ brain normally lags behind the younger brain. Added to this, all 818 of these superior performers had been diagnosed with partial atrophy of the hippocampus, an area of the brain important for consolidation of memories.

Connors reported that boron, iron and zinc improved mental activity. Boron is found in broccoli, pears, peaches, grapes, nuts and dried beans. Zinc can be found in fish, beans and whole grains. The Vitamin C in citrus fruits and salads enhances the absorption of iron. Iron helps to form ferroxyhaemoglobin, which is used to carry oxygen through the blood to the brain.

In humans, neurotransmitters like dopamine and norepine-phrine are essential for mental alertness and acuity, for high-speed calculation, and for evaluation and critical thinking. Eating protein increases the supply of neurotransmitters. Eat more protein if you wish to be more mentally alert and quick thinking. (Some of the lowest rates of dyslexia in the world are found in Japan, which has the highest per capita consumption of fish.)

Importantly for the 50+ brain, blueberries, strawberries and spinach contain chemicals which appear to reverse the deterioration in thinking ability that is due to previous lifestyle choices. (Note that, ounce for ounce, dark chocolate has ten times as many flavenols as the berries and the spinach, but it must be dark chocolate (like Malagasy, for example) not the dairy stuff! (See Appendix I for more information.)

Vitamins – to pop the pills or not?

At least ten different B vitamins can affect the neurotransmitters in your brain. For example, Anderson found that people had difficulty in thinking when their B1 levels were low.

The beneficial effects from B1, B5 and Vitamin C, and the minerals boron, zinc and selenium, are best obtained by adjusting your diet rather than taking vitamin pills. You can usefully increase the proportion in your diet of berries, such as blackcurrants, red currants, bilberries, strawberries and especially blueberries. Also, try increasing your intake of spinach, green cabbage, broccoli and watercress. Do not take iron tablets unless your doctor has investigated possible causes of your anaemia other than iron deficiency.

Food for thinking – a day plan

On days when you are involved in mainly mental, not physical, activity, try to eat complex carbohydrates (like fruit, salad and vegetables) and proteins (like fish, poultry, lentils, pulses or nuts) during the daytime. Keep grain carbohydrates, like bread and cereal, and fats, like avocado and liver, until after work in the evening. Drink before bed – but no driving – a smoothie, made from low-fat yoghurt and 80 g of fruit (especially mango) will make you sleepy. According to Dr Buxton, of the British

Nutrition Foundation, writing in the Nutrition Bulletin in May 2008, it will also contribute two of the five portions a day of fibre that you need. If you like your smoothies thick, add fat-free powdered milk.

For enhanced thinking speed and accuracy...

Mornings

If you can face protein first thing, start with it. Try eggs – boiled, scrambled, poached, or a Spanish omelette. Any kind of coldwater fish, especially oily fish like kipper or mackerel or salmon, is excellent. Try stewed fruit, berries, blackcurrants, nuts or seeds. Try soaking dried fruit overnight in hot weak black tea with a dash of fresh orange juice. This reduces the concentration of the sugar in the dried fruit, as well as producing a delicious syrup to add to low-fat yoghurt. For preference, have fresh fruit if possible. Avoid bread and cereals in the morning if you can – keep them until evening, when you should favour whole grains. Drink plenty of water on getting up, before and after cleaning your teeth, and just before leaving the house. Top up a sipping bottle of water to carry with you.

Eating a good breakfast and other myths

While it is true that children at school find it hard to concentrate and think if they feel hungry, at 50+ it matters crucially what you eat for breakfast. White toasted bread and jam rapidly metabolize into glucose and produce insulin-driven pangs of hunger well before lunchtime. Even milk and cereals (especially if sugary) will burn up in about 2 hours. To work best, breakfast should be based on protein and on complex carbohydrates, like those found in fruit.

Daytime

Again, any protein is good (especially oily fish like mackerel, herring, salmon or sardines) with dark green vegetables (like spinach and cabbage) or with salad. Try to eat vegetables raw, especially carrots, cabbage and celery. Eat the protein first. If you need afters, try fruit salad or just fruit. Avoid biscuits, bread, pasta, pizza or pastry. Drink as much cold water as you can. If you need a hot drink during the day, choose weak tea – preferably green or herbal – rather than coffee.

Evening

Wholemeal bread and cereals eaten in the evening will help you to relax and to sleep. Rapeseed oil or linseed oil will give you Omega 3 fatty acids. Corn or soya oils contain Omega 6 and Omega 9. Flax, hemp, sesame and pumpkin oils will help you to maintain the balance between Omega 3 and Omega 6. Because these oils are degraded by hard cooking, it is better to stir in a teaspoonful before serving, after the hot cooking is finished, or drizzle them into your salads or raw vegetables. Good quality non-stick pans make this easier. The wholemeal bread will give you your selenium. Pasta will give you the energy you need for physical exercise the next day. This is the time of day when puddings will do least harm to your thinking and they may help you to sleep. Try fresh fruit crumbles made with bran and oat toppings, or homemade ice cream made from a blend of low-fat yoghurt, skimmed dried milk powder and fresh fruit.

The effects of dieting, snacking and grazing on thinking

Sow wild oats when you're young and grow sage when you're 50+.

(after Winston Churchill)

Snacking and grazing

Jenkins took people with normal eating habits and divided them into two groups: one group ate the traditional three meals a day; the other consumed identical food, but 'grazed' on it up to 17 times per day. The 'grazers' maintained a more stable insulin level and had lower cortisol levels (Chapter 05). Research undertaken on students either 'grazing' or not eating at all during a thinking test, showed that those permitted to snack on raw vegetables, achieved higher scores than a matched group that was not allowed to snack.

Thinking consumes energy and needs fuel. If it suits you, have more snacks and fewer large meals. Large meals are often preceded by reduced ability to concentrate and followed by periods of drowsiness. However, do not snack on sweets or biscuits or on refined, salty carbohydrates. Snack on protein, such as low-fat yoghurt, nuts or seeds. Salads are good but are often not convenient, unless pre-prepared from finely chopped leaves, rocket, cabbage, fresh spinach or watercress, and well mixed with, say, salmon, egg, tuna, smoked fish, nuts, broad beans, lentils, peas or poultry. Raw vegetables, like carrots, celery or cucumber, are easy to nibble. Fresh fruits like apples and pears are socially acceptable snacks at any time.

Ditching diets

I took off all my clothes and straight away the doctor said, 'You'll have to diet.' I said, 'What colour?'

(Ken Dodd, age 87)

The British Association for the Advancement of Science reports that whether or not people who diet frequently lose weight, they certainly lose mental performance.

The dangers of fat-free diets!

By all means eliminate solid, saturated transfats from your diet. Transfats have few unsaturated bonds in them and so it is very hard for your body to break them down and get rid of them. They tend to be stored in your body, eventually clogging up your arteries and destroying your waistline. Stored fat cells compete with your muscles and your brain for the oxygen they need to work effectively. Transfats also interfere with two fats, Omega 3 and Omega 6, that your brain really does need.

Without unsaturated fats in your diet, your brain can't produce acetylcholine, and without this, the walls of your brain cells will become stiff and brittle, and the cells may die. You will suffer memory loss and your thinking speed and accuracy will deteriorate. Such a fat-free diet will not only kill your brain cells, it may also kill you! De Angelis found that low-fat diets increased death rates from depression, suicide and accidents. Of course, obesity and heart disease also threaten your life and your social life and so it is understandable that you might want to reduce your weight. But yo-yo dieting or a very low-fat diet are not safe ways to do it. If you use the tables in Appendix H to eat what you normally eat but choose the low-oxytoxic versions, then you may lose weight as a side-effect of protecting your brain. It is known that in countries with a low risk of Alzheimer's, where people live on low-oxytoxic food, people's body mass indices are also much lower than in countries where people eat highly oxytoxic foods .

If you want to reduce your weight or body size at the same time as protecting your brain then, according to research by Professor Fletcher in 2007, you should not buy fad diet books, especially those based on cooking and eating! Yo-yo dieting seems to be one cause of dead brain cells and depressed thinking ability. Try the 3T approach – TTT.

The 3T approach to dieting

T1 – Take Aim

Taking aim will help your body to settle slowly to an equilibrium weight, such that your body mass index (BMI) will be somewhere between 18 and 25. If it's already below 18, that's unhealthy – bad for your body as well as your brain. If it's more than 25, you are carrying more flesh than you need as a buffer against illness or hard times. Surplus body mass competes with your brain for the oxygen it needs in order to think quickly and well for sustained periods. If your BMI is already between the values of 18 and 25, ditch the diet!

To calculate your BMI, get some scales, preferably digital, that read in pounds or half kilos. Weigh yourself in your underwear (if you weigh yourself in outdoor clothes and shoes, for example in a pharmacy store, deduct 5 kg or 10 lbs). Put a hardback book or board horizontally on your head and mark off your height when standing, barefoot, with your back pressed up against a wall. Measure the height of the mark from the floor, preferably in metres. (If in inches, divide the measurement by 10, and then by 4.) Multiply your height in metres by itself. Divide this number into your weight in kilos. That is your BMI, i.e.

$$BMI = kilos \div (metres \times metres).$$

If your BMI is not between 18 and 25, then divide 20 by (your height in metres x your height in metres) and Take Aim at this target weight. The World Health Organization says that your weight can change by up to 4 kg per month without threatening your health – but slower is better. Now put away the scales for 12 months or so. Select low-oxytoxic foods from Appendix H and follow steps T2 and T3. Use the more comfortable fit of your clothes, or comments of friends, as your feedback mechanism.

T2 – Take Note

The point of taking note of your feedback is to teach your brain what moves your weight, and in particular what the things are that you do *often* that move your weight. Things you do occasionally throughout the year – parties, celebrations, holidays, trips – do not in the end determine your stable BMI. It is the things you do regularly – often by habit – that move your weight. The trick is to spot your habits, then Take Note and Take Action to break them. Habit breaking is good for your brain, whatever the habit, so food-eating habits are as good a place to start as any! The following are typical food habits to look out for and take note of. Check them out, now:

- I can't have just one, I eat the whole box.
- I've always struggled with my weight.
- I diet every year, or before every holiday.
- I am always pecking.
- I just get cravings for…
- I tend to eat on the move.
- It's just that I'm not as active as I used to be.
- I eat properly in public, but when I get home…
- I eat properly in the daytime, but during the night…
- I keep finishing the children's leftovers – waste not want not.

What habits can you add to your list?

How often do you…? Score: always = 6, usually = 4, sometimes = 2, never = 0	Score (0, 2, 4, 6)
Do the same thing on the same day of the week?	
Go back to the same place for a holiday?	
Repeat purchase and from the same retailer?	
Watch a regular scheduled television program?	
Eat the same things for the same meal, e.g. breakfast?	
Say things that are boring?	
Dismiss the ideas of other people?	
Wear the same style or brand of clothes?	
Sit in the same place in a restaurant or your lounge?	
Do things that are not good for you?	
Total score for negative habits =	

How often do you...? Score: always = 6, usually = 4, sometimes = 2, never = 0	Score (0, 2, 4, 6)
Seek out people who might be interesting?	
Forgive people?	
Surprise others?	
Vary your daily newspaper?	
Deliberately look for a challenge?	
Make changes to make things more interesting?	
Try a new place for a meal or a coffee?	
Learn something new?	
Do something you don't find easy?	
Listen quietly with full attention and empathy?	
Total score for positive habits =	

Add your positive and negative habit scores together. How did you get on?

0–25   You have good habit-breaking skills. Use them to ditch diets. Use them to bust food habits that push your BMI where you don't want it to be.

26–50 You need to strike a balance between your good and bad habits. Is there a positive that you could do more or a negative you could do less?

50+   You are habit prone. Perhaps you border on obsessive or compulsive. Do you need professional help or counselling? Discuss your score with another person (Chapter 06). A friend can often spot hidden habits. Once spotted, most habits are easy to break, given a little support.

T3 – take action

I'm on two diets at the moment. I simply don't get enough to eat on one.

(Jo Brand)

Now you have Taken Aim, and Taken Note of the habits that stand between you and your aim, you are ready to Take Action to change your unhelpful habits around eating and drinking, so that you can ditch that diet. Here are five useful questions for you to ask:

- Is this a habit that was useful in the past, but is now past its sell-by date?
- Are you good at this habit? (This might be why you are stuck – people tend to stick with what they're good at.)
- Is the habit copied from someone who used to be a useful role model who is no longer an appropriate model for you?
- How did you learn this habit? If you learned it, you can unlearn it!
- Do you see a habit as an expression of your personality? Well it's not. It might be an aspect of your 'style' of operation in some situations, but you can adapt your style to varying circumstances as you get older. The state of your brain is a lifestyle choice.

Get into the habit of breaking habits. Start by ditching habitual weight-loss dieting. Weight-loss diets can damage your brain (low-fat diets), or deprive you of mental energy, or of B vitamins or minerals that you need to think clearly and well over sustained periods. Your body will follow your mind. Try this…

Exercise 1: immediate proof that your body will follow your mind

Stand with your feet the same distance apart as your shoulders, toes turned slightly in. Extend your right arm out and in front of you, fingers at eye height. Focus on the finger tips of your right hand and rotate your trunk as far as you comfortably can and notice at what your finger is pointing. Centre your body again. Close your eyes and, in your mind's eye only, see yourself rotating further this time. Watch your hand swing well past its original stopping place. Without opening your eyes, rotate your trunk again and, in your mind's eye, see your finger going past the original stopping point. Allow your body to follow your mind. Open your eyes. Amazing, eh!

In the same way, your brain will adjust the weight of your body and your BMI as you take aim, take note and take action to break habits.

Exercise 2: fold your arms – developing your second nature

Fold your arms. Now fold them so the other arm is on top. Difficult, hey? Now relax. Fold your arms. Notice that the original arm is back on top again! You have to be quite deliberate and methodical to do things differently from the way you habitually do, especially if it's a habit of a lifetime. So never give yourself a hard time about relaxing back into an old habit. It's normal 'first' nature. Many repetitions of a 'new habit' are needed before it becomes your 'second' nature – that is where emotional intelligence comes in (Chapter 01). Repeatedly feel the good feelings you will feel when you see yourself breaking a habit.

Breaking eating habits works because your appetite is controlled by a part of your brain called the hypothalamus. It is about the size of a clementine and weighs about 14 grams. Your hypothalamus is involved in your emotional thinking (Chapter 01). That is why eating food is often such an emotionally charged matter. Harvest now the good feelings you will feel when you have ditched your diet. In the meantime, listen to your hypothalamus and eat when you are hungry. Your brain tells you that. (Do not wait until you are 'starving', because your brain will naturally go into some emergency mode and instruct your body to 'binge' – to stock up against the threat of imminent starvation.) Indications of hunger include your stomach rumbling, your head aching, being irritable, restless and unable to concentrate and having a dry or bad-tasting mouth. Many of these are also symptoms of dehydration, so always drink a glass of water first to be sure that what your brain is debating is the need for food, and not just a need for water. If you do need food – eat, and as soon as you can, whatever the timetable says! However, if your hypothalamus is signalling an emotional need – not a genuine need for food – this food will only make you fat. Check whether you are an emotional eater. Do you:

- eat more when you are alone?
- eat more when you are happy?
- eat more when you are sad?
- think about food a lot?
- feel guilty about food?
- eat when you're bored?
- eat when you're upset?
- cheat on diets?
- eat under stress?

Doing something different – thinking twice

If, for the wrong emotional reasons, you always do what you've always done, you will always have what you've always had. If you have always got an overweight body, you will always get an overweight body. To achieve something different, you have to do something different.

To do something different, you have to think differently:

- **Think twice before jumping on the scales.** Random variations – like fluids, sweating and constipation – play havoc with bathroom scales. Only use scales when you are certain – for example, from the fit of your clothes – that things are going the way you want them to.

- **Think twice** before eating. Have you had a drink first? Do you have time to eat slowly? Are you ready to take 20 minutes? Are you able to leave some food on your plate?

- **Think twice** about whether you feel stressed or low. Is it a break or some reassurance that you really need (rather than this sweet food)? A talk or a phone call to someone might take the pangs away.

- **Think twice** about eating when you're not at home. Some fast food or food that is convenient to eat on the move is very oxytoxic. But not all fast food is (see Appendix H). Fish and chips are not as bad as most fast food and some snacks have a very low oxytoxicity. Carry small apples in your pocket. Carry water in case it's water your brain needs. It may only be a taste in your mouth – carry minty sweets such as Tic Tacs or Fisherman's Friends. The mint smell will also help you to think more clearly.

- **Think twice** about using food or drink as a treat or reward or a pat on the back. Instead, buy a magazine or an expensive moisturizer (or a smaller size of jeans and smaller top!).

- **Think twice** about 'red light' food warnings about sugar, salt and chemicals. You are what you eat, and so is your brain.

- **Think twice** before shopping. Make a list. Don't buy offers if they are not on your list. Don't buy on impulse. If you really need it, it will be on next week's list. Check whether any of the following are (or should not be) on your shopping list.

Thoughtless shopping list	**Thoughtful shopping list**
Crisps	Fresh fish
Biscuits	Pasta
Pies	Eggs
White bread	Bananas
Mayonnaise	Red fruit
Cook-in sauces	Chillies
Hard cheese	Ginger
Bacon	Olives
Liqueurs	Skimmed milk
Strong cider or ale	Low-fat yoghurt
Cappuccino/lattes	Yeast
Coconuts	Fast fish and/or chips
Peanut butter	Chicken
High oxytoxic ready meals	Chicken liver
(see Appendix H)	Kidneys
	Avocados
	Nuts
	Melons
	Seeds
	Molasses
	Maple syrup
	Onions
	Leeks
	Herbs
	Blueberries
	Apricots
	Tofu
	Beans
	Peas
	Olive oil, nut oil, hemp oil
	Dark chocolate

For a thoughtful approach to managing your weight and body shape, see *Lose Weight (Not Your Mind)* by Horne and Wootton, forthcoming.

The oxytoxic index

Do not seek diets to die for. Ditch any chronic diets. These diets make you irritable, lower your ability to concentrate, reduce your mental stamina, lower your mood, cause depression, damage your self-confidence and lower your optimism. These side effects lower your performance on thinking tasks. Stressing about your weight and obsessing about food releases cortisol derivatives into your blood. If excess cortisol gets into your brain, it may damage your brain cells and wreak havoc with the chemical reactions that need to take place if you are to think clearly, quickly and accurately. Additionally, if your diet is too low in fats, the walls of your brain cells may become brittle and may die. It really will be a diet to die for – slowly, and in distress.

As far as your brain is concerned, what you eat matters more than how much you weigh. Although your brain will undoubtedly have less competition for oxygen in your blood if you weigh less, being fit is more important than whether or not you are fat. To perform well on a day-to-day basis, your brain needs enough fuel and chemicals and vitamins to catalyze the chemistry of its thinking.

Moving on from improving the day-to-day thinking power of your brain, by giving it 'food for thought' you will also be protecting it, as far as possible, from attack by diseases. We have explained how brain training can be used to create reserve cognitive capacity, in case you do get a neurodegenerative disease. What we are concerned to do next is to tip the balance strongly away from you getting a neurodegenerative disease at all. This will add life to your years, as well as years to your life.

Many degenerative diseases start when a cell or cells start to mutate, and when the mutation then reproduces. Cancers or tumours often start this way, and so may diseases like Alzheimer's. Cells can mutate if they are attacked by oxygen free radicals. Free radicals are sometimes produced when oxidation takes place. The more your food requires a lot of oxidizing, the greater the chance of you generating an oxygen free radical as a bi-product. For each category of food, we have given a common member of that category an **oxytoxic index**. Its **oxytoxic index** is a comparative measure of how much oxidation takes place in your body when you eat it. The more oxidation, the greater the risk of free radicals. So, eat when you need to eat but, where possible, favour the foods with the lower **oxytoxic indices**.

Many people want the convenience of branded processed foods as well as the benefits of fresh produce, so we have included the oxytoxic indices of many branded processed foods. There is a great variation from brand to brand. The choice is yours.

The state of your brain and your thinking power is a lifestyle choice for you to make. You may be able to make a better informed choice if you first cast your eye over the **oxytoxic index tables** in Appendix H.

A daily total oxytoxic score of 100 for women and 120 for men is found in Japan, China and Asian countries where the incidence of Alzheimer's (and some cancers) is very low compared with the US and Europe. For example, the incidence of Alzheimer's in parts of the US is seven times higher, and in Europe three to four times higher than in Japan, China and Vietnam. We do not advocate keeping a daily score, but it might be prudent to favour lower, rather than higher, oxytoxic foods. And, just in case you still produce the odd oxygen free radical, if you include some of the foods from the ORAC (oxygen radical absorbance capacity) table below. Free radicals will likely attack any of these ORAC foods in preference to your brain cells. The relative power of these brain-friendly foods to absorb free radicals is shown in Appendix I. Note that dark chocolate is at least ten times more absorbent of free radicals than any other food in the table.

Table 4.1: ORAC (free radical absorbing, brain-friendly) foods

Alfafa	Apple sauce	Artichoke	Asparagus
Aubergine	Avocado	Basll	Beans
Bell peppers	Black-eye peas	Black pepper	Blackberries
Blueberries	Broccoli	Cherries	Chillies
Cider vinegar	Cinnamon	Cloves	Cocoa
Dates	Elderberry	Figs	Ginger
Green tea	Kale	Nuts	Oats
Olive oil	Oranges	Oregano	Parsley
Peaches	Pears	Plums	Pomegranate
Prunes	Purple potatoes	Purple carrots	Raisins
Raspberries	Red cabbage	Red grapes	Spinach
Sprouts	Strawberries	Tangerines	Turmeric
Whole grains	...and dark chocolate		

The **oxytoxic index** has been created on the grounds that there is little point in dieting, if dieting reduces your ability to think well when you are alive, and only extends your life by adding 10 or 20 years in which you are almost brain dead – i.e. unable to recognize, remember or reason. Maybe your starting point in deciding what to eat should be the health of your brain.

Feeling full

How much you eat should also be determined by your brain. Your brain will tell your stomach to produce hunger pangs in response to the chemicals present in your brain. For example, if your blood contains a lot of insulin, for example, because you have overloaded your digestive system too quickly with simple sugars, your brain will scream 'hunger' and nag you until you eat (probably more sugar). During this time, it will be very difficult for you to concentrate on thinking tasks. On the other hand, your brain will produce chemicals that send messages like 'full', 'satisfied', 'sated' or 'bloated' in response to the action of swallowing, tasting and, particularly, chewing. It takes about 20 minutes for your brain to produce the chemical message 'full'. You should start by drinking water, since it is easy for you to confuse a signal for dehydration with a signal for hunger. The dehydration signal is likely to persist even after you have mistakenly eaten food to no avail. You may then eat even more unnecessary food and still not extinguish the brain call for water. After swallowing half a pint of water slowly, you may well find that you are not hungry after all. If the signals persist, try changing the taste in your mouth – try mints, Coxes apples, or a square of good quality dark chocolate. Wait a while. You may notice that your brain is no longer signalling hunger. When you are sure your brain really needs to eat, eat a nutritious balance of foods and favour foods with lower oxytoxic indices. Maintain a nutritious balance over the day.

Ensure that you eat without distractions (television, radio, books) because if you are not fully aware of the texture and smells of what you are eating, your brain may under-produce chemicals that signal 'satisfied'.

Favour hard, chewy foods and chew them deliberately and slowly – a mouthful at a time. This will maximize the production of 'full' chemical messages in your brain. Foods that have been blended or processed to make them mushy or easy to swallow trick your brain into allowing you to eat much more than is needed by your brain or body.

Brain-based cooking tips

As I'm getting older, I decided to cook more healthy meals, so I bought Gordon Ramsay's new book called 'Take Two Eggs and F*ck Off'.

(Jack Dee)

Having created the right conditions, under which your brain will tell you that you are not hungry when it has had enough to eat, it still matters what you choose to eat. You need to pick from each of proteins (meat, fish, pulses, eggs, lentils, nuts), complex carbohydrates (fruit, vegetables, salad) and unsaturated oils or fats. Your brain needs the complex carbohydrates to provide mental energy for your thinking tasks. The proteins provide many of the neurotransmitters and minerals and vitamins involved your brain's chemical reactions. Your brain needs fats to repair and maintain its brain cells, and to create replacement cells.

To reduce the likelihood that your brain will be attacked by disease, when you make your daily choice of proteins, carbohydrates and fats you should favour those foods that have lower **oxytoxic indices** and try to include at least one of the foods from Appendix I.

Make a start:

1 Use anti-inflammatory herbs and spices, such as turmeric and ginger.
2 Eat raw foods or favour ingredients or ready meals with a low **oxytoxic index**.
3 Avoid simple sugars and syrups. Favour complex carbohydrates as found in fruit, vegetables, salads and wholemeal grains.
4 Cook for the minimum time, at the lowest possible temperatures.
5 Use a non-stick pan. Wipe with a little oil on a tissue before cooking. Add a little olive, or sesame, or hemp oil *after* cooking.
6 Eat fresh fish three times a week. Cook in foil in the oven with lemon or a quick hot sear in a pan, for example sea bream fillet only 90 seconds per side!
7 Eat five to ten helpings per week of deeply coloured fruits, vegetables or salads, including at least one per week from Appendix I.

There are also some easy, low oxytoxic recipes for you to try in Appendix J.

Fitness, health and training your brain

Our low oxytoxic index enables protecting your brain and enhancing its performance to be given a higher priority than losing weight at 50+. What matters more than fatness is fitness. Fitness is of two sorts: healthy fitness – the sort of fitness that helps you to fend of illness, thereby allowing your brain to perform better and better as you get older; and sporty fitness – the sort that goes further than healthy fitness because your work requires it, or your sport demands it, or because you are mad or vain!

Healthy fitness requires only 15–20 minutes of modest exercise three to five times a week. At least three times a week, you should get a bit puffed or even slightly sweaty for a few minutes. Begin and end with simple stretches after you have warmed up your muscles by walking briskly for a few minutes first.

Sporty fitness, i.e. 4S fitness, involves S for strength, S for speed, S for suppleness, S for stamina. Get a book, a friend, a gym or a coach to give you a regime for each. Sporty fitness will help your healthy fitness too – and both will benefit your brain.

Swinging along at 50+

You are far more likely than a 16–25 year old to be able to walk upstairs holding a normal conversation without becoming breathless. You are far more likely to catch that bus.

Pilates – thoughtful exercise

The main brain benefit of aerobic exercise is the residual increased rate of supply of oxygen to your brain. The main drawback is that aerobic exercises like jogging, running, rowing and power walking can be so boring that they appear to actually numb your mind. Aerobic exercise can be leavened by trying aerobic dance classes or by playing basketball, or better still, korfball, a kind of cross between netball and basketball played in mixed teams. Aerobic workouts to music using a DVD or better still in a live class, bring variety to ease the tedium.

Fortunately, exercises you do for suppleness and posture are much more mentally demanding and so bring additional cognitive benefits to your brain. Yoga is a well-known example, but a system more recently developed by Joseph Pilates is also demanding because 'Pilates' exercises demand constant awareness of the position of your limbs and the state of tension of many of your muscles. Pilates provides a mental workout that mirrors your physical workout. This is intensified when you are copying visual demonstrations or watching your movements in a mirror. In 2003, the Pilates Foundation published an excellent guide written by Trevor Bloant and Eleanor McKenzie.

Prejudice against fat people

With extra body weight, brain oxygenation through exercise is less appealing, as more of your body will compete for the oxygen which your brain needs. This adds to the prejudicial image of overweight people as slothful mentally, as well as physically. In job interviews, overweight people are at a disadvantage even when competing for jobs where mental (as opposed to physical) agility is being sought. Unfortunately, too few interviewers know that it is physical and mental fitness that matters – not body bulk or fatness.

The positive effects of relaxation on thinking

Gelb found that the tested cognition and memory of people taught how to relax was 25 per cent higher than in a control group. He found similar gains when posture was improved prior to thinking tasks.

Movement and the mind – how to sit and stand

Avoid lifts and escalators. Seek out stairs. Do not lie if you can sit, or sit if you can stand, or stand if you can walk, or walk if you can run, or ride if you can cycle.

When sitting on a chair, push your buttocks into the back of the chair. Do not cross your legs. Place feet firmly apart on the floor, about the same distance apart as your shoulders. Imagine you were trying to crumple a rug under your feet. The same applies when standing, but relax your knees. Once an hour, rub the palms of your hands together as vigorously as circumstances allow. Keep rubbing while you count backwards from one hundred to zero.

When standing, sitting or lying down, try to imagine that your navel is a large nut connected by a bolt through to your backbone. Imagine the bolt slowly tightening as you breathe in. Keep your navel bolted to your backbone.

According to McWilliams, massage and yoga not only relax you, but can help you to control the frequency of the electrical brain waves in your head. This is because excessive stress impairs thinking and the relaxation lowers the cortisol associated with the stress. But if you are not at all stressed or anxious, the effect on your mental performance may be adverse. A quarter of students, for example, require stimulation and mild anxiety (about deadlines, presentations or prospective questioning) to get them into the zone of proximal readiness to think!

Exercise 1: Memorable yoga

To improve your mental concentration and memory, try removing your shoes and standing tall with your feet together. Breathe in deeply and transfer your weight onto your right foot, placing the sole of your left foot as high up the inner thigh of your right leg as you comfortably can with the toes of your left foot pointing down your right leg at the floor. Press your left foot against the right leg and with the right leg push back against the left foot. If you can, raise your arms upwards on either side of your head and press the palms of your hands together. Focus the eyes on something just above head height and breathe deeply in and out, counting backwards from eight. Repeat with your weight on your left leg.

Exercise 2: Respire to inspire

For creative and imaginative thinking, force every last bit of breath out of your body, especially by squeezing the muscles of the stomach and buttocks. Hold this state for as long as you can and then allow the breath to rush in and appear to fill all the cavities of your body, from your abdomen up to the upper regions of your chest. Raise your shoulders to suck in the last breath. Hold for as long as you comfortably can. Repeat three times. Use a finger to gently close one nostril and breathe normally. Jot down every new idea that occurs to you – however crazy these ideas might seem.

Now change from the slow, deep breathing rhythm that is needed for creative thinking to the quicker, shallower, upper-chest breathing that favours critical thinking. To do this, stand with knees relaxed, your feet about as far apart as your shoulders, and imagine you are squeezing a rug on the floor between your feet. Hold your arms straight out in front of you and slide your palms back and forth over each other as fast as you can without a break, while counting backwards from one hundred. Do not ease off. Try to accelerate for the last 50 counts. When you reach zero, straighten your knees and drop your head as near to the floor as you can. Use one hand to tap up the opposite side of your body, from your ankles to your head, as you slowly straighten up. Bend down again and repeat with the other hand, tapping the other side of your body. Your electrical brainwave cycle will now be much quicker. You will now be better prepared for a quick 'thinking-on-your-feet' evaluation of the creative ideas you just produced when you were breathing deeply and slowly through one nostril.

You can do this exercise in a seated position. Just push your chair clear of the desk or table.

The effects of aerobic exercise

My grandmother didn't take up serious walking until she was 57. She is 97 today and we don't know where the hell she is.
(Ellen De Generes)

Dienstbier reports that aerobic exercise enhances thinking performance. Brain activity is fuelled by oxygen. Aerobic exercise increases the supply of oxygen to the brain. Herman divided people into three groups: group one was given vigorous aerobic exercise, group two was given moderate anaerobic exercise and group three was given a placebo activity not involving exercise at all. The two exercise groups consistently showed significantly higher scores on reasoning and thinking tests than the non-exercisers. The exercise regimes were rotated around the groups and the most enhanced reasoning and thinking scores continued to be achieved in the group that was exercising aerobically. According to Bagley, anaerobic exercise is better for enhancing creative thinking, although it will improve critical and reflective thinking as well, if your overall thinking is temporarily impaired by anxiety or stress (Chapter 01).

The 50+ come out to play

In Germany in May 2007, the daily paper, *Der Spiegel*, commented that 'pensioners are taking over power, while children become extinct'. In Berlin, and next in Nuremberg, the pensioners are certainly taking over the children's playgrounds! (This would not be news in China, where public places commonly have keep-fit equipment for adults, but it is still rare in Germany.) The pensioner's playground in Berlin – Prussia Park – was designed by Finnish researchers from the University of Lapland. The playground cost only £13,500 for eight exercisers – a fraction of the cost of a typical children's playground. More are planned, after Nuremberg, based on evidence that physical and mental exercise delay dementia – often indefinitely.

Just step outside – just walk this way

Provided you are brisk enough about it, walking can provide all the low-impact aerobic exercise your brain needs without risk of injury, and without special shoes and socks and other gear you need for running. Pull your stomach in and push your hips forward. This engages your muscles – abdominals and lower back and bottom – the core muscles. No wonder you look and think better. Roll your feet outwards as you walk, so as to keep your knees and ankles in a straight line. It's not as difficult as it sounds, and all the repetition is brilliant for your brain.

Walking the talk

According to Joanna Hall, you reach your optimum speed just before you feel tempted to break out into a run. You should be able to talk to a fellow walker – but only just. Buy a pedometer and build towards 10,000 paces a day, five days a week. According to Shinsha University, interval walking is as effective as interval running – i.e slow–quick–slow. The Ramblers Keep Walking project provides a free 12-week programme with guided walks and social events (www.ramblers.org.uk).

Go through the wall

Use endurance anaerobic exercise to manage anxiety or stress (Chapter 01) , or to raise your metabolic rate to speed up the flow of oxygen to your brain, and maybe even to lose weight. You will get the calming effect of increased serotonin without eating, because tryptophan will be bumped off your body fat. In this way, you can manage your stress and lose weight at the same time, if that is what you want to do.

Tactile stimulation

Give time to hobbies that involve physical contact, tactile stimulation or intricate handwork. Try massage, swimming, rock climbing, planting, sailing, DIY, or contact sports like rugby or judo. Try painting, weaving, printing, model making, working with clay, or ballroom dancing. Walk in the rain or strong wind. Try a sauna, jacuzzi or steam room.

Exercise 3: Put your head in your hands

- Start the day with your head in your hands! Sit on the edge of your bed, or the seat of your lavatory, and support the weight of your forehead in the palms of your hands, with your fingers in your hair. Allow your chin to fall slowly onto your chest, your hands stretching the skin of your forehead, and your fingers running through your hair.
- Sit up again. This time start with your finger tips on either side of your nose. Allow the weight of your head to fall slowly through your hands, which should graze your ears until your fingers touch at the back of your head.
- Sit up again and restart with your finger tips under your ears. Again allow your head to fall slowly against the friction of your palms and fingers until your finger tips pass in front of your ears and touch at the top of your scalp.
- Repeat with your finger tips passing upwards behind your ears this time, before meeting at the top of your head. This can literally make your hair stand on end.
- During the day, brush or comb your hair as often as vanity or local custom allow.

The effects of sleep on thinking

To achieve optimum performance, people need good quality sleep. Horne found that impaired sleep reduced performance on many mental tasks. Mitler's studies of catastrophes, such as the Three Mile Island nuclear power accident and the Challenger space shuttle explosion, concluded that poor sleep quality had impaired decision making and contributed to each.

The amount of sleep people need varies greatly from one person to another. It ranges from four to ten hours. For adults, quality of sleep seems to be more important than quantity. Quality of sleep can be impaired by listening for a baby, the return of a missing teenager, or by fear of not hearing the alarm clock. Sleep quality can also be impaired by snoring.

Many people who work shifts never get the chance for a high quality sleeping pattern to develop. People who work continuous night shifts perform better at mental tasks than people whose shift patterns change. Travel across time zones and the accompanying jet lag impairs performance on mental tasks. Going to bed later than usual has a more deleterious effect than getting up earlier than usual. The time taken to re-stabilize mental activity after a disturbed sleep pattern increases with age. Even with young adults it can take up to four days. At 50+ it can take more than one week.

Getting to sleep

Remove televisions and radios from your bedroom. Try going to bed later each night until you find a time at which you ordinarily drop off to sleep without delay. Talking to a partner prior to sleep can be desirable but such conversations should not involve complicated feats of memory or planning. Use a bedside notepad to park things until the next day. The deep breathing exercises described above will help you to settle your mind and slow down your brain waves.

If you are physically tense, squeeze and then relax all your muscles in turn, from your toes, through to your ankles, calves, thighs, buttocks, stomach, back, hands, arms, shoulders, chest, neck, face and right up to your scalp. If a massage is on offer, seize the moment! If early sleep is the goal, imagine a line down the centre of the body and another across the body, intersecting at the groin. Taking each quadrant in turn, direct the massage so that the flow of pressure is towards the head or feet, away from the groin. Start by lying face down. You may fall asleep without ever turning over! If you like to make love prior to falling asleep, then ask to be massaged so that the flow of pressure in each quadrant is towards the groin. Avoid direct contact with the groin.

According to Coren, scores on intelligence tests decline cumulatively on each successive day that you sleep less than you normally sleep. The daily decline is approximately one IQ point for the first hour of sleep loss, two for the next, and four for the next. After five successive days of sleeping two hours less than you need, your IQ can be lowered by up to 15 points. This means that a person of normal intelligence could have an effective IQ of only 85, the level at which you would need special education in order to learn. Even a very 'bright' person (IQ of 120 plus) can be reduced to robotic thinking, as though on automatic pilot.

According to Griffey (writing in *The Independent* in April 2004), in the UK, in 1910, people averaged 9 hours sleep per night. In 1990, we averaged eight hours sleep per night. By 1995, according to a survey by First Direct, we were averaging seven hours and 35 minutes a night. By 2004, the average had fallen to 7 hours per night. Are we sleeping less because we are more stressed, or are we more stressed because we are sleeping less? Certainly, levels of neurotoxic cortisol derivatives are raised in our brains.

The dangers of disturbed sleep at 50+

Once you have found a convenient time at which you fall asleep easily, without reading, radio or television, try to stick to it. At weekends do not set an alarm. Notice the time when you wake naturally – however early. Record your natural length of sleep time. Notice how short your 'natural sleep time' can be, especially when you are 50+. Whenever you are forced to sleep less than your 'natural sleep time', your performance on IQ tests, and the kind of mental aptitude tests used by employers, is likely to drop. The consequences can be serious. You may be incapable of learning something you need to learn, or thinking about some emergency that is new or complex or fast moving. Your reaction to unusual events will be poor, as will the reactions of a younger person. You should minimize your driving after sleep loss or sleep disturbance. Do not negotiate, or give presentations at which questions will be asked, immediately after travelling across a time zone, particularly as you get older.

Early to bed... early to rise

A study at Southampton University, based on 1,200 men and women, showed no evidence that 'early to bed, early to rise' made anyone 'healthier, wealthier or wise'! What seemed to be important was to be a regular riser – whether early or late. It is disturbed sleep patterns that disturb health, wealth and wisdom. The 50+ tend to sleep less and to rise earlier, so 50+ brains have more hours of daily brain power available to them than younger brains. This more than compensates for the few mental tasks for which more time is required as you get older. For example, you need more time during recall, because at 50+ you have more possibilities to search and select from than when you were 25 (see Chapter 03).

15 tips for sleeping better at 50+

1 First, are you sure you really need to sleep any more or any better?
2 Don't eat or drink late into the evening.
3 Evening food should include carbohydrate and not be very spicy.

4 Evening drinks should not be caffeinated or alcoholic (warm milk is good because it contains tryptophan which will relax your brain).

5 Don't do aerobic exercise in the evening (unless it's sexual).

6 Warm baths and ritualistic cleansing helps.

7 Remove computers, radios, televisions, rowing machines and bright lights from the bedroom.

8 Substitute the above with aromatic oil burners. Try lavender or chamomile.

9 Use fresh-air ventilation and keep the temperature at around 16–18°C.

10 Use blackout blinds on your windows.

11 Try relaxation breathing and exercises.

12 Park any intrusive thoughts on a pad by your bed.

13 Don't resort to listening to the radio, or worse, the television. A relaxation tape of sea sounds or wind noise will work better.

14 If you wake early, get up and do something nice, for example have sex, eat dark chocolate, drink freshly squeezed juice or read a car magazine. You may not sleep, but you can dream!

15 If midnight insomnia is recurrent, seek medical advice.

Dead drunk or dead tired (or just dead)?

Drink driving is dangerous. Tired driving is more so, causing more than one in ten accidents.

Coren tested a group of drivers after they had been awake for one hour after their 'normal' bedtime. Their thinking processes and reaction times were worse than a control group who had drunk more that the UK drink–drive limit for alcohol consumption! In countries like the United Kingdom, where the clocks are changed by one hour in the summer, car insurance accident claims rise by 25 per cent in the first four days following the one-hour sleep loss. Out of all UK motorway accidents, 25 per cent of drivers admit to feeling sleepy prior to their accident. Add in people not admitting this for fear of self-incrimination plus the drivers who did not live to tell the tale, and the effect of sleep loss is likely to be a much more serious contributor to accidents even than alcohol. The effect is more marked in 50+, 60+ and 70+ drivers and increases with age.

The magazine *What Car* organized a test by Professor Parkes of the Transport Research Laboratory. The tired subjects fared much worse than subjects over the legal limit for alcohol.

Action:

1 Have an especially good night's sleep the night before a long drive. Don't stay up packing!
2 Do stop if you find yourself whistling, singing, opening windows, turning up the radio, hitting yourself. Drink one coffee and sleep for 20 minutes – but not longer – before trying again.
3 Try to avoid driving at night.

Power naps – do they work?

New York, the city that never sleeps, is sprouting Metro-Nap soporific salons – £10 for 20 minutes. London has snooze booths, 30 minutes' shut-eye for £27.50. Who said sleep was priceless! At 50+ you can learn to do it for free!

The effects of alcohol on thinking

Heavy drinkers risk a brain disorder called Wernicke-Korsakoff syndrome, a progressive memory deficit. Sufferers normally recover their ability to speak and walk, but do not recover their ability to think. The condition seems irreversible and untreatable. Alcohol depletes Vitamin B1, which is essential for the thinking process. As we have seen already, there are other ways to feel more relaxed and less stressed, which do not impair thinking or damage your brain. The effect of alcohol is likely to be more damaging as you get older than 50+.

Thinking and hitting the bottle?

- Minimize your consumption of alcohol, especially during the day. Between one o'clock and four o'clock in the afternoon it can have up to ten times its usual effect.
- Do not drink alcohol on an empty stomach.
- Drink plenty of water before and after drinking alcohol.
- Drink spirits only with a double mixer plus plenty of ice.
- Do not mix alcohol with analysis. Even small amounts of alcohol can lead to a dangerous combination of error proneness, over-confidence and increased risk taking.

The effects of tea, coffee, cola and caffeine on thinking

Caffeine is found in tea, coffee and cola drinks and in some food products. Caffeine can quicken your reaction time and prolong your vigilance during demanding tasks. However, there is a need to keep doubling your intake of caffeine to have the same effect. Eventually a plateau is reached. The caffeine also acts as a diuretic. You keep urinating, causing dehydration. This produces lethargy and reduces your cognitive performance. Nutritionists recommend that you drink eight to fifteen glasses of water a day, depending on your body size, the weather and your activity level. Water is preferable to strong tea, soft drinks or fruit juices. David Kerr found that the caffeine lift, or 'buzz', was an illusion. Within 30 minutes of taking caffeine, he observed that the flow of blood (and hence oxygen) to the brain had reduced by 10–20 per cent. There is, however, an antioxidant protective quality to good quality black coffee.

Coffee – good for your brain (and not that bad for your body)

For years we have recommended one cup of cafetière filter coffee each day, because the benefits to your brain, and your performance on thinking tasks, seemed to outweigh the risks to your body. Our more recent interest in brain protection, especially from degenerative diseases like Alzheimer's has unearthed further potential benefits from drinking real coffee.

Many coffees – like Arabica coffee from Madagascar – are so rich in beneficial phytochemicals that, as reported by Dr Yanagimata in the *Journal of Food Chemistry* (2004), a small daily consumption of good quality coffee (not instant coffee), may be sufficient to reduce oxidative attacks on the fat components of the cells in your brain (remember, we think that oxidative attacks are possible precipitants of neurodegenerative diseases like Alzheimer's and Parkinson's, Chapter 03). When you add this to our observation that stimulation, whether from coffee, aerobic exercise or dark chocolate, is associated with increased energy, enhanced sense of well-being, improved self-confidence and greater sociability, motivation and stamina, then, on balance, the additional protection that comes from drinking a cup a day of good quality coffee, seems worth some risks, but not if your anxiety levels, or blood pressure, are already high.

Over a period of eight years, 130,000 people who consumed at least a cup of real coffee a day were less likely to attempt suicide (and also showed a 30 per cent reduction in diabetes, liver disease, colon cancer and gall stones). In studies in Norway (*The Journal of Nutrition*, Svilaas, A. (2004), 134, pp562–68), US and Europe (*The American Journal of Clinical Nutrition*, Frost, A. (2006), 83), coffee was found to be people's number one source of protective antioxidants. Further indications of coffee's protective value against degenerative brain disease came from a longitudinal study of 8,000 people (of whom half were not coffee drinkers). The non coffee drinkers were five times more likely to get Parkinson's disease. It is not certain whether the protection came from the coffee or from low levels of dophamine in the brain, without which there is no 'buzz' from being a coffee drinker. Similar levels of protection can also be achieved by eating up to six squares a day of dark chocolate (70–75 per cent cocoa). In the same way that chocolate should be dark to confer protection, coffee should preferably be drunk without milk – skimmed milk if you must, and no sugar.

Watering the brain

- Dehydration has a major adverse effect on mental activity. Coffee, strong tea and cola, like alcohol, make things worse because they are diuretics.
- The adrenal boost from the caffeine in coffee, tea, and cola is short lived. The first buzz from the first cup is eventually negated by fatigue.
- Tap water, hot water, fruit teas or herbal teas all produce greater benefits with less detriment.

The effects of sweets on thinking

People who become anxious frequently, often crave the tranquilizing effect of the serotonin that is formed from the tryptophan released into their blood when they eat simple carbohydrates. Perhaps that is why people who are over-anxious often crave something sweet. Sweet things are usually sweet because they contain simple carbohydrates like refined sugar. For the anxious person, the advantage of refined sugar is that it is very rapidly absorbed by the body, so the calming effect is almost immediate. A serious downside, however, of eating food containing refined sugar, is that it can cause an over-production of insulin. Excess insulin provokes hunger-like pains and makes mental concentration very difficult. It also produces craving for more sweet food and so the cycle gets worse. If your diet contains too much processed or refined carbohydrate, like sugar, then the insulin-producing systems in your body may become exhausted, or even diseased. This risks Type II diabetes, heart disease, damaged eye sight and other neuropathic complications.

The effects of smoking on thinking

I smoked my first cigarette on the same day I kissed my first girl. I have never had time to smoke since.

(Toscanini, aged 87)

Smokers self-report increased mental alertness and improved performance on a host of cognitive tasks after one cigarette. However, this positive effect is soon countered by an adverse effect on the oxygen-carrying capacity of your blood. Smoking ties up the haemoglobin that carries the oxygen in your blood.

Damage to your lungs limits your body's ability to absorb the oxygen needed to support mental activity.

Stubbing out dementia at 50+

The December 2007 issue of *Health Magazine* reported research showing that if you give up smoking now, even at 50+, you will reduce your risk of dementia by 50 per cent (as well as immediately improving your thinking power in the short term!).

The effects of drugs on thinking

Cannabis – the urban myth of harmlessness

This is a dilemma because the use of cannabis for pain control is rising in the 50+ age group and certainly chronic pain lowers mental performance. However, over a three-year period, Mathews studied people who were regularly using cannabis (or marijuana) at least ten times a week. He found that regular users progressively reduced their baseline of brain activity, compared with a matched control group. Regular users show lower energy levels, lower completion rates on personal goals and plans, lower reported pleasure in anything and reduced interest in using their bodies or their brains.

Cocaine – there has got to be a better way... there is

When an endorphin molecule in your body jumps a synaptic gap and finds a receptor site, you experience pleasure. Normally the endorphin will then detach. A cocaine molecule will lock the endorphin onto the receptor site so that you will continue to experience the pleasure. You will crave for a repeat of this pleasurable experience. You are hooked. The more cocaine you use the more the blood vessels in your brain will become constricted. This constriction will impair your ability to think and will eventually damage your brain. This constriction is more likely and the likely damage more extensive as you grow older than 50+.

'Just a tick' – avoiding the brain bug

Lyme's disease is a disease once found only in African countries. It is carried by ticks which bite their prey, suck their blood and sometimes leave a red ring around the bite. Lyme's disease can cause a swelling of the brain (encephalitis), a complication from which about 1 in 50 victims die. Even if you do not die, you can be left with severe neurological damage and be unable to walk or move your joints.

Today there are carrier ticks in 27 countries in mainland Europe, including the UK (in the New Forest, Exmoor, South Downs, Yorkshire Moors, Scottish Highlands and the Lake District). If you are bitten and you get a red ring, or flu-like symptoms, you need a large and sustained dose of strong antibiotics immediately. If you wait for a blood test it can be too late for the antibiotics to be effective. Since the 50+ are more likely to be walkers, they should cover their arms, not wear shorts, and check their bodies for red rings after country walks.

Designer brains and cosmetic neurology – the effects of smart drugs

In May 2007, Peta Bee, writing in the *Times*, questioned the fairness of students who were buying drugs, like Modafinil, which enhanced intellectual performance. According to Dr Danielle Turner, from Cambridge University, Modafinil improves memory, planning, information processing, emotional and reflective thinking and decision making and seems to have only benign side effects. Peta reviewed a number of other 'smart drugs', including Ritalin, which was originally developed to treat attention deficit disorder in children. It is now claimed to improve alertness, memory and visual and spatial thinking in 50+ adults.

Mice memorized five times faster when given these drugs. That kind of memory acceleration would come in handy if you needed to learn a second language, or wanted to play a musical instrument, or needed to revise for an exam – especially if your speed of new memory formation had declined (see Chapter 03).

However, you might remember everything, but understand nothing. What matters is not what you can remember, but what you can do with what you can remember. What matters most is your ability to think, and your ability to apply your thinking.

Dark chocolate boosts the brain

Dark chocolate boosts your brain while protecting your 50+ heart from disease and your 50+ body from cancer. Eating dark chocolate can improve your learning and your memory. Improved blood flow carries more oxygen to the brain, enabling you to think more quickly for longer. Your blood vessels relax, reducing blood pressure, brain damage and risk of heart disease. In February 2007, the American Academy of Science, from two separate studies, one in the US and one in the UK, reported that dark chocolate was not an old vice, but a modern-day life saver. Welcoming the news, nutritionists pointed out that the finding applied only to dark chocolate and warned chocoholics to avoid the pale dairy stuff. In a way we have come full circle, because chocolate was originally brought from South America to the court of the Spanish Empire as a medication and brain stimulant. It was a state secret which they believed helped their intelligence and their military dominance.

Dark chocolate is high in antioxidants. Professor Ian MacDonald found the increased blood flows in the cerebral cortex persisted for 3 hours after eating dark chocolate. Dr Helen Berg of Harvard found that rates of heart disease were only a fraction of Western levels in parts of the world (such as Panama) where drinking dark chocolate was part of the everyday diet. Deaths from cancer were similarly very low. Rates for strokes and diabetes were also low. Dark chocolate contains epicatechin – a mineral so vital to health that Professor Hollenberg would like to see it classified as a vitamin. The efficacy of epicatechin is undermined by sugar and diary products. Hence the need to eat your chocolate dark!

The neuroscience of dark chocolate

A heart-felt plea

According to Dr B. Jensen, you need the magnesium in dark chocolate to decrease the coagulation of your blood. This will help your heart to deliver more oxygen to your brain. This will not only raise the thinking speed and thinking power of your brain, it will also protect your brain from the damage that is caused by high blood pressure.

Dark chocolate lifts depression

Dark chocolate contains monoamine oxidase inhibitors (MAOIs). These allow the levels of serotonin and dopamine in your brain to remain higher for longer, alleviating depression and producing feelings of well-being.

Dark chocolate – the new vitamin

Free radicals attack and oxidize the DNA in your brain, creating growth points for tumours and other degenerative brain diseases like Alzheimer's, Parkinson's and motor neurone disease. Cheng Lee at Cornell University, showed that dark chocolate is rich in antioxidants, called flavonols. Flavonols mop up the free radicals, before they can oxidize your brain. Dark chocolate is twice as rich in antioxidant flavonols as red wine as and three times richer than green tea. The flavonols in dark chocolate also make your blood platelets less likely to stick together and cause brain damage through a stroke. Cheng Lee found that a normal cup of drinking chocolate, based on dark chocolate, contained about 600 mg of epicatechin.

Dark chocolate better than broccoli

The US Department of Agriculture compared the Oxygen Radical Absorbancy Capacity (ORAC) scores of well-known brain foods like spinach, blueberries and broccoli with dark chocolate (ORAC scores measure the concentration of flavonoid antioxidants in foods):

Broccoli	890
Sprouted alfafa	930
Plums	949
Sprouts	980
Raspberries	1,220

Spinach	1,260
Strawberries	1,540
Kale/cabbage	1,770
Blackberries	2,036
Blueberries	2,400
Dark chocolate	13,120

Dark chocolate a safer 'buzz' than caffeine

Eating dark chocolate substantially increases your mental speed and energy because it contains the brain stimulant theobromine. (Dark chocolate is virtually free of caffeine when compared with the levels found in coffee, strong tea and Red Bull. Caffeine also gives your brain a temporary boost, but it can raise your blood pressure, which can be serious if it is already too high. Dark chocolate contains about 21 per cent of theobromine. Theobromine works as a brain stimulant by relaxing muscles and so dilating veins, arteries and blood vessels thereby allowing more blood to flow to the brain. The effect of theobromine is gentler and more sustained than that of caffeine. It lasts four times longer and is kinder to your heart. Theobromine has actually been prescribed for heart patients to help lower blood pressure.

Get involved

Dark chocolate contains PEA (phenylethylamine). PEA activates the neurotransmitters in your brain, which control mental attention, concentration and alertness. Your levels of PEA go up naturally, without chocolate, when you are gripped by a great movie, or are enjoying a good book, or are wholly engrossed in a football match, a work project or a computer game. Elevated levels of PEA can cause us to lose track of time. This is why time seems to fly when you are enjoying yourself. PEA is present in higher levels in 'blissful' people (Chapter 01). It is also found in dark chocolate.

The brain's BLISS chemical

Dark chocolate contains an anandamide – a cannabinoid brain chemical which is known as the 'BLISS chemical' because it is produced in the brain when you feel good (Chapter 01). The anandamide released in your brain when you feel good acts on your brain in the same way as the THC in cannabis, but because anandamide does not act on the whole of your brain, like cannabis does, you can feel good without losing your mind. You do not feel 'out of it' like you would on cannabis (or marijuana). Anandamide is a natural brain chemical that is not known to have harmful side effects, unless you would regard BLISS as harmful. In fact, BLISS is strongly correlated with good health (Chapter 01) and the anandamide in dark chocolate is the brain's own bliss chemical.

The secret of eternal youth?

According to Dr G. Cousens, MAOIs (monoamine oxidase inhibitors) in dark chocolate work by allowing increased levels of anandamine and dopamine to circulate in the brain. It is the high level of anandamine and dopamine that distinguishes the brains of children from the brains of most adults because, in general, as you get older the levels of these neurotransmitters decrease. This decrease is associated with a decrease in physical and mental spontaneity and joy. You are as young as you think and feel and the MAOIs in dark chocolate can help to keep your anandamine and dophamine levels nearer to the levels of your youth.

And so to bed

Dark chocolate produces endorphins that induce the loving feelings that often lead to sex. The same endorphins also facilitate the euphoria of the 'afterglow'.

The effects of sex on your brain and your thinking

The effects of sex on your thinking depends on whether or not your pre-sex stress levels are excessive, whether or not you have an orgasm, and what type of thinking you are concerned about.

The seven steps in the sex life of your brain

Step 1. You and your partner each need to have sufficient testosterone in your brain. Low levels of testosterone are the most common cause of low levels of libido. Stresses, fatigue, disturbed sleep, hormone imbalance due to pregnancy, hysterectomy or menopause, are common causes of inadequate levels of testosterone.

Step 2. Given you have sufficient testosterone, then a rising level of estrogen can generate a feeling of desire, triggering the release of pheromones under your armpits. These may create a reciprocal sexual desire in your partner (the jury is still out on this one).

Step 3. Sexual desires release dopamine. Dopamine helps you to think visually. Dopamine will help you to visualize, imagine and fantasize about the different possible places and ways in which you might have sex with your partner. This will further raise your level of desire and the level of nitric oxide in your bloodstream.

Step 4. The nitric oxide increases your rate of blood flow. Besides helping you to dilate the labial lips of your vaginal area, or to engorge the tumescence of your penis, the increased rate of supply of oxygen to your brain will enable you to process information faster and to assess problems more quickly. (The increased rate of oxidation will leave your head clearer afterwards for calculations, decisions and action.) Nitric oxide readies you for action.

Step 5. If the action is sexual, your oxytocin levels will rise, causing pelvic contractions and raising the possibility of female orgasm. The oxytocin heightens a sense of being wanted, safe and secure. It is sometimes called the 'trust hormone'. It increases preparedness to think of novel or riskier solutions. It aids creative thinking.

Step 6. The pleasure of sexual activity, especially following orgasm, raises the levels of serotonin in the brain. Serotonin calms agitation, stress and anxiety. Cortisol levels associated with stress are moderated, making calm, logical, decision making and calculation easier. High levels of serotonin favour creative thinking.

Step 7. With stress relieved, head cleared and visual and creative thinking empowered, there is an 'after glow' of satisfaction associated with a rise in the level of phenylethylamine (PEA). PEA produces feelings of well-being and a tendency to smile involuntarily! PEA is the brain chemical associated with romance and falling in love. It is also produced by eating dark chocolate. (Sometimes life is less complicated if you just eat the chocolate!)

Manopause and mid-life crisis – what crisis?

Menopause among 50+ women has received much coverage elsewhere, but manopause, the equivalent phenomenon for 50+ men, has not received the same attention until now. According to Dr Ian Banks of Men's Health Forum, the manopause is better known as andropause. Too low a level of testosterone in manopausal men can cause low libido, erectile dysfunction, low mood and irritability – all four of which can lower performance on thinking tasks, given that sex is good for your brain and depression is not (Chapter 01). Psychologically, the resulting gain in weight round the belly and the loss of hair on the pate is sometimes over-compensated for by buying a car with a bigger bonnet, and clothes that are too tight, and by chasing younger women in order to prove...

An alternative to big cars, and making a complete fool of yourself, is to ask your GP to check your available testosterone level – your total might be fine, but too much may be gummed up by Sex Hormone Binding Globulin (SHBG). If your available testosterone is low, consider testosterone replacement therapy (TRT). The main risk is exacerbating a pre-existing prostate cancer – but this can be checked out before you start your course of TRT. The 3G cocktail (Chapter 02) is reported to have favourable side effects on libido.

Sun is bad for you – and other myths

The 50+ have always known that they think and feel better after a bit of sun, whatever the doom mongers say about wrinkles and skin cancer. The 50+ were right! The shrinkage of telomeres, at the ends of parts of your DNA, is a marker for your biological age and, in a study of 2,160 women aged up to 79, Professors Speltor, at Kings College London, reported in November 2007 that your shrinkage is less (i.e. your body is biologically younger) after you sunbathe. The sun appears to make your body younger – no wonder you feel better. Vitamin D produces the same effect and sunshine aids the production of Vitamin D in your skin – accounting for about 90 per cent of the Vitamin D we need (15 minutes a day, three days a week is all you need). No wonder we feel older in the winter and 'our fancy' returns in the spring. Vitamin D also protects against brain diseases like multiple sclerosis.

The 50+ are well represented among those who buy homes in the sun, but they still need to apply their sun creams after 10 minutes or so to avoid the 'leather look', and to minimize the risk of skin cancer.

Summary

- Thinking ability can be enhanced through diet.
- Mental performance is affected by the sequence in which you eat food.
- You can improve mental performance by 'grazing'.
- Yoyo weight loss diets can damage your brain and your thinking. Ditch them. Fitness is more important than fatness. Protect your brain by eating low oxytoxic food and high ORAC food.
- Physical exercise and posture can enhance thinking performance.
- Dehydration impairs mental activity. Drinking alcohol makes things worse.
- There is a short boost from caffeine but the effect of theobromine in dark chocolate is more sustained.
- Alcohol impairs your judgement, memory, analysis and mental agility and dehydrates your brain.
- There is no net benefit to thinking from nicotine, cannabis or cocaine, but there is extensive, often irreversible, damage to the brain.
- Performance on IQ tests can be improved by changing sleeping habits.
- Your performance on thinking tasks can be improved by having sex.
- It sometimes easier just to eat dark chocolate!

Suggested further reading

Craven, K. (2007) 'We've got the bug', *The Independent*, 15/5/07, pp12–13.

Dharma, D. (2004) 'Brain Longevity', *The Lancet* 43, pp324–36.

Halford, P. (2004) *Optimum Nutrition for the Mind*, Piatkus.

Jaski, R. (2006) *Wit and Wisdom*, Carlton.

Thomas, G. (2003) *A Mind and Body Workout*, Octopus.

UK Mental Health Foundation (2006) 'Feeding Minds'.

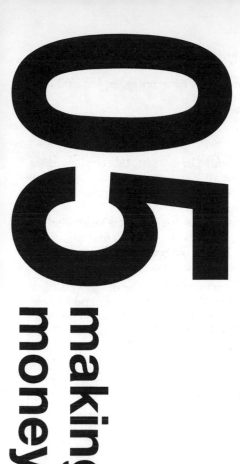

05
making more money

In this chapter you will learn:
- about your enhanced powers of critical, creative and reflective thinking at 50+
- how to exploit the enhanced development of the frontal lobes of the 50+ brain to think logically, solve problems and make decisions
- how to use superior 50+ thinking skills to earn a better living working for someone else, or to make more money working for yourself.

We know the science.
We have predicted the threat.
It's time for action.

(Governor A. Schwarzenegger, Jan 2007)

Introduction

At 50+ your country needs you! Or, at least, its economy does. Professor Hart of the UK Small Business Research Centre has discovered that new business start ups by the 50+ generation are adding £24 billion to the national economy. He adds that when economic regeneration is powered by the 50+, it is more likely to succeed in boosting local economies. In the UK, in 2007 alone, according to research by Yellow Pages, the 50+ generation accounted for 16 per cent of new business start ups.

None of this is surprising when you look at the thinking skill set and mind set that is needed to succeed at work, or in businesses, and when you see how all its components improve strongly with age, as long as you don't retire and as long as you stay fit and healthy.

Research on men in Boston, USA has shown that you are more likely to stay fit and healthy, and keep 'ahead at work', if you don't retire. If you follow the low oxytoxic diet and physical and mental exercise regime suggested in Chapter 04, the chances are that at 50+ you are currently less than halfway through your potential working life. So stop smoking, drink one coffee and eat no more than one quarter bar of dark chocolate a day! Stay ahead at work, earn a better living and live a better life. Death is not what it used to be, so aim to die on the job! Work till you drop – you deserve that better death.

Because 'work' in today's knowledge economy usually means brainwork, staying 'a head at work' today means thinking ahead. Fortunately, the older you get, the better you become at thinking ahead. Applied thinking requires critical, creative and reflective thinking, and all three improve with age.

Applied thinking

Applied thinking involves the use of critical, creative and reflective thinking.

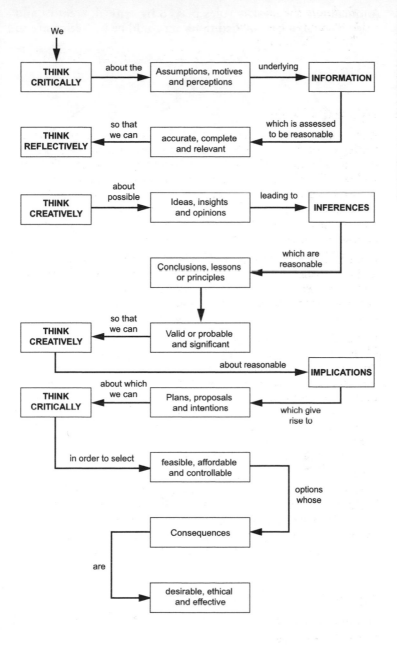

Figure 5.1: The process of applied thinking

A mnemonic for the key roles played by critical, creative and reflective thinking in applied thinking could be by 'seeing eye to eye':

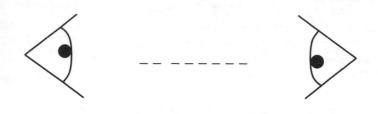

We are always seeking to get from one word whose initial is **I** to another word whose initial is **I**, via another whose initial is **I**, i.e.

Applied thinking	=	Critical thinking	+	Creative thinking	+	Reflective thinking
Which is getting						
from...		Information		Information		Information
via...		Inference		Inspiration		Insight
to...		Implication		Implementation		Intention

When thinking critically at work, or profiting from experience, or for checklists of key actions to take to improve your creative thinking, consult Appendices A–F and read *Teach Yourself Training Your Brain*, Horne and Wootton (2007).

Applied thinking – ten questions to ask...

Concerning the believability of Information:

1 Which words or phrases are ambiguous or imprecise?
2 What assumptions are not admitted?
3 What assumptions are admitted?
4 Why is this being said or written?
5 What statistics are offered?
6 Are the statistics skewed?
7 What is omitted?

8 Who might construe this information differently?
9 What concepts underpin the collection, or analysis, of this information?
10 Is their use valid?

Concerning the reasonableness of Inferences:
1 What internal contradictions can we see?
2 What counter-examples can we think of?
3 What opinions are being offered as facts?
4 How authoritative, or biased, are the sources?
5 What evidence is offered?
6 What conflicting evidence is offered?
7 What flaws are there in their reasoning?
8 Have counter-arguments been considered?
9 Is their evaluation fair and their rebuttal convincing?
10 Does the conclusion overstretch the evidence available?

Concerning the practicality of Implications:
1 If the implied action were taken, would it so change the situation that it would invalidate the assumptions on which the argument for action is based?
2 How controllable is the behaviour of the actors in the situation?
3 Are the skills present which will be needed to take the implied action?
4 Are all the consequences beneficial? Judged by what criteria?
5 Are there unwanted side effects?
6 Does the implied action confer the greatest benefit to the greatest number?
7 Does the implied action waste the least resources?
8 Does the implied action do least harm?
9 Thinking about resources, how feasible are the implied actions?
10 What risks are associated with the implied action? What is the probability of the risk and the extent of the consequence? Is the worst case acceptable, and by what criteria is acceptability judged?

At 50+ you can go on getting better

Aristotle said: 'You are what you habitually do'. If you change what you habitually do, you will change. If, at 50+, you habitually ask questions like the ones that follow, you have already become a great thinker. If you continue to add such questions to your conversational repertoire (Chapter 06), you will continue to become even clearer in your thinking.

Ten questions clear thinkers often ask

1 Could you elaborate a little?
2 Can you give me an example?
3 How could we check that out?
4 How are those two things connected?
5 How does that follow from what you said earlier?
6 Why do you think that is important or significant?
7 How can that information help us to make progress?
8 Can you think of a different way to explain that to me?
9 Can you be more precise? How much, how many, how often?
10 What do you think X would say in reply to that (where X can, for example, belong to another race, culture, gender or socio economic group)?

Your intellectual virtues at 50+

When we hear people like you, at 50+, habitually asking the questions like the ones above, we envy your persistence, integrity, empathy, courage and humility. We envy your confidence to think for yourself. These are intellectual virtues. These are the intellectual virtues that help you, at 50+, to reduce hypocrisy, indifference, cowardice, arrogance, injustice and conformity in the world. One way your more developed virtues and habits of mind show themselves is in the way in which you question what other people have written.

Ten ways to question what you read

1 Why do I think the author wrote this?
2 What question is the author trying to answer?
3 Are there any clues to the author's intentions?
4 What kind of information is being brought forward here?
5 Why am I expected to believe that this information is true?

6 What assumptions are being made explicitly, and also implicitly?

7 What principle, general truth or conclusion does the author want me to accept?

8 Are all the inferences reasonable and supported by valid reasons or examples?

9 If I accept these conclusions, what actions are implied that I, or others, should take?

10 What would be the consequence for others if these actions were taken?

Ten rules for applied thinking at 50+

1 Ask yourself what assumptions you are making.

2 Articulate as clearly as possible the criteria you are using to make judgments.

3 Remember to own what you feel, as well as what you think.

4 Treat initial reactions, your own and other people's, only as tentative positions.

5 Enquire whether other people share your perceptions.

6 Empathize with the feelings and thoughts of other people.

7 Decide whether you have enough justifiably believable information to support a tentative conclusion. (Could more information be gathered easily? What kind of information is needed? Is there a reliable source that is readily available? What credibility would the source have and why?)

8 Recognize that all interpretations, including your own, are subjective.

9 Admit the limitations of your information, or of the time spent gathering or checking it.

10 Contextualize your conclusions. Don't claim universal truths or principles.

Ten ways to spot flaws in the arguments of younger people

1 Check whether the arguments offered contradict what has been said elsewhere.

2 Check whether evidence offered is out of date, unreliable, uncorroborated.

3 Check whether correlations are being offered as though they were causes.

4 Are assertions being offered as facts?

5 Does the argument contain non-sequitors?

6 Ask whether there are possibilities that are not being considered. (There are usually more than two possibilities.)

7 Ask: 'On what does this all hinge? What is the crucial point of the argument? On what does it turn?'

8 Ask: 'What is the *sine qua non*? What is it that would invalidate a key conclusion, if it were shown to be untrue?'

9 Judge the parts of the argument you regard as pivotal as to the soundness of the assumptions on which it rests.

10 How strong is the reasoning that leads from these assumptions to the conclusions you are being invited to accept – dubious, weak, telling or compelling?

Thinking rules at work

Thinkers can't retire

Louis Armstrong said that musicians cannot retire as long as they have music in their heads. In the same way, thinkers cannot retire as long as they have thoughts in their heads. In the twenty-first century, thinking is work, so you cannot retire from work while you still have thoughts in your head.

So, don't retire, simply earn a better living at work. At 50+, some of the rules at work have changed. The basis on which most businesses – and even charities and publicly funded and provided services – now compete has changed since the 50+ first started work. In Western economies, the basis of competition has moved from brawn to brains. Even the machines have microchips to 'mind' them. Even in the so-called 'knowledge' economies, the knowledge of employees is no longer a sufficient basis for the comparative advantage of one organization over another. Databases are too quickly changed, updated and redistributed to all who are willing to pay for them to remain a source of competitive advantage. Knowledge is now perishable.

It is how well employees can think about what they know that gives one organization an advantage over another and, in all the different ways that it is important to be able to think at work, your 50+ brain is so much better than younger brains. Your 50+

brain continues to get better by the day, until well into your eighties, as long as you follow some basic rules:

Rule 1   Wake to increasingly bright light, artificial if necessary, and current affairs radio if you can stand it. If not, pre-selected music that has a strong rhythm.

Rule 2   Eat breakfast – fruit and/or non-dairy protein (egg or fish). Keep grains such as bread, toast and cereals until the evening and then choose whole grains. Drink plenty of water from the moment you get out of bed. Load up like a camel. Drink one cup of high quality black coffee. Never add refined or granulated sugar to anything – especially in the morning. Eat sitting down without distraction and with full awareness of taste, texture and chewing. (See Chapter 04.)

Rule 3   As you go through your morning routine, keep swapping hands so that, for example, you do some things with your left hand that you normally do with your right and vice versa. Do two or three eye exercises and put your head in your hands. (See Chapter 04.)

Rule 4   To get to work, prefer running and cycling over walking, walking over driving and public over private transport, park and ride over ride, shared car over single usage. Carry a refillable water bottle and keep sipping before you get thirsty. When you arrive, favour stairs over lifts or escalators. If you have a choice, choose an office on a higher floor.

Rule 5   Think (and talk) on your feet. Sit as little as possible. Moving about and talking both aid brain work and help you to remember what has been discussed and decided. Use a whiteboard to log discussions and take down the key points at the end, preferably as a visual map. Do your thinking aloud, on your feet, and away from your computer. Do not work near fax machines or photocopiers or printers, and use fresh-air (not air conditioning) for ventilation.

Rule 6   Lunch, if you need it, follows breakfast rule 2, but add in salads and/or vegetables to your fresh fruit as additional sources of complex carbohydrate. Add a teaspoon of olive oil or nut oil or hemp seed oil for your dressing. If you are a grazer, graze. Favour nibbling plain nuts, not salted, and not peanuts. Fresh fruit is better than dried fruit because the sugar content is less concentrated and has a slower release, and the juice helps to keep up your hydration. Take a walk in the park – 20 minutes – whatever the weather (well almost!). If you are going to stay after 5 p.m., take another walk at break time. It will re-oxygenate your neurons and moderate excessive levels of cortisol in your brain.

Rule 7   Talk, think, write – then talk some more. Then walk the talk. Under-promise and over-deliver. Try to show that you are enjoying it. Even if you have to force yourself to smile, your brain chemistry will change to follow suit. That change in your brain chemistry will help you to think well, which will put a genuine smile on your face and in turn on the faces of other people around you. This will lift general levels of morale, mood and optimism, which will, in turn, favour improved performance (Chapter 01).

Rule 8   Dress the part – whatever signals success, confidence and competence in your organization. Think of people that you think are on the top of their game. How do they dress? Is there the odd thing you could copy and still feel it was not to false for you? Grooming is never amiss. Have the best hair cut you can afford and just before you need it! Stay on top of tooth stains, dry lips, clean cut nails and deodorant. After your midday walk, do a few eye stretches and a hand rub (Chapter 04), and you will hit the afternoon ground running, while all around you struggle with their mental work.

Rule 9   Have a plan – a private plan discussed with a few confidantes: a long-term plan for what you want out of your work, and a short-term plan for what you want to get done this week. When random things happen (which they will) that do not fit with your plan, reel in the slack and hold firm until the next random wind, or tide, turns in your favour.

Rule 10   Do not gossip, whine, whinge, bitch, take sides or play politics and do not spend more time than you have to with people who do. They will take up valuable working space in your brain and preoccupy your thoughts, distract your concentration and lower the mental energy you want for your own work. Defend people who are sniped at by others. Be loyal. Compliment others whenever you can do so sincerely.

You can usually find something about them, or their work, that you genuinely like. Ask questions. Show genuine curiosity and interest in other people's work and projects.

Rule 11   Listen, say 'please' and 'thank you', and don't swear or use religious names in vain. If there are ethics or laws peculiar to the sector you are in, be sure you know what they are. Don't lie. Keep adding to your contact/network list, and keep cycling through it to refresh the connections every few months. Adapt your approach for each person. Everyone is different.

Rule 12   At 50+, your predictive thinking is much more accurate than a younger person's. So think and lead. Act as if you have already taken that step ahead. Wear the demeanour, and talk up the talk associated with the next step.

Rule 13   By all means feel angry – it will fuel your mental energy, whereas sadness will sap it. But do not lose your temper. At 50+ you will be less patient and more easily provoked. Squeeze every last ounce of breath from your body and allow fresh breath to rush in to fill the vacuum. Do this three times and your temper will expire with your breath. Do not make gratuitous personal remarks. Avoid sniping and cynicism. Cynicism is corrosive. It will corrode you, as well as your workplace and thinking space.

Rule 14   Cultivate, nurture and develop close relationships with people at work (Chapter 06).

Rule 15   Read the *Rules of Work* by Richard Templar.

Rule 16   If you're not in management, at 50+ you probably should be (if you can stand it!). At 50+, you have the attributes needed for successful management, much more so than younger people. At 50+, you know how to spark emotional engagement in people; how to not take meetings too seriously; how to spot dead wood and freeloaders and have them transferred; how to let younger people make mistakes and help them learn from them; how to accept your limitations (though you have fewer at 50+ than when you were younger); how to encourage others; how to spot good people; how to take the rap from time to time – especially to shield younger staff (they will love you for this rare management attribute); how to get your people good kit; how to pour oil on friction; how to celebrate a success every week; how to respect individual differences; how to listen to the ideas of younger people; how not always to need the last word on everything; how to be positive; how to protect creative people from necessary control systems; how to risk saying 'yes'; how to ask young people for solutions as well as problems; how to work early and hard as an example; how to enjoy yourself at work; how to use your superior predictive and creative thinking to be proactive about change; how to use superior reflective thinking to learn from mistakes – yours and those of younger people; how to use your superior planning skills to have a plan B as well as a plan A; how to increase the chances that you will get lucky (chance favours your reduced fear of failure at 50+); how to recognize excessive stress; how to know when to let go of an idea or a person; how to visualize success; how to go home before it's time and to have a good home to go to; how to keep learning from your superior experience at 50+; how to concentrate on doing a few out of the many things that you can do better at 50+.

You can apply for a better job now you're 50+

In all psychometric tests, you are likely to out-perform a young person. Likewise, if an assessment centre includes tests of group work, leadership, problem solving, prediction or creativity, at 50+ you will normally out-perform a young person. However, at 50+, one of the few things you might be less good at, compared with a younger person, is thinking fast on your feet. This can be a problem in selection tests and selection interviews. Your counter-measure, at 50+, is better preparation. You need to leave the panel in no doubt that you are looking forward to meeting their customers and clients; to meeting and working with some new people; to feeling you are contributing to improving their profits or the service they provide and contributing to their growth and reputation. Here are some questions to prepare and rehearse. Be sure to do it aloud.

A. Why do you want this job?

The panel will want to be sure that at 50+ you still have 'fire in your belly' – that you really want the job. Think now. Which of the following reasons might you have? Practise giving that reason – out loud.

- It fits in with my life and career plan, in that...
- It will enable me to help people by...
- I will be better off financially because...
- There will be more opportunity to work on my own and I will enjoy this greater autonomy and responsibility because...
- I will enjoy the chance to travel because...
- I will enjoy the chance to learn about...
- I will enjoy the greater scope for creativity in...
- It is important to me to have work that I am proud to talk about to others, that I can feel is socially useful, like...
- It seems that there will be more opportunities for working as part of a team and that is important to me because...
- It sounds like it will be busy and stimulating, with plenty of variety. I like it when you never know what you might be faced with – when every day brings something new to solve or learn about.
- I like the fact that I will have to learn new skills, like....
- I am attracted by the opportunity of further training in...
- It will be good to make use of my experience in persuading, negotiation, problem solving...
- It will good to put new ideas on... into practice.
- It will be good to make use of my experience in...
- I like the thought of going home every day feeling satisfied that I have made a practical contribution to...
- It will be good to get back to...
- I much prefer to be in a job where my pay will be directly related to my performance – that way I know I will be well rewarded.
- I can see that there will be lots of opportunity for extra responsibility and that there are clear promotion routes.

B. How do you see yourself developing, if you come to us?

Emphasize that the immediate tasks described seem challenging and that your first task will be to tackle these to create a firm foundation for future action.

C. Why did you leave your previous job?

Do not be negative about the employer you left. No panel will want to recruit disloyalty. Emphasize the new challenge and learning opportunities of the new job and the improved financial reward. If you do not mention this, the panel will suspect you are not being frank with them.

D. What is wrong with your present job?

It has become too easy, no longer a challenge. You feel under-stretched and ready for something more challenging and more financially rewarding.

E. What have you tried to do to make your present job more demanding?

Refer to proactive proposals you have made and changes you have initiated: 'It's just that scope for this is limited by...'. Or, you hadn't been planning to leave: 'It's just that the opportunity provided by this job seems so much more appealing because...'.

F. Can you give an example of how you handle criticism?

Stress that you haven't had a lot of practice! Explain that it would depend partly on whether or not you felt the criticism was justified and how it was delivered. Cite an example of how you have benefited from criticism.

G. Give an example of how you reacted to not getting your own way

Explain that you consulted widely and then put your reasons and some other options in writing for management to think about before asking for a meeting to discuss your concerns. Describe your feelings and your reasons for finally accepting that your ideas could not be implemented for the time being.

H. How would you rate your present manager?

Emphasize what you like about her/him and how she/he could perhaps build on her strengths to become even better.

I. Ideally, what would you like to be paid?

My current salary is... and by next year it will be... Obviously I am expecting to improve on this. One of the things that has attracted me about your position is the extra responsibility and clearly I am expecting this extra responsibility to be rewarded as I show that I am capable. I know that you would not offer me the job if you didn't think I could do it well, so I am expecting an offer of at least...

J. Do you think you are under-paid in your present job?

The present pay is fair for the present job – it's just that you have outgrown it as you have gained expertise and experience and demonstrated that you can do more.

K. Where do you expect to be in three years' time?

Emphasize how you expect to be applying the new learning and experience you will have gained.

L. Do you have any questions for us?

Yes, you do! You must, if you are serious about the job. However, do not dwell on:

- the salary
- the holiday entitlement
- sharing an office
- the need to arrive late, or leave early, because of…

You can sort out such matters after you get the job offer. Rehearse asking the following questions, and ask at least two, but no more than six of them:

- How has the vacancy come about? (Is there anything I should know?)
- What do you do to encourage internal promotion?
- What will be my immediate priority on starting?
- Where would you see me in five years' time?
- How does the organization hope to change in the next five years?
- Do you have any reservations about my ability to do this job?
- When can I expect to hear from you?

The primary purpose of your questions is to convey further information about yourself that will increase your chance of being offered the job. Banish negative thinking about your prospects (Chapter 01). Be prepared to display several forms of your 50+ intelligence (Chapter 02). Visualize yourself enjoying the interview and being offered the job. Feel the good feelings of achievement you will feel doing the job well. Form close relationships with people you meet during the selection process, including the other candidates (Chapter 06).

Making better decisions at 50+

Managers are professional decision makers. They are expected to get more decisions right than wrong – which, at 50+, you generally do. They are expected to get most of the big ones right. Fortunately, at 50+, you are very good at making up your mind. You are very well equipped for decision making.

What should I eat? What should I wear? Who shall I talk to? Should I re-marry? Shall I apply? Having these kinds of choices to make is important confirmation to you that you are free – that you have freedom as an individual and that you are a member of a free society.

You are rarely freer to choose than when you're 50+. Parental pressures may be fading, financial demands may be lessening, and some responsibilities may have flown the nest. At the same time, your knowledge, life skills, experience and thinking powers are burgeoning.

While you are able to take better decisions at 50+, the decisions may take you longer to make. You just need to start thinking about them sooner (your superior predictive thinking will help you to anticipate the need for decisions) and you will tend to think about them for longer (this results in more thoughtful, better thought out decisions). For example, at 50+ it will take you longer to absorb and hold in your short-term memory any new information that is relevant to the decision that you need to take, but your enhanced visual thinking means that you can use cognitive mapping and systems thinking to help you.

At 50+, you have a great deal of life-acquired knowledge and experience to review, to see if it can usefully bear on the current decision you need to take. At 50+, you also now know that opportunities of a lifetime need to be taken during the lifetime of the opportunities.

At work, you will be paid more for your preparedness to take decisions and for keeping your head when younger people all around you are losing theirs! If you are a manager, you are not expected to get all of your decisions right, but you are expected to decide and not to dither. At 50+, when you do get the occasional decision wrong, you will be more philosophical than a younger person – you will be less disabled by regret or guilt. You will be more able than a younger person to move on to take the next decision. You are more likely to get the big ones right, and that's why employers will pay you more.

The make-up of your mind

Can neuroscience help you make up your mind? Decisions are made up of a number of mental processes, such as information processing, new memory formation, logic, visual thinking, prediction, emotion and empathetic thinking. Nearly all of these mental processes are very much better developed in the 50+ brain than they are in younger brains. The exception is new memory formation, which is slower, but Chapter 02 gives you the mental moves you can make to ameliorate this.

Dos and don'ts of decision making

1. Do imagine...

Use your visual thinking to picture what things will look life after your decision is implemented. Looking at that picture in your mind's eye, how do you feel (Chapter 01)? According the Professor Gilbert of Harvard, younger people routinely over-estimate, or under-estimate, the strength of the feelings they will experience – either positively (too optimistic) or negatively (too pessimistic). The 'forecasts' of the 50+ are consistently more realistic, often based on similar situations of which they have had direct experience.

The 50+ are less constrained by anxieties arising from fear of loss. Professor Kahnemen, of Princeton, reported in *Psychological Science* (vol. 07), that the 'price' of loss aversion in the general population was about 1:2, i.e. people will only risk losing at the level of one, if they stand to gain at the level of two. Because they are more likely to have had more experiences of 'it was not as bad as I feared', the 50+ are less loss averse, and so can contemplate a wider range of options in coming to their better decisions. At 50+, you are better at remembering different ways of seeing the world so that it can continue to be an acceptable place for you to inhabit. You know better than most that the worst may never happen. Even if the worst does happen, you know, based on your experience, that you will survive.

2. The 50+ have guts as well as instincts

So trust your instinct! In the same edition of *Psychological Science*, mentioned previously, Janine Willis of Princeton reported that 50+ subjects were able to decide on another person's likely trustworthiness, competence, aggressiveness or long-term likeability within one-tenth of a second. Given ten times longer, i.e. around one second, they retained confidence in their first decision. This helps the 50+ to compensate for their slower speed of new information processing.

According to Professor Dijksterluis, of Amsterdam, writing in *Science* (vol. 311), rather than allowing information overload to impair their decision making, the 50+ default to a well-honed and well-informed gut instinct. The gut instincts of the 50+ are better guarded against the ever-present danger of emotional override that was investigated by Joseph Arvai and reported to the Advances of Science conference in San Francisco in February 2007. Arvai found that when most people are confronted with decisions about what to do about terrorism or violent crime, they generally allowed their emotional reactions to by-pass any rational review of the information relevant to their decision.

3. Feel the fear (but not the anger) – before you do it anyway!

Arvai's finding on the dangers of emotional override does not mean that all information needs to be factored into decisions – only that you should not allow emotions to by-pass due consideration of as much relevant information as time allows. At the moment of decision, brain scans show that your limbic system – the centre of your emotional thinking – is always active. Damasio found that damage to the limbic system produces chronic indecision, even about what to eat or drink, or even whether to get out of bed. This does not mean that the impact of all emotions is helpful. Anger, for example, rarely is. Fessler found, for example, that men (not women) made poorer gambling decisions when they were angry.

4. Self-serving bias

It is good to know that your brain is generally on your side – often protecting you from unknown risks by making you anxious about unfamiliar actions for which you do not yet have well-rehearsed or learned neuron traces in place. (Often these can be safely rehearsed or put in place by simply visualizing in advance the hoped for successful actions – see Chapter 04, the body rotation exercise.)

One disadvantage of having a self-serving brain is that it tends to introduce bias when you try to weigh up information in decision making. Your brain is predisposed to notice, attend to, give weight to, or favour consideration of information that fits in with preconceived ideas or familiar views. This may be another reason why 'thoughtful conversations' (Chapter 06) are such an aid to accuracy and clarity of thought, as well to the longer-term creation of increased cognitive capacity. What your 'thoughtful companion' is able to do is to act as a devil's advocate, or to ask questions which are not constrained by your own brain's desire to confirm its own wisdom. De Bono has suggested that you can bypass your brain's self-serving bias by orchestrating an internal dialogue between different aspects of yourself, and explicitly calling up pessimistic black-hat thinking.

5. Oh, that sinking feeling

The 50+ brain is more able than a younger brain to make use of 'that sinking feeling' – to decide to ditch things, or to drop the subject, or to walk away and move on. At 50+, when 'you get that feeling that you've been here before', you are better able to say, 'I've been here before, let's quit ahead, or quit now, before it gets worse'. Younger brains might persist long after they should have aborted the mission. Younger brains are often victims of what Arks and Blomer called 'the sunk cost syndrome' under which, if you've spent a lot of money on a meal, you are inclined to finish it even if you are full already and don't even like it. (Then you really will get that sinking feeling!) Even though you have sunk, or invested, a lot of money in that meal, you really should just leave it! It's the same with that expensive suit that you'll never wear again – donate it to a charity.

6. Look both ways, before you...

The 50+ are more inclined to do this, and so avoid the 'framing effect' of which Ray Dolan, from UCL London, wrote in 2006 in *Science* (vol. 313). The framing effect was discovered using an NMR scanner to note the involvement of the amygdala in decision making. People tend to decide between otherwise identical plans in favour of those that are framed in terms of their positive outcomes, and decide against otherwise identical plans that are 'framed' in terms of their negative outcomes, e.g. their cost. This framing effect is neutralized when people are asked to look at the plans both ways. The 50+ are more likely to look at things both ways.

7. Everyone agrees...

The 50+ are much less likely to decide 'X', just because everybody thinks 'X'. The young have a stronger need to conform to peer or social pressure, or to defer to authority or 'expert' opinion.

8. Short listing your long list before you decide

In a seminal work on decision making in 1976, Herb Simm distinguished between 'maximizers' and 'satisficers'. 'Maximizers' are people who need to consider all possible options before they can decide. Satisficers are people who decide quickly in favour of the first option that meets their threshold criteria. The 50+ have generally learned to be good 'satisficers' in decision making. That is why they are successful at selecting 'soulmates' or 'life partners' or 'thoughtful companions' (Chapter 06). The 50+ are more 'Quakerly' in their decision making, seeking decisions that are 'good enough' or 'serviceable'. Schwartz found that 'satisficers' are subsequently less dissatisfied with the outcomes of their decisions. 'Maximizers' were far more likely than the 50+ to feel anxious or depressed or frustrated by the results of their decision making.

Bullshit baffles brains

Business jargon

At 50+, it is important not to let bullshit baffle your brain at work. Business bullshit can be an elegant, colourful, light-hearted language that bonds the cognoscenti into 'in' groups that have fun and compete successfully. But sometimes, business bullshit covers up a lack of brain power, and it can be used to bluff or intimidate outsiders. Don't be bluffed or intimidated.

If you don't know what some of these mean, have a look on the internet. Alternatively, ask work colleagues if they understand some of the terms – many probably won't. You will probably discover that you are much more managerially 'literate' than your younger colleagues.

Empower	Framework	Driven	On message
Tick the boxes	Brainstorm	Best practice	Synergy
Quality	Ducks in a row	Offline	Flight path
Skill set	Mind set	Basket case	Disconnect
Customer-facing	Trajectory	Suits	Can do
Dissing	Joined-up thinking	Game plan	Bottom line
Empire building	Give me the numbers	The deal	Back to basics
Win–win	Process	Looking good	Close of play
Takes no prisoners	Level playing field	Lessons	The extra mile
Mushroom manager	Seagull	Handbags out	Cherry pick
Fast track	At the end	Wannabe	Low-hanging fruit
Strategic	Feedback	Workaholic	Seeking alignment
Park it	Learning curve	Scope it	Best practice
Comfort zone	Stakeholder	Focus	Touch base
Pocket science	Don't make waves	Don't rock the boat	Survivor
Template	Bench mark	Barrier to	Free rider
Grasp the nettle	Big picture	Ball park	Blue-sky thinking
Gravitas	Grown up	Outside the box	Go for it
Off the wall	Customer-focused	Halo effect	Hidden agenda
No sweat	Hearts and minds	Proactive	Move the goal
Lean	Knowledge worker	Post-its	Lick and promise
Lifeblood	Holding nerve	Jumping through hoops	Keep it simple
Manage expectations	Key learning points	Lifeblood	Nu surprises
Ramp it up	Pull-out stops	Long haul	Manage upwards
Hit the ground running	Wake up – smell the coffee	T over A	The elephant in the room
No pressure	Cool	On a roll	Within our gift
Working breakfast	Power nap	Prioritize	Silo management
Proactive	Deliverables	Profile	Back to back
Free time	Off the radar	Robust plan	Sink or swim
Feed back	Huddle	Talking shop	Squeaky clean

Straight	With the bark on	Verbal diarrhoea	Window
Bite the bullet	Work ethic	To task	Bring to the table
Fall on sword	Go nuclear	The nuclear option	Work–life balance
Work smarter	Don't do difficult	Keep your powder dry	Lock, stock, barrel
Do easy	You can if you think you can	Loose cannon	
Likely landmines?	Long-terms aims	Short-term gains	Scratch where it itches
You scratch my back…	On-side	Mission critical	TQM
RD	On-track	In play	Coal face
On a charge	Pre-emptive	Stir pudding	Sharp end
Dancing round handbags	Blitz	Scattergun approach	Take flak
Dove tail	Seamless	Do you read me?	Explore options
Get act together	Get wagons in a circle	Wait for the cavalry	Walking wounded
Weapons grade	Bite the bullet	20–20 hindsight	Save bacon
Scenario	A bridge too far	Rising tide	At the end of the day
A shambles	Shit hits the fan	Shit or bust	Plate spinning
Balls in the air	Between a rock and…	Sign off	A big ask
Blood bath	Stick to knitting	Sub-optimal	Soft landing
Catch 22	Drill down	Systematic	Dive deep
Get granular	TLC	In the pipeline	Enough on a plate
Fence mending	Flaky	Bear with me	Manage expectations
Fluid	From day one	Genie out of the bottle	Teflon management
Big picture	Hobson's choice	Competitive advantage	Continuous improvement
Off the scale	Knock on	Last chance saloon	Ground rules
Less is more	Let's not go there	Future facing	First principles
Lose the plot	Name and shame	Nesting	Go for it
Hardware	Helicopter vision	Nightmare	White noise
Non core	Leading edge	Lateral thinking	Blue sky

Reengineering	No-win situation	Mission statement	Quick fix
Read riot act	Rearranging deckchairs	Out of the loop	Head count
Heads roll	Orchestrate	Push the envelope	Proposition
To target	Step change	Results driven	Reinvent ourselves
Magic bullet	Holistic	Flesh out	USP
Value added	On the same wavelength	Scoping it	Squaring the circle
Brand	Badge	Wow factor	Differentiation
Band width	Iconic	Off-brand/ off-message	Segmentation
Door opener	Feel-good factor	Paradigm	
Game plan	Viral	Impacting	Vehicle
A must	Ramp it up	Heavyweight	Mega
Must have	Niche monster	Ratchet up	Mood music
Simply the best	Champions	All systems go	Heroes – show me the
The Peter Principle	Check in/check out	Fine tune	Road map
Free loader	Core competence	Knowledge worker	Get into gear
Mentor	Open-door policy	On autopilot	Green light
To land	Personal development	Skill set	A square peg
Reinvent the wheel	A steer	Tailspin	Flat structure
Succession planning	Away day	Up to speed	Bread and butter
A bung	Down-size	Right-size	Let go
Class act	To come of age	Cover all bases	Step up
Hyper	A jobsworth	A curved ball	The boy done good
Dream team	Early bath	Even keel	Movers and shakers
Nerdy	Key player	Spin	Scapegoat
The game plan	In two minds	Dead men walking	Own goal
A lightweight	Take to next level	Sticky wicket	Drive
Lifestyle choice	Plain sailing	Hardball	Bottom line
Sea change	One game at a time	80/20 rule	Top level

Swings and roundabouts	World class	Bean counter	The numbers
Tweak	Upside	To wash its face	Massage figures
Creative accounting	Front-end loaded	Basket case	The city
Bang for bucks	Built on sand	Apples with apples	Double whammy
Critical path	Cost effective	A red line	OD/ID/PD
Seed corn	Slippery slope	Line in sand	Levers
Drivers	Slush fund	Bridge the gap	Done deal
In the black/red	Playing the percentages	Got legs	To nail
Touchy feely	Up the ante	Access	Connectivity
Cut and paste	Down time	Fire walling	Fuzzy logic
Hand holding	Multi task	Portal	State of the art
User	Word of mouth	AKA	B2B
Dinky	ROI	Smart	Swot
TQM	Cooking with gas	Jerry built	Proof of pudding
Pigs might fly	Rule of thumb	Run it by	Smoke and mirrors
Blue in the face	Whistling in the dark	Salmon run	Pear shaped

---

Beware of 50+ business consultants

Would-be client: 'What do you charge?'

50+ consultant: 'To initiate consultation, £1,000 for three questions.'

Would be client: 'Isn't £1,000 for three questions a bit steep?'

50+ consultant: 'Yes, and what is your third question?'

TEXT messaging

Many people today use mobile phone text messaging to communicate with their friends, peers and, increasingly, work colleagues or opposite numbers in customer/supplier organizations. The following selection will give you an idea of what these messages are communicating (source: Ellis Wootton, 13 years old!):

GR8	Great	121	One to one
BBFN	Bye bye for now	2D4	To die for
KIT	Keep in touch	2nite	Tonight
THNQ	Thank you	4get	Forget
NTHING	Anything	4give	Forgive
RUOK?	Are you OK?	BRB	Be right back
R	Are	COZ	Because
8	Ate	G2G	Got to go
B	Be	H8	Hate
B4	Before	Jk	Just kidding
BCNU	Be seeing you	Np	No problem
QT	Cutie	Nutha	Another
D8	Date	Nm	Not much
DNR	Dinner	OMG	Oh my god
EZ	Easy	PLZ	Please
XLNT	Excellent	PPL	People
F8	Fate	Tb	Text back
4	For	2DAY	Today
FYI	For your information	2MORO	Tomorrow
L8	Late	WAN2	Want to
L8R	Later	WOT	What
Lol	Lots of love/laughs	Y	Why
M8	Mate	U	You
PLS	Please	U+me	You and me
PCM	Please call me	Ur	Your
Q	Queue/cue	UR	You are
R8	Rate	VG	Very good
C	See/sea	W8n	Waiting
CU L8R	See you later	Wan2	Want to
SPK	Speak	T	Tea
THX	Thanks	2	To/too

Making money by minding your own business

Being young and in business was greatly over-rated. Every failure was devastating. Later on, I realized that you always get another go if you want to.

(attributed to Mary Quant by Felix Dennis)

In 2007, 16 per cent of the successful new UK businesses were started by people aged 50+. This is not surprising because the mind set – or set of thinking skills – which you need to run a business successfully is highly developed in the 50+ brain. Luck helps, but thinking reduces the need for it. Luck favours the prepared mind, just as chance favours the brave. (Watch *The Dead Poet's Society* or almost anything else with Robin Williams in it.)

Why run your own business? To make money, rather than just earn a good living. Then you can give the money away, if you want to. But also, perhaps, to have more free time – i.e. time that you are free to spend how you choose, perhaps on writing books, sponsoring artists, volunteering to work with disadvantaged groups, hanging out with friends, or phoning relatives. When you run your own business, your time is your own. When you are earning a good living, your time belongs to others. Money is like sex. Thoughts about sex and money can pre-occupy your brain, for example not having enough, not getting enough, how to get to more. The beauty of having enough is that it frees you to think about other things and other people.

How much money is enough?

Arbitrarily, between £15 million and £40 million is enough money. Alternatively, enough for whatever you need to spend it on, or more than you can give away in a lifetime. So make a start. No task takes longer than a task one does not start. Listen to your wealth-wanting drum and ignore some conventional wisdom. Conventional wisdom, unlike 50+ wisdom, is replete with reasons for not doing things. There are the odd nuggets in conventional wisdom – but they are hard to separate from the fool's gold. Think things out for yourself from first principles. At 50+, you are well equipped to do so.

Minding your own business – the best cure for retirement

In the twenty-first century, wealth comes from the mind and the imagination.

(Steve Forbes – a billionaire)

Setting up your own business will be such a welcome learning curve. Anyone not busy learning is busy dying. Your own business may well fend off Alzheimer's. As a minimum, it should prevent the hardening of your neural arteries. Nobody can retire you from your own business. You can work till you drop and so die a good death. At 50+, you have less to lose, less to fear and less to prove than a younger person – all are major advantages when you start your own business. It will be hard – but no worse for that. It will sometimes get hairy and scary – but it will often be fun.

After a few failures, you will eventually have a small success – and one small success will breed another. All that is needed is applied thinking, and at 50+ you are better prepared for the steps that prevent others. At 50+, you are prepared to take the steps from knowing to doing. In your own business, you are not prevented from taking the steps from knowing to doing – as so often you are when you try to earn a good living from someone else.

Team working isn't working

Employers are often fond of teams, groups and meetings. These are purpose-designed to make thinking difficult, and therefore action is often absent or ill advised. Fear of failure and avoidance of blame stalk most meetings. Only knowing and thinking and doing gets it done.

Knowing and thinking,
Is not enough.
Only knowing and doing
Is real applied thinking.
Only knowing and doing,
Gets it done.

(Terry Horne (2007) after Felix Dennis)

The fear of failure

Let's do it (or at least let's agree to forget it, and thereby create headspace for our next thought). As Dylan said: 'When you got nothing – you got nothing to lose.'

Does your business idea risk utter destitution? At 50+, that is unlikely. Public embarrassment is likely to be your worst-case scenario. At 50+, you are more philosophical about being embarrassed than you were when you were younger. Nevertheless, it is a real fear. It will still wake you up in a cold sweat at 4 a.m. It can still be a nightmare. But it is only a nightmare. At 50+, you have the thinking skills to harness fear. Harnessed fears can fuel your mental energy. The fear of failure prevents many bright young people from becoming your competitors. This is good for you, because there is only room for just so many people to make £15–40 million. At 50+, your fear is a gift – something you can overcome as your potential competitors cringe.

Boldness not bravery

The more I prepared, the luckier I got.

(Gary Player – golf champion)

At 50+, you will hesitate – that is prudence, born of experience. As Goethe knew well, until one is committed there is always hesitance – the chance to draw back. But once you are committed 'providence moves all'. All sorts of things appear to help. Events seem to stream from decisions once taken – all manner of helpful and chance meetings conspire to carry you forward on the tide which you have taken. You have set out on your own and that feels so good after years of being a corporate team player. Team spirit is what comforts good losers. It shackles people to desks for a good living wage. In many professions, like teaching, there will be other rewards – but in commercial organizations, working in groups or teams will compromise your thinking and compensate you in only very small ways for your loss of individuality and your lack of personal fortune.

Fortune, it is said, favours the brave, but at 50+ you know that good fortune is a combination of preparation, preparedness and opportunity. Goethe asked only for a degree of boldness – not even bravery. Boldness can, of course, lead to failures and to losing some battles, but at 50+ you care less about what people will think. At 50+, you know that if opportunities are taken, they need not be taken perfectly. In fact, they do not necessarily need to be taken very well! As long as your execution is good enough, i.e. better than that of a potential competitor, your tide can still lead you on to fortune.

Exercise – see yourself rich?

Expel all the breath from your body and allow the air to rush in and fill your body. Repeat this three times. Close your eyes and picture yourself living your life according to its possibilities. Picture yourself and hear yourself phoning through a large donation to a charity. Picture the difference in the world before and after your donation. Watch yourself spending the rest of the day. Who are you with? What are you doing? What are you talking about? If you can picture it, you can do it!

You don't need great ideas

For the 50+, ideas are not a problem. At 50+, creativity is well served by the breadth of knowledge and possibilities and potential creative associations that can only come with living long enough to collect them. But, in 'The Hollow Men', T. S. Eliot warned, 'between the idea/and the reality/between the motion and the act/falls the shadow'.

At 50+, you are less afraid of shadows. Shadows can be illuminated by clear thinking. The question is only whether the light is worth the candle. The 50+ are quicker to dispel dross. Time is more precious and they more readily cut to the chase. Pick one serious idea and keep going. Don't give in.

Never give in.
Never give in.
Never, never
Never give in.
In nothing great
Never give in.
To nothing,
Save conscience,
And good sense.

(after Winston Churchill)

Five common errors in minding a business

History is full of ideas, irresponsibility, obstinacy, and errors.
(Popps)

1. Invalid premise or assumption

Critical thinking starts with justifiably believable information. This involves taking so-called 'facts' and assessing the credibility of their sources and the validity of any underlying assumptions. At 50+, you are better equipped to check things for sense, because you have more of it. You are better able to judge sources, because you have more experience on which to base your evaluations.

2. Over-optimistic predictions

Running out of cash (not profit or orders) is by far the most common cause of business failures. In fact, the more orders you have and potentially the more profit you expect, the more likely you are to run out of cash and to wind up bankrupt and out of business. In the US it can be a badge of honour for a budding business person; in Europe it is more embarrassing.

Numerical thinking is the essence of good business. You must hone your ability (and propensity) to estimate and quantify your visual and verbal thinking (see Chapters 06, 08 and 10 in *Teach Yourself Training Your Brain*, Horne and Wootton, 2007). Even if lack of cash planning does not doom your business, it may result in you having to sell equity (or shares) in your business to others in return for a cash injection. Any loss of ownership (even one share!) threatens one of your primary reasons for being in business, which is to make lots of money for yourself (to give away again, or whatever). The implementation of all new business ideas must be on the basis of a positive cash flow – or it (and your wealthy ambitions) are doomed. Cash, not profit, is the lifeblood of any business. If your numerical thinking is weak, the situation is not terminal, but you will need to employ the services of someone for whom they are strong.

3. Digging the same hole deeper

When your business idea is in a hole, it is hard to know when to stop digging – when to give up, abort, abandon and start digging somewhere else altogether. How do you decide when to abort? The sooner the better – it is never to soon to fail. Success is the ability to move seamlessly from one failure to the next, looking back without regret and forward with hope. Take your learning with you and there will be a better outcome next time. There is no shame in trying and failing – it is only a matter of timing. An idea before its time may fail – what might have worked last year may not work this year. An idea that failed last year may now be an idea whose time has come. Cut the cord, before a failing-to-succeed-now idea pulls you under. That way, you may live to breathe life back into the idea when the winds and tides of fortune are more propitious.

Errors on the surface flow
For pearls dive later
And below

(after Dryden)

4. Basing big actions on little thought

A good tailor measures twice and cuts once. A good business person thinks twice before acting at all. At 50+ you are better equipped to think creatively of a big idea, and better able to think critically about whether it checks for sense against your experience, of which you have much. Use your visual, predictive and superior numerical thinking to plan actions based on your big idea. Plan the first small step in great detail. Take the first small step and evaluate all the new information that this will always flush out. Re-think if necessary. Re-plan if necessary. Think big and act small and then think big again.

5. Not sharing the profits

You will need to find, nurture, encourage and trust the most able people you can persuade to join you – even if it means paying them more than you pay yourself out of the business. You will make your money when you sell the business. Pay good people out of the business (but not out of the proceeds of selling it – you risked your money for that, the return is yours). You started your business to make money, remember. Take it for yourself and then give it away – don't share it with employees. Incentivize their performance out of the business, not out of the sale. They are earning a good living out of your business. If they want to make money, let them start their own business. Maybe you can help them into their business. Don't let them help themselves to yours.

Do you have a head for business?

Are you an entrepreneur? What are the characteristics of entrepreneurs?

Persistence

Persistence is not to be confused with stubbornness. Stubborn people persist in the face of plentiful evidence that they should not. The phrase 'never give in' was useful to Churchill in the context of the Second World War – but 'never' is a dangerous word. Sometimes it is better to surrender a position, an idea, your shares and move on. Live to succeed another day. Start digging somewhere else. Acknowledging a mistake and making a new plan is not a sign of weakness, it is a sign of good thinking.

Diversification

No matter how good your 50+ idea, and no matter how successfully your well-thought-out plans are bearing fruit, 50+ entrepreneurs know that time will pass and fruits will perish. 50+ entrepreneurs start diversifying almost as soon as their first idea has taken root, let alone borne fruit. Partly driven by 50+ creativity, partly by their 50+ experience that nothing lasts forever, they begin to spread their risk, to licence, to franchise, to diversify. Try to keep your diversification closely related to your business, so that you can capitalize on cross promotion, economies of scale and other synergies.

Learning

50+ entrepreneurs are incurably nosey; they learn from their experience and from that of other people. The 50+ have learned what questions to ask and how to listen to the answers without interrupting or arguing (Chapter 06). Courtesy helps the 50+ to learn more easily and to make more money more quickly – especially in America. Do not agree to listen to someone for less than 20 minutes – it is rarely possible to 'dive for the pearls' in less than 20 minutes. Likewise, it is hard to concentrate and do justice to what someone is saying for much more than 20 minutes. So there you have it: 20-minute meetings, interviews, presentations, visits – whatever – 20 minutes.

Betting lucky in business

- Do not describe or characterize yourself as unlucky or people will not invest in you, personally or in your business.
- Thank your lucky stars for lucky breaks you have had.
- Do not make plans that need luck for them to succeed.
- Accept and take advantage of the lucky breaks that you will get.
- Do not be distracted by looking at greener grass.
- Just do it. You will probably get away with it. If you don't, apologize.

Negotiating in business

- State fair terms and stick to them.
- Don't barter, it makes you seem dishonest from the outset.
- Your second thoughts are probably your best. Stick to them.
- Do not let your goals or hopes drift upwards out of greed – you are likely to confuse the other side and, if you fail to agree, you will both lose out.
- Do your homework on the likely best hopes and goals of others and their likely walk-away position. Do the same for yourself. If there is overlap, you can agree. If there's not, you can't, so don't negotiate. Then it's down to power. If you cannot increase your power, back off. Settle for the best you can and move on.
- Adjourn frequently to take advice, but don't let advisors take the decisions. It is you who must live with the consequences. Think the consequences through visually and empathetically.
- Be courteous and, if possible, humorous, if not then self-depreciating. Creative thinking is usually required to find mutually beneficial win–win solutions and this is helped by good humour (Chapter 01).
- Once you've agreed, honour your agreement. Do not try to squirm or renege afterwards. If you don't agree, adjourn and return another day. But once you agree, that's it. Honour it and don't weasel. If the other side try it on, don't retaliate. Your word is your word, whether given to a good person or to a knave.

Felix Dennis holds up Francis Bacon (1561–1626) as a model:

If you would negotiate with any man (or woman), you must think about their nature, so to lead them; their goals,

so to persuade them; their weaknesses, so as to awe them;
or to those who have power over them, so to control them.
With cunning persons, interpret them, but do not believe
what they say. Say as little as possible in return. Do not aim
to reap all at one sitting. Ripen your fruits by degrees.

The joys of ownership

In Chapter 01, we discovered that making lots of money brought
'yacht envy', not happiness. However, the more realistic pursuit
of BLISS involves an S for Satisfaction, of which a key element is
possession – the ability to say 'this is mine'. This is one of the
reasons that running one's own business is so deeply satisfying,
quite apart from the autonomy, independence, status, power and
physical possessions that you buy if you make a lot of money.
The fact that you own the business is intrinsically satisfying.
Being an owner-manager feels completely different from being
an employee-manager. All the more important, then, that you
fight tooth and nail to retain your ownership or equity. To
become very rich you must own most, preferably all, the shares
in your business. You may need to become as possessive about
your own business as Gollum was about his 'precious' ring in
Lord of the Rings (J. R. Tolkien). According to Felix Dennis,
ownership is not just the most important thing – it is the only
thing. Only when you are the owner can you afford to be
reasonable.

The Virgin brain and The Body Shop brain

Think about Richard Branson and Anita Roddick. If you took away
all their money, it would not be long before they were each of them
rich again. This is because you haven't taken away their ability to
think and that's what made them rich. (Paul McKenna – friend of
Richard Branson and Anita Roddick)

The perils of partnership

The relative shares of the partners need to reflect who is putting
in the capital and who is doing how much work in the venture.
Choose partners who are brilliant at what you're not good at –
even if they constantly show you in a bad light by comparison.
A partnership is not like a marriage, in which you may be
prepared to die for your partner and let them share all. In your
own business, the making of money comes first. If you are

fortunate in your partners, friendship or even affection may follow, but the needs of the business to make money comes first. Bad partners can take hours of precious time to convince to do something, or not to do something. The perils of partnership can easily outweigh the advantages, if you make a bad choice of partner.

Going public

Unless it is your final cut and run with the money, don't go public if you can afford to stay private. You will lose many of the joys and freedoms for which you set up your own business in the first place. Your actions and even your private life and conversations will become constrained, quite properly, by a whole raft of regulations designed to protect the public.

Ten lessons on employing others in your business

1 Whatever title you retain, or take, be sure that it empowers you to attend all management meetings, and try to do so at least once a month.
2 In your absence, your chief executive should stand in for you and be responsible for ensuring that you receive prompt verbatim minutes.
3 Do not allow anyone to be appointed, or removed, from the senior management team, including any directors, without your agreement.
4 Do not allow anyone to relocate any office.
5 Do not allow anyone to dispose of any asset.
6 Insist on approving any changes to the product or marketing plan.
7 Insist on approving any written information about the company, its policies, products or services.
8 Insist on signing off bank transactions above a significant threshold.
9 Insist on approving all press releases.
10 Make clear the target figures for growth and return on assets, but allow others to suggest how best these might be achieved.

Ten tips for a brain-based businesses

1 Allow money to be the measure of how well the business is doing. Publish the financial scores. (Ring fence money for investment. Separate it from money for costs.)

2 If you get a good offer, sell out while the going is good.

3 Look after your suppliers as well as you look after your customers.

4 Minimize secrecy.

5 Advertise regularly for new staff – whether you need them now or not. Interview yourself. Applicants are an excellent source of market intelligence.

6 Actively seek to train and promote junior staff.

7 Back up managers who make decisions – even if they make some mistakes. If they make too many, sack them.

8 Favour one-on-one meetings over group meetings. Manage individuals. Use a conversational management style.

9 Share profits with employees and decide on bonus payment personally.

10 Reduce overheads by 10 per cent at the end of each year.

The neurochemistry of making money

When you want something, your brain releases dopamine into your blood. This creates a craving – the 'must have' feeling. When you get it, your brain releases serotonin – a 'feel good' chemical. It can be addictive. If doing deals and making money becomes your main source of serotonin, you will never have enough. You will be 'driven', but never satisfied. Money cannot fill a psychological black hole, for example to feel 'safe'. The fear produces adrenaline which drives the pursuit or the chase. The serotonin of success soothes, but not for long!

Critical thinking at work – a wealth warning

Now that you know how to use applied thinking, at work to earn a high salary, or to make a lot of money by working for yourself, it maybe worth thinking about the tensions between a healthy mind and a wealthy bank balance.

According to the philosopher Francis Bacon (1625), even when wealth is not a direct impediment to virtue, wealth is an encumbrance on your journey through life. You are unlikely to give it up, because you will think it too valuable. Yet harbouring it will inhibit spontaneous ease of travel. You will need often to watch over your wealth, constantly needing to check it and to conceal it from the envious eyes of others. In these ways, wealth can be a burden not a blessing

The process by which you acquired your wealth may develop habits of mind of which you are not proud. Becoming wealthy in your life may preoccupy your mind and the minds of others with thoughts of what will happen to your wealth when you die. This can impoverish the quality of relationships while you are still alive. The pressure on you to share out your wealth before you die might become very tiresome. Your best hope is that having had all the fun, learning, stimulation and sense of achievement of using your 50+ thinking power to acquire wealth by keeping your head at work, you will have thereby acquired the wisdom to give it all away, wisely!

Summary

- Applied thinking aims to change things, to make the world a better place.
- Applied thinking is supported by critical, creative and reflective thinking, all of which are more highly developed in the 50+.
- Applied thinking empowers people who are 50+. The 50+ are less impressed than younger people by power or celebrity.
- Applied thinking is not negative. Its intention is to support the person whose ideas are the subject of the critical thinking.
- Applied thinking develops in its wake courage, intellectual independence and social self-reliance, more commonly found at 50+.
- The superior applied thinking of the 50+ generation rests on their superior critical, creative and reflective thinking and this argues against their early retirement and in favour of their earning a better living at work or, importantly, making even more money for us all by minding their own businesses.
- In a knowledge economy where competitive advantage goes to those who can think well, about what they know, the elderly do no need to be a burden to be cared for by a younger generation. On the contrary, the 50+ generation can earn the wealth not only to look after themselves, but also to fund the

long periods of education needed by the young. If the 50+ do continue to work until they are 80+, they will never be a burden!

Suggested further reading

Baggini, J. (2006) *Do You Think?* Granta.

Dennis, F. (2007) *How To Get Rich*, Ebury Press.

Edmunds, E. (2005) *Bullshit Bingo*, South Bank.

Horne, T. and Doherty, A. (2003) *Managing in Public Services*, Routledge.

McKenna, P. (2007) *I Can Make You Rich*, Transworld.

Middleton, J. (2006) *Upgrade Your Brain*, Infinite Ideas.

Templar, R. (2007) *The Rules of Work*, Pearson Education.

Thompson, A. (1999) *Critical Reasoning*, Routledge.

Wootton, S. and Horne, T. (2003) *Strategic Thinking*, Kogan Page.

www.newscientist.com accessed 05/05/07

06 lust, love, sex and intimacy at 50+

In this chapter you will learn:

- to exploit your superior verbal intelligence at 50+
- to use internal dialogues to augment your thinking power
- to use thoughtful conversations to develop intimate relationships as well as your brain
- about the neurochemistry of friendship, love and sex.

Logic is little more than knowledge of a language with which to talk about it.

(Charles Lamb, 1801)

Introduction

Before you begin reading this chapter, look back at Figure 0.3 on page 8.

Neuroscience points strongly to the effectiveness of oral rather than written work as the better way to connect up your brain and extend its cognitive capacity. An important resource is conversation. Thoughtful conversations have an added bonus. Thoughtful conversations develop closer, more intimate relationships. Close personal relationships are a rich source of BLISS (Chapter 01), further adding to your ability to think well and clearly express what you think, both orally and in writing. Talking better, thinking better, writing better, and acting more effectively become a virtuous circle, leading to increased cognitive capacity (Chapter 02), and increased success at work (Chapter 05), adding further to your state of bliss (Chapter 01).

Given the centrality of talking to your education, personal development and successful living, it is useful to be able to feel comfortable in social situations, because these provide rich and varied opportunities for you to practise thinking aloud.

Verbal intelligence is the ability to ask yourself questions that help you to think well and then to answer them! Both operations involve remembering, selecting, using and then connecting words together. These operations make up an 'internal dialogue' – a thoughtful conversation that you have with yourself inside your head.

Whatever other thinking modes you also use (see Appendices A–F), you are limited by the ability of your internal and external dialogue to communicate to yourself and others the results of your thinking. That may be why psychologists since the 1900s have measured vocabulary, verbal reasoning and verbal IQ. Early psychologists realized that verbal intelligence was closely correlated with success in the world of business and in other professions where it was important for you to think clearly and to clearly communicate your thinking to others.

Good thoughts – spoken or written in the right words – have power to persuade, inspire or seduce, or just to influence events. At 50+, you have more words and more word power, and therefore more thinking power than when you were younger.

The neuroscience of word play

Most of the verbal action takes place on the left side of the brain, which is the side that is active when you are cheerful or optimistic. Perhaps that's why having a chat cheers you up (Chapter 01). Broca's area of the brain handles grammar and speech. Wernick's area of the brain handles sound and meaning. (See the diagrams on page 198.) These areas of the brain are on the opposite side of the brain to that which handles visual images. That is why you stand a better chance of getting and keeping the whole-brain attention of an audience if you can use words to tell a 'graphic story', i.e. a story that conjures up a 'big picture' in the mind of the listener. The linguistic left of the brain functions better when levels of oestrogen are higher. Levels of oestrogen are generally higher in typical female brains. Typical female brains display a superior command and use of language than typical male brains (see Appendix G).

Seeing the funny side at 50+

Robert Ornstan discovered that while normal verbal thinking (internal dialogue) takes place substantially on the left side of your brain (if you're righthanded), word play (as in puns, jokes, humour, double entendre) is more likely to involve the right side of your brain. People who have a stroke in the right side of their brain often lose their sense of humour.

Conversation and brain training

Levelt discovered that you use three distinct areas of your brain when you talk to someone else. You connect lots of neural pathways, even before you get to the content of what you want to say. As you search for the next word you need in your spoken sentence, your brain accesses the smell, colour and sounds that are associated with the word you are seeking, thereby calling up even more neural connections. That is why a word can be on the tip of your tongue before you finally say it.

In the meantime, your brain will be finding back-up synonyms and holding them in reserve, in case you cannot find the exact word that's on the tip of your tongue. All this happens, word by word, throughout your conversation. Small wonder thoughtful conversations are such a good mental workout. Small wonder paired learning is the learning method of choice if you want to develop the capacity of your brain, as well as your skill in using it.

Your brain can generally find, and provide sounds for, between 120 and 180 words a minute, i.e. up to 10,000 words an hour. It is a myth that this slows down when you get older. True, the older you get, the more possible words you have to choose from, but this can be worked around. Having more words at 50+ is an asset for verbal thinking, and for any thinking tasks that involve creative and reflective thinking (Appendices E and F).

Reading is important, but...

Reading can play an important part in training your brain. Reading is a useful source of new information, which your brain must struggle to map, connect, cross check, and then integrate with information already dispersed in your memory. But reading is not as good at developing your brain as talking and listening. Thoughtful conversations about old and new information involve more of your brain than just reading, and so conversations increase your general cognitive capacity, as well as helping you to consolidate new information in your memory.

At the moment in the UK, under the government's literacy scheme, valuable brain development time is lost teaching children to read too many words. The government literacy scheme requires children to read 158 prescribed words by the age of seven. In 2005, Jonathan Solity, from Warwick University, analysed over 900,000 words used in adult's and children's books. Solity discovered that only 100 words were needed to read most books in English. (The extra 50 per cent of time needed to learn the extra 58 words added only about 2 per cent to a reader's understanding. This time could be better spent developing a love of reading, by giving children a wider range of stories and topics.)

Don't be boring at 50+

A gossip talks about others.
A bore talks about himself.
A conversationalist listens,
To you.

(Anon)

Tests of verbal thinking, verbal IQ and verbal reasoning

In 2007, The National Association of Graduate Recruiters in the UK reported that it had failed to fill one-third of its vacancies for graduates, because of a lack of suitable applicants. Facing a general decline in literacy standards, and a decline in the ability of even graduates to think clearly and to express clearly what they think, employers have been forced to employ recruitment consultants to pre-screen graduate applicants by using psychometric tests. In future years, they will need to seek more people of 50+ to make good their shortfall!

The advice for what to do on the day of a verbal thinking test is the same as in Chapter 02 (on IQ tests). The specific brain training you need for verbal thinking tests is to practise answering the following eight types of question that are used in psychometric tests of verbal reasoning and verbal IQ:

1 find the synonyms
2 find the antonyms
3 double meanings
4 double uses
5 missing word pairs
6 mistaken use of words
7 verbal analogies
8 redundant words.

If you need to brush up on any of these types of questions, read *Teach Yourself Training Your Brain,* Horne and Wootton (2007).

The neuroscience of word games

Crosswords and alphabetics

Alphabetics puzzles are English crosswords in which you use all 26 letters of the English alphabet, but use each letter only once.

Example 1

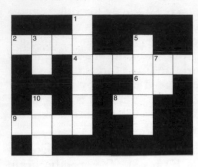

Across
2. A receptable for cereal
3. A hoot of a bird
4. Something you can get from an accident
6. Abr. advertisement
8. Master of ceremonies
9. You might wear under your shirt

Down
1. To promise
3. Pulls a plough
5. Noise a duck makes
7. Road abr.
10. Turkish hat

Hint: If you list the alphabet and cross out each letter as you use it, this process of elimination helps to reduce the final few words to anagrams.

Answer

Although they appear simple, alphabetics are good for developing spare cognitive capacity because they use many parts of your brain simultaneously.

For example:

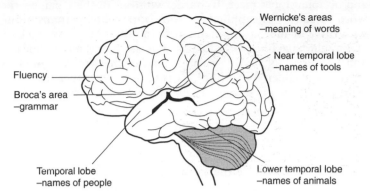

Word games can also develop 'fluency' or 'speed'. For example:

- Try to write down as many mammals as you can in one minute.
- Now try to write down all the words you can that begin with 'B'.

Password and association games

In password-type games, which are played two against two, you try to get your partner to guess what word you have in mind by giving, as one-word clues, words of associated meaning. If I had the word 'pickle' in mind, I might, in succession give words like 'onion', 'vinegar', 'fix', 'acetone', 'jam', 'mess', 'ploughmans', 'predicament'. If my partner guesses the word I have in mind, i.e. 'pickle', after only one clue, we score 10. Thereafter we can only score 10 minus the number of clues I have to give before my partner guesses the word I have in mind. For this game, Broca's area of the brain is important and so is the angular gyrus:

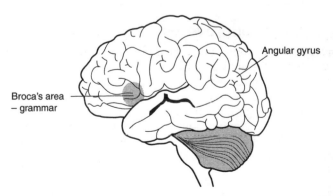

The angular gyrus is the area where the left temporal, parietal and occipital lobes meet. In harder versions of these games, the word to convey is supplied by your opponents, perhaps along with three or more forbidden clues. In our example of 'pickle', you might have been forbidden to give as clues 'onion, 'vinegar' and 'preserve'. N.B. Any form or part of the words in mind is always 'forbidden' or 'taboo', as is the use of proper names or trade names, in any of the variety of password games.

The games are called 'password', because your partner can always say 'pass' – meaning, 'I'm not sure yet, give me another clue'. A good fun variant is when you play in groups and all groups have the same word in mind. Members of each group take it in turns to give their partner a 'clue', in the hearing of everyone. This opens up the possibility of laying 'trails' of association to put the other players off the scent, while still using words that you believe your partner will eventually associate with your word.

Another game to try, in a larger group, for example in a minibus or on a long coach or train journey, is the 'Association Game'.

The Association Game

One person starts with a word. The next must follow, without hesitation, with an associated word. The first person to stumble breaks the round and starts a new round with a new word. Any player can challenge any association offered by another player. If the explanation is not satisfactory, the successful challenger starts a new round. If someone uses a word that has already been used earlier in the game, they can be challenged for repetition. This game develops quick thinking, creativity, imagination, concentration and memory.

Paired words or proverbs

Both sides of the brain are involved in these types of games. They involve dividing words into pairs, or groups, using some given rules. It involves what psychologists sometimes call 'divergent' – as opposed to 'convergent' – thinking. 'Divergent' thinking is good brain training for creativity and imagination, i.e. very good for creative, visual, spatial and symbolic thinking. This form of brain training helps with the production and interpretation of metaphors, similes, symbols, parables, poetry and figurative and creative writing.

In more complex versions, definitions are made up of rare or unfamiliar words picked from a dictionary and opponents have to guess which are 'true' and which are 'false', or which 'words' pair with which definitions. The trick is to make the definition you invent sound plausible. One example is the 'Dictionary Game'.

The Dictionary Game

You need a dictionary, preferably two, and writing materials. Create two teams. Each member of the team chooses an obscure word and writes its meaning on a piece of paper. The dictionaries are then put away. The rest of their team writes out false definitions. Teams take it in turn to read out a word and a set of possible meanings, including the correct one. If a nominated member of the opposite team spots which is the correct definition and guesses right first time, they score 10 points. If the team confer, they can still score 6 points provided they guess correctly the second time. A third guess that is correct scores 2. Anyone whose false definition is selected scores 4.

Different people group and match words using very different organizing principles, schema, frameworks or associations. The trick is to get to know how your partner's mind works – to tune into your partner's way of thinking. Matching by function normally takes place on the left side of your brain, and visual or metaphorical matching on the right side of your brain. Puns, double meanings and most sexual innuendo come from the right side of your brain. A 'Carry On' film is a right-brain workout!

Recent research has refined Broca's original view that 'we speak with our left brain'. About 95 per cent of right-handed men are left-brain dominant for syntax (sentence structure) and semantics (meaning). Sally Shaywitz has used NMR scanning to show that women are not so strongly lateralized for language and talking as men are. In a study with two matched groups of around 20 men and 20 women, all 20 men revealed blood flow in the left frontal lobe while talking, but all the women showed equal blood flows in their left and right hemispheres. We can begin to see why 50+ women do so well in a 'knowledge or thinking economy', once freed from societal prejudice. Stereotypical female brains have more areas of the brain involved when they talk than do stereotypical male brains. Lefthanders and ambidextrous people generally have more active language areas in their brains.

PET scans show that getting people to explain how 'squirrels invest' or why 'beginners are green', takes place on the right side of the brain of right-handed people. During the Dictionary Game, the right side generates possible options, which the left side evaluates and selects. The right side adds intonation and gestures and physical expression, which are usually illegal in most word games, but 'de rigueur' in charades or the 'Adverb Game'.

The Adverb Game

This is good with children, or as an icebreaker at adult parties. Person A and person B leave the room. A gives B a mystery adverb – a word that describes how something is done, for example 'quickly', 'thoughtfully', 'confusingly', 'seductively'. A and B return to the room and B's task is to get the audience to guess the mystery adverb. The person who first guesses becomes A in the next round and gives another B person a new mystery adverb. The audience guesses the adverb by taking turns to ask B to carry out various actions in a way that would be described by the mystery adverb, for example 'Open an envelope this way'. Person B would then have to demonstrate how they would open an envelope quickly or thoughtfully or seductively... The audience can be divided into competing teams who take turn to demand an action and to guess the mystery adverb.

Both Howard Garner and Ellen Wiiner have reported that people with right-brain stroke damage (or who have severe lateral dominance) do not respond to 'hints' or indirect requests ('gosh, that meal was good but it's created a lot of washing up' equals 'will you please help me wash up these dishes'). The critical, creative and reflective thinking which supports applied thinking proceed via Inferences, Insight or Inspirations, and these involve the right-hand side of the righthander's brain. This underlines the crucial role of brain training in securing whole-brain development. Most government educational regimes strongly favour literal left-brain development. However, laughter, health, mood, thinking and BLISS all need you to involve your whole brain – left and right. The world needs the thinking power of more creative, more optimistic, less unhappy people. (According to the World Health Organization, suicide and self-harm have now become the world's major health threat.)

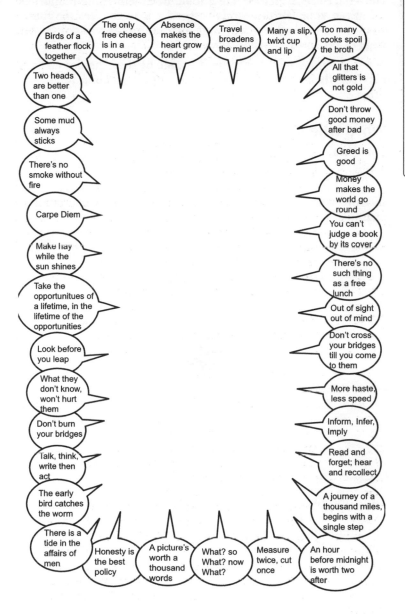

At 50+, your right brain can hold the many contradictory ideas and images generated during a joke, or an emerging humorous situation; your left brain finally 'gets' a joke or 'sees the funny side' of an otherwise depressing situation. Take a look at the page of proverbs on page 203.

Try pairing the ones that mean the same by drawing dotted lines between them. Then find pairs that appear to contradict each other and join them with solid lines.

Word wheels

On a brain scanner, word wheels have been shown to activate similar areas to literal crosswords (cryptic crosswords 'electrify' many more brain circuits).

In word wheels, the words don't just interact, they overlap. For example:

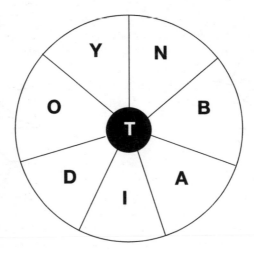

Using the given letters no more than once, make as many words as possible of four or more letters, always including the central letter. How many did you find? We found 25 (see bottom of the page).

(Answers: adit, anti, antibody, atony, bait, bandit, baton, bint, biota, boat, botany, dainty, dint, doit, into, iota, oaty, obit, obtain, tidy, tiny, toad, today, toady.)

At first glance, the word wheel above seems to be filled with random letters, but on closer inspection the collections can be divided into English words. If you talk aloud about the letters and the possible words you can make, your brain scan will show more activity, in more regions of the brain, leading to greater residual cognitive development. In healthy brains, word wheels activate your Broca's area; your Wernicke area; a part of your left frontal lobe that hears the melody in your speech or singing; a corresponding part of the right frontal lobe that hears the pitch and the rhythm of your speech – so you can see, hear, understand why it is important to think aloud. Counting round the circle involves the part of the brain associated with calculation and the angular gyrus is active as you read and re-read the letters.

The verbal superiority of the 50+ brain

David Selacter's work on memory underscores the need of the 50+ to do brain training in order to unleash and exploit their superior potential as verbal thinkers. Selacter illustrates:

> *I cannot remember what I ate for dinner a year ago, because I have had dinners since then and it would take a while to review them all before deciding which was the one I ate a year ago. The 50+ have had many more than 364 dinners!*

The superior, more extensive vocabulary of the 50+ requires longer to review before selecting the most apt word (and all its associated sounds, shapes, meanings, intonations, pitch, tunes and rhymes) – no wonder learning and reciting poetry and drama are so good for a child's brain development.

The role played by verbal superiority in the overall superiority of the 50+ brain is better understood as we turn to the central role of internal dialogue.

Thinking as internal dialogue

> *To think is to talk, if only to yourself!*
>
> (Wootton, 2003)

Up to and including the 1980s, references to intra-personal conversations were rare. Since the 1990s, the idea of thinking as an internal dialogue has been widely discussed. Key among the implications of this idea is the importance of vocabulary and hence of brain training exercises, puzzles and games that develop your vocabulary. Clearly you cannot think – as an internal dialogue – about things for which you have no vocabulary. Neither can you manipulate mental concepts for which you have no labels. Learning to talk clearly will aid clear thinking, and clear thinking will aid clear writing. In the worlds of business and social policy, government and the caring professions, this will enable effective action to be taken. Because of the superiority of the 50+ vocabulary, the role of the 50+ in the management of business and public services will become pre-eminent as we become a brain-based economy.

Internal dialogue – physical fitness and psychological well-being

Since the 1990s, doctors and sports scientists have shown a lot of interest in the mind–body connection, especially in the survival rates for major surgery and cancer and in the times taken to recover from sports.

Internal dialogues appear to coordinate and connect the work of different parts of the brain, such as the sensory cortex and the motor control functions. Internal dialogues, the conversations you have with yourself, determine how you view your own body, the importance you attach to it, the respect with which you treat it, and whether or not you allow other people to abuse it.

Thinking aloud

John Steiner observed that people often introduce their internal dialogues into conversations with other people. They 'fly kites' or 'float ideas'. Consciously, or unconsciously, these people are seeking reactions: 'Will it fly? Or will it sink like a lead balloon?' While it is clear that thinking aloud, with or without others present, exercises much of the brain, it is less clear that all thought necessarily involves the use of language. With or without language, the brain can manipulate more complex symbols than words. Images, metaphors, schema and symbols, as in systems thinking for example, can all be used to aid complex thinking. Caruthers has recently decided that normal spoken and written language is definitely involved in thinking processes such as believing, desiring and reasoning. Words join images and sounds as symbols which can be manipulated during the thinking process.

> **'Keep your head, when all around you are losing theirs'**
> **(Kipling)**
>
> Since the 50+ vocabulary is more sophisticated, the 50+ can talk about more complex things more precisely. If you learn to talk more fluently, you will be able to think more quickly. You will be able to think faster under pressure and to talk more calmly under duress. You will be able to 'keep your head, when all around you are losing theirs'.

How to have a 'thoughtful conversation'

Thoughtful conversations simultaneously improve the quality of your present thinking and develop your subsequent ability to think quickly and accurately, provided that you:

- Convey non-verbally that you are listening to and taking seriously the other person.
- Look out for things that puzzle you, rather than for things with which to disagree.
- Respect the other person, even if you disagree with them.
- Give good reasons for any opinions you express.
- Ask for clarification of what is puzzling you.
- Ask others for reasons and examples.
- Avoid intimidating language like, 'It's obvious that...' or, 'Nobody in their right mind...'.
- Use ideas as temporary 'sky hooks' to hoist up the level of the discussion.
- Stay open to the possibility that you may be wrong, or misinformed.
- Remain tenacious in your desire to get to the bottom of things.
- Avoid disguising statements as questions.
- Connect what you say to what has been said earlier.
- Realize that people need help to understand how proposed future actions flow from current opinions and how these, in turn, are based on other information.
- Delay, for as long as possible, coming to firm conclusions about what is being discussed. (When there is time – and there nearly always is – float ideas tentatively. Agree to come back to the matter in ten minutes, or later that day, or that week.)

- Remain tolerant of the opinions of other people. (People do not like to enter 'thoughtful conversations' expecting to be judged by someone older and wiser.) Try not to interrupt their train of thought, however woolly you find it. As a minimum let them finish their sentences. A conversation is not a competition.

30 useful things to say in thoughtful conversations

1 My concern is…
2 Why do you say that?
3 What do you mean by that?
4 How would that affect… ?
5 What can we agree on?
6 How is this different from… ?
7 How is… consistent with… ?
8 What leads you to think that?
9 How are you able to prove that?
10 How can you be sure about that?
11 I'm sorry, I didn't quite follow that.
12 Can you explain the relevance of… ?
13 What assumptions are we making here?
14 OK, so where does that take us to next?
15 Can you just take me through that again?
16 Have you considered the possibility that… ?
17 Do you have any evidence to support that?
18 So am I correct that what you are saying is… ?
19 We appear to have two or three quite separate ideas here.
20 Is it possible to check any of these things out? If so, how?
21 Can we just agree again what we know to be the case?
22 While I can accept… , what does not seem to follow is…
23 How is that connected with what you just said about… ?
24 When you said ABC, you seemed… (label the emotion).
25 You seem to be very certain of that. Can you help me to understand why?
26 You seem to be starting from quite different assumptions. What are they?
27 Can you give me a concrete example of how it might work out in practice?

28 You might be right, but I don't quite follow how you got there. Please explain.
29 What would have to happen before you reconsidered your point of view?
30 I have lost the thread. How does that connect with what you were just saying?

Think like a man

Should you choose a man or a woman as a 'thinking companion'?

One of the best ways to improve your verbal thinking, and to expand your overall cognitive capacity, is by choosing carefully those with whom you have 'thoughtful conversations'. Favour constructive, challenging, tentative, non-judgemental 'thoughtful' companions, who are interested in exploring ideas as well as facts. At 50+, it is especially important to avoid cynics and people who complain all the time. They will drain your spirit as well as your energy. At 50+, avoid people who only want to preach arguments they have already rehearsed. When choosing your 'thoughtful companion' or 'critical friend', should you choose a man or a woman?

The answer is that it all depends on what sort of brain you have, and what sort of brain your potential partner has. While typical male brains (TMBs) do think differently from typical female brains (TFBs), very few men are 100 per cent TMB and very few women are 100 per cent TFB. (You can get an indication of the male–female balance in your brain by answering the questions in Appendix G.)

Female intuition still going strong at 50+

Roger Gorski found more activity in the corpus callosum in women. This is the bundle of nerves that connects the left- to the right-hand side of the brain. This means that even when talking, which is a predominantly left-brain activity, women may still be accessing right-brain associative play on the meaning of the words said or heard. This is what may give their conversations a more intuitive or 'off the wall' feel. Furthermore, neuroanatomist Sandra Wikelson, who has performed several hundred autopsies since 1977, reports that the corpus callosum in women does not shrink with age.

Building close relationships – intimacy and a 'meeting of minds'

When conversations between two people are thoughtful, not only does the thinking benefit, so does the relationship. Research by Steven Duck and Anne Giradot, replicated in 2003 by Doherty and Horne, found that relationships between work colleagues, friends or sexual partners became closer, the greater the extent of the disclosure between them. When the disclosure moved from information to thoughtful opinion, the relationship intensified. When empathetic thinking and shared 'visions' of the future were added, intimacy often resulted. Humour and creative thinking (and maybe dark chocolate) sometimes completed the route to bed! The 50+ are more creative than younger people, so all you need to do is buy the dark chocolate and keep your sense of humour!

In a virtuous circle, creative thinking profits from relationships that are secure, and creative thinkers have been found to be more sexually attractive.

Making thoughtful relationships closer

- Make disclosures related to your partner, and to the present time and place.
- Keep disclosures in balance with your partner, not under- or over-disclosing.
- Add opinions to the information you disclose.
- Add feelings to the opinions you disclose.
- Begin more sentences with 'I… (notice, think, feel)'.
- Build trust by aligning your actions with your opinions.
- Try to match any intimate self-disclosures made by your partner.
- Avoid having 'secrets' and things that 'you just don't talk about'.
- Are you sufficiently self-aware and honest to match the openness of your partner?

(taken from Horne and Doherty, 2003)

Don't argue!

At 50+, you have less patience and are less inclined to 'tolerate fools gladly'. Latent envy of youth (usually misplaced) can fuel uncharacteristic aggression towards younger people who have made the mistake of being adversarial. Resist your reputation to 'take no prisoners'! This is important. But for some 50+ people, it can be difficult. Some younger people are so competitive that nearly every discussion becomes an argument and an argument that they must win. At 50+ you will normally win the arguments but you may be losing friends. At 50+ having friends is more important than winning arguments. It is easier to pick arguments than find new friends.

Winning the argument at 50+

In order to prevent arguments, I prefer to do all the talking myself.

(Oscar Wilde)

According to Roger Drake, in a face-to-face argument, you are more likely to win if you move slightly to your right. This moves your opponent's eyes to their left, thereby activating the right side of their brain, which is less confrontational and more open to novelty and change. Also, you are more likely to change another person's mind if you whisper into their left ear, and thereby talk to their right brain.

Check out how argumentative you are. Consider the following 20 statements and write your score in the unshaded boxes.

Score: rarely true = 2, occasionally true = 3, often true = 4, always true = 5

	Y	X
I try to avoid arguments if at all possible.		
In the middle of an argument, I feel excited.		
I generally come out best in an argument.		
A good argument clears the air.		
Only afterwards can I think of what I should have said.		
An argument is an intellectual challenge.		
I don't like people who are argumentative.		
I don't like to just let things go.		
It takes skill to avoid getting into an argument.		
I will always stand up for myself and defend my corner.		
I feel sick if I sense an argument brewing.		
There's nothing like the cut and thrust of debate.		
Arguments leave me shaking and upset.		
It's nice to make a point and have a counter-argument.		
Arguments create problems and never settle things.		
Each time arguments happen, I say 'never again'.		
I feel very energetic and fired up when I argue.		
I avoid arguments at all cost.		
Arguments are good mental exercise.		
If I argue, people won't like me.		

Your score is Total Y minus Total X.

= Score

How did you do?

People who can make good use of verbal thinking in thoughtful conversations, or who make good 'critical friends', generally score between two and six. The 50+ are usually too 'nice' or too 'polite' to argue and hence have low scores. Sometimes low scorers are from Asian cultures in which any kind of confrontation is to be avoided. The 50+ who score above 6 are often too argumentative, too competitive, too abrasive or too adversarial. In general, the 50+ are more likely to have the confidence to concede; they know that life's too short to sweat over small stuff. They are more inclined to keep their powder dry for important matters of principle.

So, I'm too competitive, too adversarial, too argumentative, so what!

If you win arguments and lose friends you will be the loser. Having close friendships is strongly correlated with good health, creative thinking and real-world achievement. The connection between friendship and physical health is not well understood. Perhaps it is a bi-product of reduced cortisol, and of increased endorphin and serotonin when friends talk to each other. Both of these changes in the chemicals in your brain are associated with enhancements in your immune system.

Close friendships are a safe haven from which creative excursions can be made, and creative thinking is strongly correlated with success in professions like science, engineering, medicine and management, as well as in the more obvious areas of art, advertising, marketing, media and journalism.

Clearly there is more to forming close thoughtful relationships than balancing excessive compliance and excessive argumentativeness. For example, everyone would prefer partners (and neighbours and work colleagues) who are reasonable – and you are much more likely to be reasonable if you can reason.

It's *how* you row that matters!

In a 2006 yougov survey of couples, where one or both partners were thinking of splitting up, the number one reason for dissatisfaction with the relationship was disagreements over money. But the second reason, way ahead of disagreements over sex, children, alcohol, coming home late, the in-laws etc., was dislike of the way the other person argued. People disliked the *way* their partners argued, more than *what* they argued about. Linda Waite, who has been tracking crumbling relationships since 2000, says about half of slow rumbling, grumbling, crumbling relationships eventually break down altogether. Yet half improve and describe their relationships as 'now happy'. So you can learn to argue better – the prognosis is not good if you don't!

The neurochemistry of love, lust, attachment and sex

When we are talking about love here, we are talking about romantic love. Romantic love, lust and attachment each have separate neurochemical systems. Each can react without the other. However, lust, love and attachment are a common sequel. Lust is a temporary urge for sexual gratification. Romantic love is a sense of elation in the presence of, or at the thought of, one particular person. Attachment is a sense of peace and security conducive to having children.

Writers on youth and age, love and sex

I never enjoyed youth so much as I do now that I am 50+. (after George Santayana)

But enjoyment and love are not the same thing. Love as a young person is as nothing compared to the love of an old man for his wife. (after William Durant)

The yearning for love and romance persists – it outlasts even the capacity for sex. (after Joseph Heller)

The neurochemistry of one-night stands

Lust is associated with increased testosterone in the brain. In 50+ men, this occurs daily in the morning and is more noticeable in autumn. In pre-menopausal women, it occurs monthly at the time of ovulation. But testosterone levels can be stimulated at other times. Testosterone levels can be stimulated in 50+ men by the sight of a cleavage, the flash of leg, by pornography or by an offer of sex. In women, testosterone is stimulated by affection, words, deeds or humour. It is stimulated in both sexes by danger, novelty and dark chocolate. You should be aware of the risk that what you might think of as 'lust only' sex can easily precipitate romantic love and the desire for attachment.

Myths about male and female orgasm

In 2005, Professor Holstep in the Netherlands investigated what happens in your brain when you have an orgasm. He got couples to make love while their brains were scanned using a PET scanner. (Laboratory conditions had to be improved before some partners could rise to the occasion! Lights were lowered and socks issued to those who got cold feet.)

Contrary to myths that the parts of the brain involved in verbal and emotional thinking needed to stay engaged for women to have good sex, female brains (as well as male brains) experienced major neurological shutdown as orgasm approached. The orgasms released endorphins – endorphins help creative thinking and reduce depression and anxiety, thereby enhancing speed and accuracy of thinking.

Intercourse – verbal and physical

It may be no coincidence that the word for physical and verbal communication is the same – i.e. intercourse.

She: 'How can I stop him thinking all the time?'

Friend: 'Castration?'

Physical communication patterns in bed, mirror verbal communication patterns elsewhere. For example, sulking will turn up as withholding sex, controlling will turn up as dominating sex, anger will turn up as punitive or humiliating sex, teasing as… teasing, and so on. Think about it.

On carrying a baby at 50+

Fearing genocide, the inhabitants of a Muslim village fled during the night. To escape they would need to cross a cold high mountain. They took a little-known path. The path was very steep and very high and very cold. The mothers carried their babies. The fathers helped the older children and the older people struggled on alone. Eventually, some of the older people began to sit down by the edge of the path, exhausted by the cold and the lack of oxygen.

The older people said: 'We are exhausted. We have become a burden. We are slowing everyone down. We will all be caught. Leave us here. You can carry on more quickly without us.'

The mothers said: 'We too need to rest. With every step our babies are becoming heavier and heavier to carry.' And so, the mothers gave, to each older person, a baby to carry. The mothers said to the older people: 'Look, instead of just sitting down and dying in the cold, please carry our babies as far as you can, before you sit down to die. Your bodies will at least keep our babies warm and you will give us respite to regain our strength so that we can reach the summit tomorrow.'

The older people clasped the babies tight against their chests, and started walking. And you know, the older people never stopped! They climbed all the way over the mountains, still carrying the babies. The babies had given them reason and reason had given them strength.

(A story told to Fakhrun and Danya by Abbu, when Danya was two years old. It is based on a true story originally told by Ruby Lee.)

Social situations at 50+

How comfortable are you in social situations?

Either before, during, or after a social interaction (perhaps with someone you would have liked to get to know a little better), how often did you have thoughts similar to those below? Write your score in the unshaded box.

	In social situations I have thoughts similar to...	Score 1–4	
	Score: 1 = I rarely had thoughts similar to this. 2 = I sometimes had thoughts similar to this. 3 = I often had thoughts similar to this. 4 = I very often had thoughts similar to this.	A	B
1	I'll throw caution to the wind – in for a penny, in for a pound.		
2	I wish I could just avoid the whole situation.		
3	We could get on really well.		
4	We probably have a lot in common.		
5	Come on, what's the worst that could happen?		
6	I must make a good impression or I'll let myself down and afterwards feel terrible.		
7	I don't have to put myself through this.		
8	This is going to be awkward, but I can handle it.		
9	What is there to lose? Its worth a try.		
10	I'll probably come across as really stupid.		
11	If I blow this, I'll never be able to fail again.		
12	This will be a good opportunity to...		
13	I'm just not good in these situations, something always goes wrong.		
14	I'll try breaking the ice by asking/talking about...		
15	These kind of situations scare me to death.		
16	I'm afraid they will think I'm...		
17	I'm beginning to feel more relaxed now.		
18	I'll panic if I can't think what to say.		
19	I will feel really awkward if...		
20	Whatever, I'll handle it somehow.		
		Total As:	
		Total Bs:	

How did you get on?

What did you get for your A and B totals?

Total A measures how **positive** you feel about social situations.

Compare your score with typical scores for men and women:

Male A score	Female A score	Percentage scoring this high
27+	30+	15%
25+	28+	30%
23+	26+	50%
21+	24+	70%
20+	23+	85%

Total B measures how **negative** you feel about social situations.

Compare your score with typical scores for men and women:

Male B score	Female B score	Percentage scoring this high
27+	22+	15%
25+	21+	30%
22+	18+	50%
20+	17+	70%
17+	15+	85%

So, what does your score mean?

A high B score means that you probably agree with whoever said: 'Better to remain silent and look a fool, than to open my mouth and remove all doubt!' People with high B scores are nervous about social situations and you make yourself even more nervous through self-defeating internal dialogue.

A high A score, on the other hand, shows that you do not have excessive social anxiety (a little is good, it revs you up ready for the social fray!). You see yourself as quite socially adept. Even if you sometimes don't get the reaction you would like, it is no big deal to you. You are more likely to think: 'Nothing ventured, nothing gained.'

Men and women also seem to behave differently when they have high B or low A scores. 50+ women are more inclined to carry on regardless – tolerating their discomfort and anxiety, and making the (often enormous) social effort. Shy 50+ men, on the other hand, are more likely to become, or remain, isolated and develop low BLISS scores, and lead less successful lives. If, at 50+, you are in the bottom 15 per cent for A and the top 15 per cent for B, you are likely to prefer staying at home, maybe watching television or having a drink alone. This is not very satisfactory for you, or for a society that is in urgent need of the superior brain power of your 50+ brain. The good news is that this is not irreversible and you can change things.

Now, what to do about your score?

Look at the statements that you are making that contribute to high B or low A scores and stop making them, especially to yourself in your internal dialogue. If you rehearse them, and myelinate them, they might become self-fulfilling. Take the following five steps:

Step 1.   For two weeks, smile, give eye contact and say 'hello' to any stranger who smiles back. This can be at work or at a class, or at the checkout. You may get the odd quizzical look, but research evidence suggests that people will usually smile back.

Step 2.   For the next two weeks, practise adding small talk to the initial smile, eye contact and 'hello'. Waiting in a queue, or a line, is a good time to practise. Try a comment about the weather, some new feature in the shop, the price of things, a local sports result, a programme on television last night, or an item on the news. If you are served by the same person more than once on successive weeks, try 'How have you been keeping?' You will be surprised that people often seem glad to reply in some detail – about a trip or an illness in their family. This can then be followed up the next week – 'How was your trip?' 'Is your mother recovering OK?'

Step 3.   Set yourself a target of finding one good or complimentary thing to say to at least one person each day. This can be quite a daunting target to start with, especially as evening approaches and you still haven't met your quota! You may have to ring someone or go and buy something such as milk at the local shop. Soon it will feel more natural and you can raise your target. People tend to like people who like them – show them that you like something about them – if only their hair colour or cut. Comment if they have a new tan – did they get it on a trip? It is natural to take interest in when and where, and where else they have enjoyed...

Step 4. Make the first move with invitations. Ask a co-worker what they usually do for lunch. It may seem OK to ask if you can tag along or to recommend somewhere different they might want to come and try...? If you and your neighbour are in the garden on a sunny day, invite them round for a cold drink, or to give advice on a sickly plant. Talking about a good film on television last night may lead to a new film release that looks good and would they like to come along and see it? Not everyone will say 'yes', not everyone will like you, just as you don't like everyone you meet. That's why you have to keep going to find the odd person you do like and who does like you.

Step 5. Now you have got neuron traces in your brain that are familiar with smiling, giving eye contact, saying 'hello', starting small talk, showing interest, making suggestions and accepting 'no' and sometimes 'yes' – it is time to move into a circle or group where there is high chance that there is someone with something in common with you, or even a shared love (or pet hate). Try joining an assertiveness class, or a language class, or a book club, or a hill walking club, or an art or craft class. Why not volunteer to work in a charity shop? Book shops readily reveal people's interests and can prompt conversation and joint endeavour. Prepare a few sentences that you could say at your class or group or to a particular individual. Write them down or record them. Rehearse them and forget about them. Later that day or evening, you will find it easier to speak up. Nobody will notice how nervous you were, and someone may later take you up on what you said. Never assume that anyone making the effort to speak to you is doing so without good reason. They may like you, or find you interesting, attractive even. If you are 50+, who can blame them? You are likely to be one of the most interesting people in the room and if you did have a high negative B score on social anxiety, you are probably sensitive and unthreatening – just the sort of person a person like you would want to get to know.

(*The test design with norms and percentiles, was originally published by Carol Glass in* Cognitive Therapy and Research.)

The nuns are at it again

I want a few friends at the end. With my vast store of aged wisdom, it seems a pity not to speak it all, so keep me from the recital of endless detail and give me wings to get to the point. Oh, and seal my lips on my aches and pains – they are increasing as I get older and my love of rehearsing them is getting sweeter as the years pass. I dare not ask for grace enough to enjoy the tales of other people's pains, but help me at least to listen with more patience.

I do not wish to be a saint – for they are hard to live with – but a sour and cynical old person is the crowning work of the devil. Give me the ability to see good things in unexpected people and give me, please, the grace to tell them so.

(from a seventeenth-century nun's prayer)

Intimacy and trust – can you get close to others or let others get close to you?

Having made the acquaintance of others, some of whom you may now be meeting quite regularly under circumstances of mutual interest and congeniality, your brain and thinking will already be benefiting from the opportunities you now have to think aloud, to have thoughtful conversations. If you were able to use the opportunities provided by these thoughtful conversations to develop a closer, more intimate and trusting relationship with one or two of your acquaintances, your brain would benefit even more. Discussions based on deeply held beliefs might become possible and this would involve the many parts of your brain connected to your amygdala, as well as the parts of your cerebral cortex dealing with words and logic and perhaps imagination. The sharing of important past events, or even childhood experiences, will cause your hypothalamus to activate 17 or more additional areas of your brain associated with your long-term memory. The question is, can you do it? Can you tolerate closeness and intimacy? Can you sufficiently trust another person?

Do you agree or disagree with the following statements?

Thinking about the following statements I would give a score of… 1 = strongly disagree, 2 = mildly disagree, 3 = mildly agree, 4 = strongly agree	Score 1–4
1 Closeness can lead to good feelings and bad feelings.	
2 The desire for closeness with someone usually follows feeling attracted to them.	
3 I can usually see another person's point of view.	
4 When I can be open and close to another person, I feel good.	
5 When another person is attracted to me, I usually want to get closer to them.	
6 Generally, I find it equally easy to get close to men or women.	
7 I feel close to others when I can discuss my sex life with them.	
8 The closer I feel to someone, the more accepting I am of them as they are.	
9 It is important to me to have some close relationships in my life.	
10 Close relationships have usually brought me great satisfaction.	
11 I can reveal my deepest feelings to people I trust.	
12 Being able to express how I feel makes me feel close to someone.	
13 I like it when other people tell me how they are feeling.	
14 I like feelings of closeness to others.	
15 I like to share my feelings with other people.	
16 I do not react negatively to demands from people close to me.	
17 I am not worried about being dominated in a close relationship.	

18 Sex and intimacy are not the same thing.	
19 I am open and not normally secretive.	
20 I am not worried about rejection in trying to get close to someone.	
21 I do not resist closeness or intimacy.	
22 I do not always need to be in control all the time.	
23 I find it easy to have more than one close relationship in my life.	
24 I can become close to people with whom I initially have little in common.	
25 I am not worried that I might lose my individuality in a close relationship.	
26 I am not worried about maintaining my personal space.	
27 I feel a strong need to share my thoughts and feelings with someone else.	
28 When people become close they always listen well to each other.	
29 I am not afraid to talk about sex and my sexual feelings.	
30 I am not worried about being too trusting of other people.	
Capacity for closeness, trust and intimacy score:	

How did you get on?

What was your total score for capacity for closeness and how does it compare with other people's?

The percentage of people who score	is
75+	85%
80+	70%
86+	50%
90+	30%
100+	15%

So, what does your score mean?

According to Dr Treadwell, on whose work (reported in the *Journal of Personality Assessment*) our test is based, the lower your score, the greater you are at risk of alienation, loneliness and impaired health as well as impaired thinking. But very high scores are not entirely unproblematic. Many of the 50+ will remember having insufferable 'encounters' with people who were members of 'encounter' groups and 'sensitivity training' groups in the 1970s. The graduates of such groups often graduated with a missionary zeal to find and convert others to the joys of 'authentic' close relationships. Their indiscriminate openness was often unwanted. That said, you should hope for a score that allows you readily to be close to your spouse or long-term partners or old friends. You deserve to have at least one person who 'calls you friend', who believes in you, gives you hope and who you need too. Even so, over-disclosure or unreciprocated levels of disclosure, can actually threaten a relationship if the level of disclosure becomes too burdensome for one partner, or if one partner lacks sufficient self-knowledge or self-awareness to be able to reciprocate.

Now, what to do about your score

If your score was less than 70, ask yourself whether you close down all your relationships, because, according to Horne and Doherty (2003), 'closeness in a relationship – at work, or at play, is a function of the extent of and depth of the disclosure'. If you feel lonely or isolated or just 'grey and empty', it may, in part, be due to a lack of closeness, particularly if it usually falls short of emotional disclosure.

If your score was 105+, you might be overwhelming some people with your intensity.

If your score differs from that of an existing (or potential) partner by more than, say, 20 points, that might highlight some unbalance ahead. Both reserved, or both intense, may work, but very disparate positions portend a great deal of frustration, about feeling 'over-disclosed', 'making all the running', and about 'carrying the whole emotional burden of the relationship'.

How satisfactory is your 50+ relationship?

We have looked at how you can get into (or back into) a relationship at 50+, and the importance of balanced disclosure, closeness, intimacy and trust, not only for the health and survival of the relationship, but also as a supportive framework for the kinds of thoughtful conversations that develop the cognitive capacity of your brain. Is your brain getting this kind of nurturing in your present close relationship(s)? How satisfactory is your 50+ relationship with partner X? Please answer the following questions about your relationship with X and ring the score beneath the word that most closely fits your answer.

1.	How many major problems are there in your relationship with X?			
Possible replies	Very many	Some	Few	Very few
Score	1	2	3	4

2.	How much do you love your partner?			
Possible replies	Not a lot	Somewhat	Quite a lot	Very much
Score	1	2	3	4

3.	Does your relationship with X still live up to your original hopes?			
Possible replies	Hardly	Partly	Mostly	Completely
Score	1	2	3	4

4.	How often do you think: 'I wish I had never got into this relationship?			
Possible replies	Nearly all the time	Often	Sometimes	Almost never
Score	1	2	3	4

5.	How good is your relationship with X compared to most?			
Possible replies	Poor	Bearable	OK	Excellent
Score	1	2	3	4

6.	In general, how satisfied are you with your present relationship?			
Possible replies	Not satisfied	It's tolerable	It's good	Extremely satisfied
Score	1	2	3	4

7.	How well is partner X meeting your needs?			
Possible replies	Not well at all	Not well enough	Well	Extremely well
Score	1	2	3	4

Your total score for your relationship with X:

How did you do?

What is your total score for your close relationship with X at 50+ and how does it compare with the way other people rate their close relationships?

The percentage of people who score	is
18+	85%
21+	70%
23+	50%
26+	30%
28+	15%

(Source: The design, norming and percentile scoring for this test was based on original work by Susan Hendrick, reported in the Journal of Marriage and Family.)

So, what does your score mean?

We have to note that Susan Hendricks worked largely with married couples and the scores she normed correlated with much more detailed inventories of satisfaction with married life. At 50+, one of your close relationships is likely to be with someone to whom you are married. Hendricks' scale does pretty well at predicting which co-habiting couples will still be together one year ahead.

You might find your score a bit unnerving. You have to remember that at 50+, you are probably more resigned to, or more realistic about, your relationship than younger people who may still have idealized views of themselves and their partners. By definition, the norms are for couples who are together and prepared to talk about their relationships. They will therefore be skewed towards a more favourable view – so don't be too alarmed if most of them appear to be reporting that they are more satisfied with their close relationships than you are with yours. Most people will be reluctant to admit to themselves, let alone an interviewer, that they have had to accept second or third best for their close relationship. So, at 50+, you need to take the scores of younger people with a pinch of salt – they may have inflated the averages with which you are now comparing yourself. It may be more instructive to get your partner to complete the test. Long-term couples tend to give similar (high or low) ratings for their relationships. If you are reluctant, or afraid, to have such a discussion with your partner, it does not bode well for the ability of your relationship to nurture your brain and your verbal thinking power!

Such a reluctance to engage in verbal intercourse may mirror, or contribute to, a reluctance to engage in sexual intercourse. This chicken and egg can be very difficult to sort out at 50+, when there can be other physical or hormonal reasons for a decline in satisfaction with the physical side of a relationship. Since it is a two-way street, one can 'affect' the other. It may surprise you to know that, at 50+, there is not a strong correspondence between frequency of sex and satisfaction with the relationship, though total absence is sometimes an indicator that all might not be well. Neither is frequency of arguments negatively correlated with satisfaction (what seems to matter more than how often you argue, is *how* you argue). However, what does correlate with satisfaction is frequency of sex minus frequency of arguments, i.e. if you are going to argue, having sex is an important way to make up and repair damage to self-esteem or confidence in the relationship. Awareness of the pattern may be helpful, lest you or your partner end up picking fights when you would be better off picking your moment for a cuddle that could lead to some sexual satisfaction, the chemistry of which is good for your brain as well as your relationship.

A good sex life at 50+ is not only good for your brain, it is becoming more widely expected. When the 50+ were young, it was rare to see 50+ stars in films enjoying sex. Now it is commonplace. Granny sex is mainstream, and 50+ stars like Helen Mirren, Harrison Ford and Meryl Streep are regarded as very sexy and sexual without extensive artifice. Many male stars go on into their late seventies. This can create expectations and pressures on your 50+ relationship. Hundreds of books have been written on how you can improve! But most of them focus, mistakenly, on physical techniques. They point out, rightly, the aphrodisiac power of novelty, and advise you to try new settings, new outfits and surprising homecomings. These techniques will rejuvenate your sex life for a while but, by definition, the novelty will wear off! A more enduring solution is to work on the quality of your verbal intercourse.

Verbal intercourse not only improves your capacity for internal dialogue when you think, it mirrors and rehearses the talk for your sexual intercourse later. At 50+, men, especially, report an increased desire to have sex for different reasons from when they were young and enslaved to their testosterone. At 50+, men want to express love and affection through sex and to feel the reassurance of having that reciprocated. At 50+, it is more about love than lust. At 50+, the key to improving your sex life is to spend more time talking to each other and doing things together. Try making deliberate and specific attempts regularly to revitalize any feelings of love, respect and admiration for your partner as they arise. There will probably be many genuine opportunities each day. Make it a goal to seize at least one. So how much do you know about sex at 50+?

Sex at 50+

I still have two abiding passions – model railways and women. Now that I am 89, I am finally getting a bit too old for model railways!

(Pierre Monteaux, orchestral conductor, aged 89 years)

The quality of your thinking about some aspects of your sex life may be limited by the quality of the information on which that thinking is based. At 50+, you are likely to know more about sex than a younger person – will probably have had more (sex, that is). But you know may not be up to date in terms of social attitudes or well informed by recent science. It might be as well to check out what you do know about sex, now that you are 50+.

Tick your best answer for the 20 questions in the following sex Check Test and then check to see if you were right. If you do well, fine. Follow up on the ones you got wrong. If you do badly, fine. Get a book and discuss what you discover with your partner.

Sex Check Test

1.	**Bisexuality: studies have shown that...**	
A	It does not exist	
B	It is commonplace	
C	Bisexuals are homosexuals in denial	

2.	**Dressing up: studies have shown that dressing up for sex...**	
A	Indicates mental disorder	
B	Is intended to degrade, belittle or humiliate	
C	Is normal and commonplace	

3.	**Menopause: studies have shown that a women's sexual behaviour after menopause is determined by...**	
A	Her residual levels of oestrogen	
B	The attitude of her partner during menopause	
C	Her attitude towards sex before menopause	

4.	**Effects of age: studies have shown that as men get older...**	
A	The urgency of their sex drive slows down	
B	They require more physical stimulation by their partner	
C	They take longer to recover between orgasms	
D	All of the above	

5.	**Testosterone: studies have shown that male testosterone**	
A	Declines from age 40	
B	Disappears in mid 50s	
C	Remains high until late 90s	

6.	**Pornography: people who use pornography...**	
A	Become confused about fantasy and reality	
B	Show a temporary increase and interest in sexual activity	
C	Develop deviant or coercive interests in sex	
D	Come to regard their partners as sex objects	

7.	**Sex therapy: the most effective therapies are based on...**	
A	Thinking, i.e. cognitive therapies	
B	Psychoanalysis	
C	The use of surrogate partners	
D	Medication	

8.	**Getting it up: erectile dysfunction is not caused by...**	
A	Age-related arthritis	
B	Slipped discs	
C	Diabetes	
D	Alcohol	

9.	**Most common male sex problem: studies found it to be...**	
A	Premature ejaculation	
B	Erectile dysfunction	
C	Low desire or interest	

10.	**Menopause: studies have found that female menopause causes...**	
A	Hot flushes and sweating	
B	Painful dryness of the vagina	
C	Insomnia, irritability, lack of concentration, impaired thinking	
D	All of the above	

11.	Age and fertility: the most common cause of infertility is...	
A	Age-lowered sperm count in the male partner	
B	Age-lowered estrogen levels in the female partner	
C	Increased toxins in the environment	
D	A removable blockage in the fallopian tube	

12.	A baby at 50+?: studies have shown that you will maximize your chances of conceiving your child if you have sex	
A	5 to 10 days after the first day of the menstrual cycle	
B	5 to 10 days before the first day of the menstrual cycle	
C	3 days before and 3 days after the menstrual cycle	
D	5 days before and 5 days after the day the egg is released	

13.	Female orgasm: studies have shown the best sexual position is...	
A	Man on top	
B	Woman on top	
C	Rear entry	
D	Side by side (spoons)	

14.	Age, gender and masturbation: studies have found...	
A	That both women and men masturbate and sometimes when they are together	
B	That masturbation continues throughout life to death	
C	That many people masturbate and have regular sex with a partner	
D	All of the above	

15.	Sex vs. love: studies have found that...	
A	Male love is diminished by frequent sex	
B	Male satisfaction with sex is not enhanced with love	
C	That for a man, sex does not need to involve love	

16.	**Female ejaculation: studies have found that...**	
A	Between 10% and 40% of women ejaculate liquid on orgasm	
B	The vagina sweats during intercourse, producing a clear liquid	
C	That the clear liquid is a sign of a urinary tract infection	

17.	**The clitoris: studies have found that...**	
A	The clitoris can become erect during love play and intercourse	
B	That the clitoris is often concealed prior to erection	
C	That the sole purpose of the clitoris is to provide pleasure	
D	All of the above	

18.	**Contraception: the risk of conception is lowest using...**	
A	A cervical cap	
B	A sponge	
C	An inter uterine device (IUD)	
D	Oral contraception	

19.	**Risky contraception: studies have shown that there is the greatest risk of conception when using...**	
A	A cervical cap	
B	A diaphragm	
C	A condom	
D	An inter uterine device (IUD)	

20.	**Age and risk to babies: studies have found the biggest contributor to birth defects in Western countries is...**	
A	Malnutrition	
B	Age of parents	
C	Cigarette smoke	
D	Cocaine	
E	Alcohol (even one unit)	
F	Sexual activity during pregnancy	

Answers

Score 1 for a correct answer.

Question	Answer
1.	B
2.	C
3.	C
4.	D
5.	A
6.	B
7.	A
8.	A
9.	C
10.	D
11.	D
12.	D
13.	B
14.	D
15.	C
16.	A
17.	D
18.	D
19.	D
20.	E
	Total score

How did you get on?

How many of the 20 sex check questions did you and/or your partner answer correctly? Follow up on any areas of doubt. Keep talking. It's the talking that develops your brain. The by-product is better sex and with better sex come brain chemicals that enhance your thinking skills and your thinking power.

A sex warning – don't say we didn't warn you!

What is undoubtfully good for your brain, might not be so good for your body. Graham and Lynne Jones (in *I love Sex*) report that sex had been a suspected cause of acne, thrush, cervical cancer, blindness, body odour, whooping cough, gout, sore throat, loss of teeth, tennis elbow, Achilles heel and housemaid's knee.

Some of these might be due more to 'how' than to 'how often'!

'Guessing the truth'

When she was a mother
It was the role that she loved best.
A fullness and fulfilment rose
To fill her heart and breast.
And that's the truth – we guessed.
She could not put her arms around
Their innocence and youth,
To keep them safe
From her own death
And that must be the truth.
For there is no more hostelling,
She's walking all alone.
And they now fly throughout the world,
Her little ones have flown.
Yet wind still blows across this hill,
A sound she loved to hear,
And she would love it still,
If she were here
And still, upon this hill.
For when she was a mother,
It was the role that she loved best.
And that's the truth.
We guessed.

(An unhappy and happy conjunction of Pam Ayres,
Ann Murray, Simon Wootton and the thoughts of
Carolyn Horne at 50+, Terry Horne 2008.)

In Chapter 06 we have been concerned about the capacity for thoughtful relationships because relationships affect your general health and your predominant mood, and both of these affect the ambient chemistry of your brain. The chemicals present in your brain determine your brain's ability to think well, and to resist degenerative disease. Also, close, intimate relationships are a vehicle for thoughtful conversations.

Thoughtful conversations help you to develop spare cognitive capacity. If your brain has spare cognitive capacity, you may be able to continue to think well, even if you do contract a degenerative brain disease like Alzheimer's. Thoughtful conversations rehearse your ability to express clearly what the world now needs – the clear thinking of its most powerful brains – the brains of the 50+.

Summary

- Verbal thinking and overall IQ are governed by internal dialogue.
- Internal dialogue is limited by your vocabulary and fluency.
- The 50+ have a more extensive, precise vocabulary than young people.
- Embedding your verbal thinking into conversations with others improves your ability to think for yourself by yourself and develops intimacy in a relationship.
- Brain 'chemistry' matters, in lust, love, attachment and sex.
- You can deepen your relationships, and achieve closeness and intimacy, through thoughtful conversations and the 'meeting of minds'.

Further suggested reading

Bragdon, A. (2005) *Learn Faster, Remember More*, Geddes and Grosset.

Bryon, M. (2001) *Graduate Selection Tests*, Kogan Page.

Bryon, M. (2003) *Civil Service Tests*, Kogan Page.

Carter, P. (2005) *IQ and Psychometric Tests*, Kogan Page.

Cox, E. and Rathvon, H. (2007) *Mensa Cryptic Crosswords*, Stirling.

Fisler, H. (2004) *Why we love: the brain chemistry of love*, Henry Holt.

Gamon, D. (2005) *Mental Muscles*, Geddes and Grosset.

Horne, T. and Doherty, A. (2003) *Managing Public Services*, Routledge.

Howard, P. (3rd edn) (2006) *Manual of the Brain*, BAAD.

Tolly, H. and Thomas, K. (2006) *Verbal Reasoning Tests*, Kogan Page.

part

two

brain workout

introduction

This brain training workout has two components: a series of 14 blocks of exercises (or circuits), and 14 cryptic crosswords. For some people, doing regular circuits in the gym is the best way to improve their performance in the field. For others, 'the game is the best coach'. You can try either the series of exercises, or the cryptic crosswords, or both. Since each circuit is composed of the same mix of exercises, some easy and some difficult, then your score should improve between Circuit 01 and Circuit 14. In the case of the 14 cryptic crossword puzzles, you should find that you can do them more easily as you work your way through from Circuit 01 to Circuit 14. That is because the puzzles are of similar levels of difficulty and you will get better with practice.

Solving a cryptic crossword simultaneously involves traffic between many different areas of your brain as you try to: use logic; recollect obscure bits of general knowledge; make creative associations between the bits you remember; count letters and spaces; hold several possibilities in your short-term memory; decide on the most likely possibilities; analyze the best way to cross-check your decision; and, finally, manage your motivation and frustration! All these separate aspects of your brain development are intensified if you do the puzzle, or discuss the puzzle, with another person. Cryptic crosswords don't just test your brain power – more importantly, the attempts you make to solve the cryptic clues leave new neural traces and connections in your brain. These new neural connections create new cognitive capacity that improves your performance on other thinking tasks and also helps to protect your improved performance against disease by creating reserve cognitive capacity.

Dr Barry Gibb – neuroscientist

(talking about the new Nintendo DS Range of electronic brain trainers, *Times 2*, 29/09/07)

If you think of the brain as a machine, you would not expect it to function for 120 years without good maintenance. For good maintenance, the brain needs purpose-designed stimulation – such as films, music, books and well-designed brain training activities. 'Neurobic' activities help to keep your head fit in the same way that aerobic exercises help to keep your muscles fit. Brain training exercises can help you to make the most of what you've now got. Because these brain training exercises are carefully graded, you can evaluate how much better you become over time. You will be able to gauge for yourself how much your thinking speed and accuracy have improved.

(Barry Gibb is author of *Rough Guide to the Brain*)

In his book *Mind Sculpture*, Professor Ian Robertson, reports on the way brain training exercises sculpt the mind. Professor Robertson invites you to look at your right hand and mentally number your fingers 1–4 (forefinger 1, middle 2, ring 3, little 4).

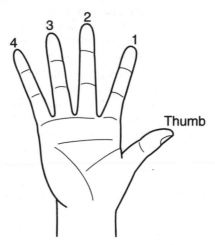

figure 0.1

If you now touch the thumb of your right hand against your fingers in the pattern 4-1-3-2-4, you will be able to do it about 30 times in a minute. (Also notice how many times you can do

4-1-2-3-4 in a minute.) If you practice 4-1-3-2-4 for 20 days, you will then be able to do it about 80 times in a minute! Moreover, under a CT scanner, it will be seen that the neurons involved in this brain training are enlarged. The number of synaptic connections will have increased and the myelin insulation will have thickened. If you now attempt the activity which you have not practised, i.e. 4-1-2-3-4, you will find that it too will be easier and faster, even though you have not practised it! This is because residual synaptic connections and neural pathways created by your 4-1-3-2-4 training are now available to help you with other brain-based activities. That is why Elbert found that learning the guitar, the violin or the cello, helped verbal thinking. The same part of the brain – the planum temporale – was involved in both activities. According to Professor Robertson, music practice is a form of brain training. It helps to create an intricate web of connections between your neurons.

Even more startling evidence of the ability of your brain to transfer the benefits of one type of exercise to performance in another was reported by Yue, who found that four weeks of physical exercise could increase muscular strength by 30 per cent, compared with control group who did not exercise. But a control group who only sat on their couches and visualized the muscular effort showed a gain in strength of 22 per cent – the power of visual thinking! So, even if you cannot immediately understand why some of our brain training exercises use the parts of the brain they do, be confident that they will add to your general cognitive capacity. You will be able to carry out other thinking tasks with greater mental strength, speed and suppleness. According to Moran, basketball ace Michael Jordan and Golf Master Jack Nicholas were both able to improve their shooting and putting by doing brain training which involved visual and emotional thinking.

Some of Glen Gould's sublime Beethoven piano concerto recordings were, he said, only ever practised in his head. For you, listening to Glen Gould's music may improve your performance on certain thinking tasks, but there is no evidence that listening alone will change your brain. For that, you would have to play or compose the music yourself – or at the very least imagine yourself doing so.

Active engagement and challenge appear to be necessary for improved mental fitness. A useful analogy might be pushing yourself beyond your comfort zone by using a heart rate monitor during aerobic exercise.

Try reading the following list of ten words beginning with 's':

shore, sandal, Sunday, sweater, single
stand, similar, silent, soya, Sony

And now, as quickly as you can, write any word beginning with 's' in each of the 10 boxes below:

Sound your new words out aloud, as you write them in their boxes. (Notice the different impact on your brain compared with quiet reading.)

A brain scan would only show a tiny increase in blood flow and brain metabolism when you read the first list, but a surge of widespread activity as you sounded out the second list that you created (see Fig. 3.2, page 93). Chess Grand Masters show relatively limited brain flows when playing chess against junior players (they largely use memorized responses to the moves made by their young opponents). However, even a Grand Master's brain leaps into life when asked to teach or coach the junior player. As a rough rule of thumb, your brain activity will involve more widespread formation of more neural pathways as you progress up the following hierarchy:

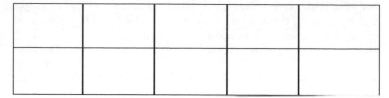

Teaching
Coaching
Creating   **Increasing brain activity**
Learning
Knowing

Hence the brain developing power of paired learning, or of acting as a 'critical friend', or of being a 'thoughtful companion'. So, please take every opportunity to work on brain training exercises with someone else.

Try not to skip a puzzle if you find it hard. Discuss it with someone else. Be persistent. The churning is the learning – especially if done aloud and especially if done with another person. Professor Timiras found that mechanical memory training, done in isolation, produced only a short-term gain in overall mental performance. The gain faded unless there was constant repetition, recall and re-enforcement. (The benefits were more persistent with people whose brains had been damaged by a stroke or a head injury.)

T. S. Eliot said older men (and women) should all become explorers. We agree that being forced to embrace novelty bears fruit in adult brain development. We think this accelerates when explorers return to tell the tale. Travel is in the telling.

As an old man, Confucius advised his country men: 'work your brain every day for else you will lose it'. Confucius would not be surprised by brain scans today which show adults gaining new synapse and new neural development as they work their brains.

Neuroscientists were prompted to look for evidence of continued brain development in adult brains by Rosenzweig's observations of mice. Young mice that were set problems or puzzles to solve added new neurons at rate of 4,000 a day, compared with 2,400 a day in a control group that was not set problems or puzzles to solve. Not only was the rate of production of new neurons 66 per cent faster, the new neurons had more dendrites and longer axons, i.e. Rosenzweig's problem-solving mice were each day developing neurons that were better equipped to make the interconnections that support intelligent behaviour and which increased their reserves of cognitive capacity. Even more exciting for 50+ brain trainers was Rosenzweig's discovery, since replicated by other researchers at Sack and Princeton Universities, that the same effect was found in old mice. In the old mice, many of the new brain cells appeared near the hippocampus – a vital centre for directing new memory information and new learning. Elizabeth Gould, at Princeton, was able to separate the developments caused by purely mental exercises from developments caused by physical exercise. The mental brain training had the most powerful effect – more powerful even than physical exercise and diet (Chapter 01). The effects were enhanced when the activities were carried out in social situations, rather than in isolation (Chapter 06).

Within each of the brain circuits in this part of the book, we have included some puzzles that will specifically target the left side of your brain. This is because such work stimulates centres that hold positive emotions. As you know from Chapter 01, elevated mood enhances mental performance. PET scans show that you laugh on the left side of your brain (and cry on the right). Damasio discovered that your right frontal lobe is active when you feel sad, afraid, disgusted or angry. That is why some activities have been included specifically to stimulate the left side of your brain. Visual puzzles favour the right-hand side of the brain. Verbal puzzles the left.

Now, turn either to the first circuit – or to the first cryptic crossword (these are located after each circuit). Keep a note of how many of the circuit puzzles, or cryptic clues, you can solve. You are encouraged to discuss sticky problems with other people, if you wish. You will progressively be able to solve more of the problems, more quickly. Have fun!

Recommended reading

Cobb, J. (1995) 'Education reduces incidence of dementia and Alzheimer's – the Fremingham study', *Neurology*, 45, pp1706–12.

Coffey, C. (1999) 'Education and brain size – creating reserves', *Neurology*, 55, pp188–97.

Damasio, A. R. (1997) 'Neuropathology of emotion and mood', *Nature*, 386, pp768–70.

Gibb, B. (2007) 'Does brain training work?', the *Times* 2, 29 September 2007, p9.

Gould, E. (1999) 'Learning enhances neurogenesis (new brain cell formation) in adults', *Nature Neuroscience*, 2, pp259–65.

Korni, A. et al (1995) 'Functional MRI evidence for Adult Motor Cortex Plasticity during motor skill learning', *Nature*, 377, p155–58.

Moran, A. (1996) *Psychology of Sports Performers*, Psychology Press.

Robertson, I. (1999) *Mind Sculpture*, Bantam.

Rosenzweig, M. (1996) 'Effects of training in adult brains', *Brain Behaviour Research*, 18, pp56–66.

www.brainwaves.com (Look for 'Building mental muscle and left brain power' by Bragdan, A. and Gamon, D. Also 'A photo quiz for the mind's eye'.)

Yue, G. (1998) 'Strength increases from imagined contractions', *Journal of Neurophysiology*, 67, pp1113–23.

The Titanic was built by professionals, the Ark was built by amateurs.

(Terry Horne)

circuit 01

Q1 Are you afraid to start? Make your way from Fear to Hope, changing one letter at a time.

HOPE

_____

_____

_____

_____

_____

FEAR

Q2 When does some coffee taste like soil?

Q3 The letters A, B, C, D, E, F each represent a different digit in the range 0–8. Which letters represent which numbers? (There are hints and clues below.)

A	+	B	=	A
C	+	A	=	D
D	+	C	=	EB
EB	+	D	=	ED
ED	+	EB	=	AD
AD	+	ED	=	CA
CA	+	AD	=	DF
DF	+	CA	=	EEB
EEB	+	DF	=	EGF

Hint: First line gives B = 0; third line gives E = 1 since 2 digits cannot add to 20; seventh line is 42 + 26 = 68).

Clue: C = 4, A = 2, D = 6

Q4 The *only* Bond girl who appeared in three Bond films, in 1974, 1983, 1985, now divides her continuing career between the US and her native Sweden.

_ _ _ _ / _ _ _ _ _ (4, 5)

> Hint: Surname belonging to someone from Eden.

Q5 Can you get yourself up from being idle to become one of the academic stars at a university (one letter at a time)?

_____

_____

_____

LAZE

> Hint: Start in a daze get it finished.

Q6 Every block in this pyramid contains a number which is the sum of the two on which it rests. What are the missing numbers?

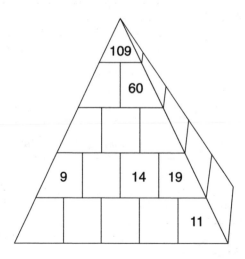

Q7 Complete the Sudoku.

			3			8		1
				5	6	7	3	
4	3	7		9	8	2	6	
1		3				5	7	8
6	4	8	5			3		
	9						4	2
3	6	1		2	5			
	8	4			1			6
9	7			8	4	1		3

On every circuit, questions 8, 9 and 10 will be about numbers – their significance in nature, mathematics, science, religion, mythology, art or history – all proven bastions of the 50+ mind.

Q8 _ _ _ _ _ _ _ tons of TNT is used as a measure of explosive power.

Hint: As in a 3-megaton bomb (from Greek 'mega' = very large).

Q9 Jesus is said to have sent out _ _ disciples, and this number of wives await in heaven.

Q10 The _ _ s brought boom and bust to Wall Street, and brought fascism, brilliant jazz, penicillin, cars, TV, flights and votes for women. The era of James Joyce, Franz Kafka, George Bernard Shaw, T. S. Eliot, Al Jolson, Charlie Chaplin, Buster Keaton and Houdini.

Hint: It is the most common 'score' and two of them combine to give perfect vision.

When you have worked out the title of the next four films, try to rent, buy, borrow and watch them. They are all a brain workout. They all involve emotional, visual and verbal thinking, plus either logic to aid your critical thinking, or humour to aid your creativity.

Q11 After tempting fate by numbering it 13, NASA control room became the brain of America, trying to work out how to get Tom Hanks back.

☐ ☐ ☐ ☐ ☐ ☐

Hint: Aphrodite's friend?

Q12 A new direction in settling accounts.

☐ ☐ ☐　☐ ☐　☐ ☐ ☐ ☐ ☐ ☐

Hint: Not backwards.

Q13 A definite start to one who plays ivories (black and white not Merchant).

☐ ☐ ☐　☐ ☐ ☐ ☐ ☐ ☐ ☐

Hint: Musician.

Q14 Beginning gravely and ending self-consciously, he needed a hand in the middle to free his country without a fight.

☐ ☐ ☐ ☐ ☐ ☐

Hint: Peace-loving Hindu, freed an Asian subcontinent but created partition.

is to ... as ... is to A, B or C?

A

B

C

Hint: Mirrors.

How did you get on?

Score 3 for each correct answer.

(Score an extra 3 points if you did not use the Hints).

Enter your total here

1 in 2 people can expect to score 10 or less when they start.

1 in 40 people can expect to improve their score to 70+.

Cryptic tip 01

Every cryptic crossword clue gives you at least two ways to find the answer.

One is to find the synonym for part of the clue, i.e. a word meaning the same.

The other way is to find the answer through a play on the words that are to be found in the rest of the clue.

For example:

> Male goose is all mixed up in danger. (6)

We find the answer twice: once because a male goose is a gander; and the second time because 'gander' is to be got from the letters of 'danger' all mixed up.

The first task is to spot and separate the word (or few words) for which the synonym is required. In these cryptic tips we will put these in upper case: MALE GOOSE. Normally, several possible synonyms might be the answer. Untangling the play on the remaining words in the clue will normally reduce the number of possibilities to only one possible answer. This will be confirmed when the answer fits in with the cross letters from other clues in the crossword.

The second task is to spot the instructional words that tell us what kind of game is to be played with some of the remaining words in the clue. In the example above, the cryptic operation was an anagram of 'danger', and this was signalled by the words 'all mixed up'. There are many different ways of signalling a particular operation. For example, anagrams may be signalled by words like 'confused by', 'rearranged', 'all shook up', 'stirring'. The possibilities are many, and spotting them becomes easier with experience and practice. When giving cryptic tips, we will show the operation in italics: *all mixed up*.

The third task is to identify the words on which the cryptic operation is to take place. In our cryptic tips we will embolden these words: **danger**. So a cryptic clue has three important parts:

THE WORDS FOR WHICH A SYNONYM IS REQUIRED

+

a cryptic operation

+

the words on which the cryptic operation is to take place.

Cryptic crossword 01

ACROSS

2. The loans get mixed up at the hairdressers (5)
4. 'It's Ben about a vegetable' (4)
6. The thirteenth friend of Aphrodite is misspelt in apology (7)
7. An uncertain approach to Dante produced music that was slow moving (7)
11. Goosey is in danger (6)
13. What nudity creates can be messy (6)
15. Within lust I erased sounds of crying (4)
17. Because it was stabled incorrectly it exploded (7)
18. Specimen maples were chopped up in error (6)

DOWN

1. Indian guru began astonishingly and ended self-consciously after getting a hand in the middle (6)
2. You can find a solid fuel replacement in a lost over (5)
3. You break the chain to go there for all the tea (5)

5. To get your own back in Geneva (6)
8. An error in pouring made a candle lighter (5)
9. Burned by the sun, it somehow lightens the load (9)
10. Caution alters sale (7)
12. Editor gives rise to a commotion (6)
14. Although he displayed flair, he was weak (5)
16. Use a gas to make the filling for a hot dog (7)

> Hint: 'Sounds like' = the synonym indicated 'sounds like' or rhymes with the answer.

Recommended reading

Haselbauer, N. (2005) *The Mammoth Book of IQ Puzzles*, Robinson.

Greeff, F. (2003) *The Code*, Foulsham.

I live in a place where people still point at aeroplanes.
(Terry Horne)

Q1 Using only 0, 1, 2, 3 or 4 only once in each line, complete the grid, so that each vertical, horizontal and diagonal has one and only one of each of the numbers 0, 1, 2, 3, 4.

1		4		
			1	
2				
		0		
0				4

Q2 How could you make sure a ghost was horizontal?

Q3 Fill in the numbers in the bottom row.

6	6	12	18
30	48	78	126
204			

Hint: Numbers get bigger from left to right, and progress similarly one to the next.

Clue: Last number > 800.

Q4 The world's first black supermodel. A *Cosmopolitan* cover girl in 1976, she is now president of a worldwide business empire.

_ _ _ _ _ _ _ / _ _ _ _ _ _ _ (7, 7)

Hint: First find the hills in Hollywood and then a famous doctor.

Q5 The protein in eggs is so good for your brain you can rise to be a poet.

_____?

_____

_____

_____

_____

EGGS

Hint: Full of electrifying energy you can make mistakes and hear that you will be behind, before you become like Shakespeare.

Q6 Every block in this pyramid contains a number which is the sum of the two on which it rests. What are the missing numbers?

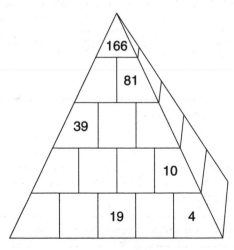

Q7 Complete the Sudoku.

1				6	5		8	9
			8		9	1		6
		9	1	3	7	2	4	
			3			9		
	3		5		6			
		6	2	8	1	3	5	7
	6		7	1	8			3
	9	1			2	8		
8		5			3	6	2	1

On every circuit, questions 8, 9 and 10 will be about numbers – their significance in nature, mathematics, science, religion, mythology, art or history – all proven bastions of the 50+ mind.

Q8 After working well on the farm, George decided to write another book in 1948 and digitally reworked that year.

— — — —

Hint: He not only wrote when down on the farm, but when down and out in Paris (and London).

Q9 Sexual position, __ __ was the number of votes required to elect George Washington as the first president of the USA and is the record number of children born to one mother, Shuya, who was Russian (in a hurry?).

Hint: Two of Shuya's children died, 67 survived.

Q10 To talk __ __ to the dozen is to talk very fast and busily, leading perhaps to this number of nervous breakdowns (Rolling Stones). By the Second World War, the average age of a combat soldier was 26, but in the Vietnam War it fell to this number. In 1642, King Charles I rejected this number of propositions for transferring power from the throne to Parliament, thereby precipitating the English Civil War.

Hint: The last year you were a teenager.

When you have worked out the title of the next four films, try to rent, buy, borrow and watch them. They are all a brain workout. They all involve emotional, visual and verbal thinking, plus either logic to aid your critical thinking, or humour to aid your creativity.

Q11 Did this Society meet in a morgue? Membership definitely confined to bards, perhaps in water.

☐ ☐ ☐ ☐   ☐ ☐ ☐ ☐ ☐

Hint: *Carpe diem* – another Robin Williams triumph.

Q12 Floated on precious water.

☐ ☐   ☐ ☐ ☐ ☐ ☐ ☐   ☐ ☐ ☐ ☐

Hint: Henry Fonda in his golden age.

Q13 A sadomasochistic study penned by feathers.

☐ ☐ ☐ ☐ ☐ ☐

Hint: Begins with a long wait and does not end in heaven.

Q14 Not warmed up before the race.

☐ ☐ ☐ ☐ ☐ ☐ ☐ ☐ ☐ ☐ ☐

> Hint: Hilarious exploits of an Olympic bobsleigh team short of practice in the West Indies.

Q15 Three surviving soldiers divided their remaining bullets equally between them. After they had each fired four bullets, the total number of remaining bullets was the same as they each had after they had divided them. What was the original number remaining before they were equally divided between them?

> Hint: If the total originally divided was T, then each had 1/3 of T. Therefore T/3 = Total left after shooting 3 x 4 bullets.

How did you get on?

Score 3 for each correct answer (score an extra 3 points if you did not use the Hints).

Enter your total here ☐

1 in 2 people can expect to score 10 or less when they start.

1 in 40 people can expect to improve their score to 70+.

Cryptic tip 02

It can be helpful to compare normal crossword clues with cryptic clues. Here are some comparisons:

Answer	Normal clue	Cryptic clue
Mamba	Venomous reptile	*Shortly* **mother** took **academic manager** to see a VENOMOUS REPTILE
Brainy	Intelligent	INTELLIGENT **female support I** take *briefly* to **New York**
Brawn	Strength	**Pressed beef** *makes* you STRONG

Note how 'shortly' or 'briefly' often indicate that abbreviations are involved. In the above examples, 'briefly to New York' = NY and 'shortly mother took academic manager' = Ma + MBA.

These examples illustrate how the normal clue is always somewhere in the cryptic clue – usually near the front or the end of the wordplay part. This makes cryptic clues easier to solve than apparently more straightforward normal crossword clues, because cryptic clues are normal clues plus extra information to help you uncover the synonym that is the answer.

Cryptic crossword 02

ACROSS

5. Mixed up loves remove the problem (5)
6. Grassing up disturbed senator is betrayal (7)
7. Goat can provide material for Roman cloak (4)
8. Equip badly to take offence (5)
9. Sadomasochistic film has long wait plus sick endings (6)

11. That is to say the laymen are confused (5)
15. Intelligent female support taken briefly to New York (6)
17. Inserted are components of one who lives there (8)
18. The sluices spewed an alternative to Farenheit (7)

DOWN
1. Being not warmed up before races led to hilarious film about a Caribbean bobsleigh team (4, 8)
2. Bad dream about carrying a weapon (5)
3. Passed out defiant after riotous assembly (7)
4. Pressed beef gives you strength (5)
10. Warbled drunkenly and had a fight in a bar (7)
12. Shortly mother took the management graduate to see a venomous snake (5)
13. You can recreate amenity whenever you want (3, 4)
14. Deranged escorts provide sexy constraint (7)
16. The mnemonic making an ass of you and me is also known as that which makes one smile (6)

Hint: Anagrams are often indicated by 'confused', 'mixed up', 'components of', 'mistakes', 'deranged', 'mistaken', 'badly', 'wrongly' etc.

Critics know the way but can't drive.

(Tynan, K.)

Q1 We have adapted an old proverb for our new book on thinking. We have removed the vowels. What might the proverb be?

THNKTWCCTNC

Q2 You dreamed a town hall is haunted. Who was there?

Q3 Use some or all of the operations indicated on the line to make each equation balance (=10). Use square brackets to embrace curved brackets.

(A) Using no more than six 1s, $10 = ( ) \times -$

(B) Using no more than six 2s, $10 = ( ) \times \times +$

(C) Using no more than six 3s, $10 = ( ) \times \times + \div$

(D) Using no more than six 6s, $10 = [ ] ( ) ( ) \times + + - \div$

(E) Using no more than six 7s, $10 = [ ] ( ) ( ) \times + + + \div$

(F) Using no more than six 8s, $10 = [ ] ( ) ( ) \times + + \div$

(G) Using no more than six 9s, $10 = ( ) \times + \div$

Hint: For example, in line C, $10 = (3 \times 3 \times 3 + 3) \div 3$.

Clues: In line A, you can use two 1s to make 11.

Q4 Pictured in a red bathing costume, the poster sold 8 million copies. Her *Cosmopolitan* cover in 1977 created a 'flick' hairstyle that was copied around the world. A prince polished her halo! She has a continuing career in TV, film and theatre.

_ _ _ _ _ H / _ _ _ _ _ _ T (6, 7)

Hint: If you push it you might get her surname, but it will get you into hot water in Germany.

Q5 Rather than quit and stay at the bottom, you could raise your word game.

_____ SPAR _____

_____

_____

_____

QUIT

Hint: Dress up for the barbeque and turn the rod that reaches across.

Q6 Every block in this pyramid contains a number which is the sum of the two on which it rests. What are the missing numbers?

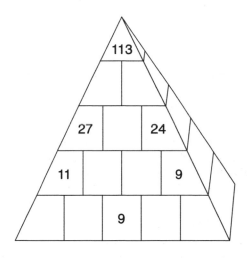

Q7 Complete the Sudoku.

1		3	5	4	6	7		
		7			8	2	3	
5	8				7		4	6
	1		3			8		7
		6				4	1	
		1		4			5	3
		1			2	9		
9				7	3		6	
		5	6	9	1	3	2	

On every circuit, questions 8, 9 and 10 will be about numbers – their significance in nature, mathematics, science, religion, mythology, art or history – all proven bastions of the 50+ mind.

Q8 Acting independently on __ __ . __ __ . __ __ __ __ , Thomas said that it was self-evident that all men were born equal and with the right to life, liberty and happiness.

Hint: __ __ . __ __ . 1 7 7 6

Q9 19 __ __ : Russia invaded Czechoslovakia and there were riotous student protests in Paris and Mexico City; anti-Vietnam War demonstrations in London; the assassination of Martin Luther King and Robert F. Kennedy in the USA.

Hint: __ __ years elapsed from the formation of the 3rd French Republic before it was invaded by Germany in 1939.

Q10 'She was only __ __ , only __ __ . She was too young to fall in love, and I was too young to know' – so sang Sam Cooke. Singers from Chuck Berry to Julie Andrews have said how sweet it is to be this age. A double is the most popular checkout in darts and we are awake for this average number of hours a day.

> Hint: There are this number of chess pieces in a set, ounces in a pound and named points on a compass.

When you have worked out the title of the next four films or TV shows, try to rent, buy, borrow and watch them. They are all a brain workout. They all involve emotional, visual and verbal thinking, plus either logic to aid your critical thinking, or humour to aid your creativity.

Q11 The post has come – sounds like you might have a partner.

☐ ☐ ☐   ☐ ☐ ☐   ☐ ☐ ☐ ☐

> Hint: What comes in the post that has the same sound as male?

Q12 A medic we don't recognize was first shown on the day President J. F. Kennedy was assassinated.

☐ ☐   ☐ ☐ ☐

> Hint: Knock, knock. Who's there?

Q13 If she was inside and went this colour before she went to hell she would need to be examined as she left.

☐ ☐ ☐ ☐   ☐ ☐ ☐ ☐ ☐ ☐

> Hint: If it is true that Eve was naked inside the garden, she might have been blue with cold.

Q14 What do Roy Orbison and Richard Gere have in common?

☐ ☐ ☐ ☐ ☐ ☐   ☐ ☐ ☐ ☐ ☐

Hint: To say this about Julia Roberts (who played the lead) would be an understatement.

Q15 Which of A, B, or C fits in the bottom corner?

Hint: In the columns, the number of sides in the top two squares = the total in the bottom square.

How did you get on?

Score 3 for each correct answer.

Score an extra 3 points if you did not use the Hints).

Enter your total here ☐

1 in 2 people can expect to score 10 or less when they start.

1 in 40 people can expect to improve their score to 70+.

Cryptic tip 03

As you may have realized by now, one of the most common ploys of the cryptic clue-setter is the anagram. We have already identified some of the common words that indicate that this is the cryptic operation required. Here is a fuller, but by no means exhaustive list:

abnormally, alterations, agitated, all over the place, (all) at sea, breaking (up), camouflages, capsize, changed, chewed, concocted, conversion, converts, cooked up, disguised, dealt, drunken, extended, loosened, erupts, misplaced, mislaid, manoeuvred, minced, mixed, moved, out of, randomized, rebuilt, re-laid, rearranged, remodelled, remade, reordered, recipe for, recovered from, redesign, reformed, rescheduled, restored, revised, ruptured, reshaped, somehow, sort, restoration, resorted, stormy, strangely, spoilt, switched, transfer, troubled, in turmoil, turned into, twisted, unravel, unusually, upset, variation of, wrongly.

If you suspect an anagram, check the number of words in the answer and look for a word in the clue with that number of letters.

For example:

- **Rene's** *upset* is an INDICATION OF CONTEMPT = sneer
- **Men test drive a** *convertible* to obtain PROMOTION = advertisement
- *Troubled* **masters sense** NEED TO RESIT = reassessment
- GREEK LETTER **is** *mixed up* **with a note** to *a short* **mother** = sigma
- MAINTENANCE OF POWER **at mains** *exchange required* = stamina
- PAINFUL SURGERY **yet Dr isn't** *confused* = dentistry
- **Hat** and **pipe** *mislaid* AT THE END = epitaph

Cryptic crossword 03

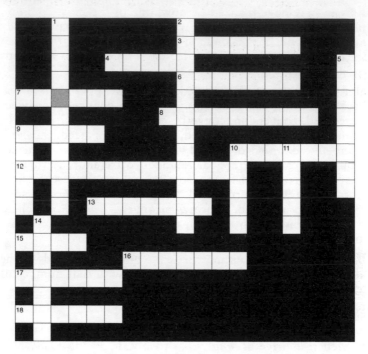

ACROSS

3. Hat and pipe both mislaid at the end (7)
4. Greek letter is mixed up with a note to a short mother (5)
6. Taken with mittens in which the last shall be first (7)
7. How could so confused a medic be so popular on TV? (2, 3)
8. Potentially painful surgery yet Dr isn't confused (9)
9. Rene's upset is an indication of contempt (5)
10. A gas Sue strangely cooked up turned out to be a common accompaniment of eggs (7)
12. Men test drive a convertible to obtain promotion (13)
13. Maintenance of power mains at exchange required (7)
15. Stand up at the Albert Hall was a romp (4)
16. In tears about the spoilt truffle (7)
17. The essence appeared in a tureen (6)
18. Billy Bunter's irritated retort to a bounder (6)

DOWN
1. Adam's partner was wrapped in azure velour to entitle this film (4, 6)
2. Troubled masters sense another test (12)
5. Capsizing cripples sailing ships (8)
9. Going backwards on trams can make you clever (5)
10. Dusty restoration of a place to write (5)
11. Spy on spoon in disguise (5)
14. Inventor rebuilt reactor (7)

Before I learn to write legibly, I have to learn to spell correctly.

(Terry Horne)

Q1 Fill in two missing words such that the sentence makes sense. The two words you add should each have five letters and be anagrams of each other.

He climbed __ __ __ __ __ , from which vantage point he hoped better to see the route along he hoped his raft would __ __ __ __ __ .

Q2 How would you be able to tell whether a three-eared person was known as Captain Kirk?

Q3 Create a set of letters corresponding to the set of numbers given. Rearrange the letters to give a word that relates (crossword style) to the clue given. The numbers represent alphabetically the positions of the letters in the alphabet, i.e. 1 = A, 2 = B, C = 3... Z = 26.

(A) 20, 9, 18, 5, 19	One never tires of going through their passage
(B) 18, 5, 19, 5, 20	One can reset the text so as not to waste words
(C) 12, 1, 19, 20, 5, 4	It lasted well when preserved in this way
(D) 14, 5, 1, 18, 9, 20	If you ever get near it you will not forget it
(E) 12, 1, 19, 20, 20, 5, 5	If you mess up the last tee, you will be sleepless there

Q4 Well known for her dramatic husky voice, she played the lead in *The Thorn Birds*. A *Cosmopolitan* cover girl in 1977. Continues as a successful film director, writer and fund raiser.

R __ __ __ __ L / __ __ __ __ (6, 4)

Hint: Her first name hides her pain. Her surname would be useful in an emergency. Dr Stephen knew Christine, who led to John's demise.

Q5 Cute as you are now you can rise to have many people with whom you are popular.

_____ ?

_____

_____

_____

_____

CUTE

Hint: Incisive, cool and able to store lots, these vehicles get you to the gig where the people are.

Q6 Every block in this pyramid contains a number which is the sum of the two on which it rests. What are the missing numbers?

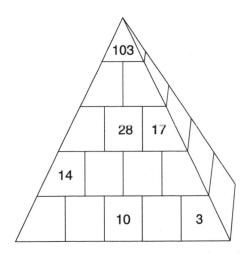

Q7 Complete the Sudoku.

1	2					6	9	
	5						3	
8	9		2	3			7	5
2	4		3		5	7		
	6		4			5	2	
		8			2	3		1
		2	7		9		5	
	3	4			1			
9		5				4	1	7

On every circuit, questions 8, 9 and 10 will be about numbers – their significance in nature, mathematics, science, religion, mythology, art or history – all proven bastions of the 50+ mind.

Q8 What do a salad dressing, a dome and a Roman mile have in common?

— — — —

Hint: The first number to be punctuated.

Q9 The number of men on a dead man's chest. Andy Warhol said 'I'll be world famous for __ __ minutes.' Goethe said, 'Nobody looks even at a rainbow for more than __ __ minutes.' A cake from Northern Ireland that contains __ __ marshmallows and __ __ digestive biscuits. This century had a 100 years war, Joan of Arc, the Spanish Inquisition, War of the Roses and Beijing as the new capital of China, and the first condom!

Hint: This square will magic the number to you.

8	1	6
3	5	7
4	9	2

Q10 __ __ is no longer a statutory retirement age in the US, new life expectancies have changed all that.

Hint: This square can magic the number you need.

17	24	1	8	15
23	5	7	14	16
4	6	13	20	22
10	12	19	21	3
11	18	25	2	9

When you have worked out the title of the next four films, try to rent, buy, borrow and watch them. They are all a brain work out. They all involve emotional, visual and verbal thinking, plus either logic to aid your critical thinking, or humour to aid your creativity.

Q11 Should always be dark.

☐ ☐ ☐ ☐ ☐ ☐ ☐ ☐

Hint: This is the French spelling because it was a French film. Should not be eaten dairy or white.

Q12 Finally succumbed to the cold hard force of nature, despite the fact that a giant of a man was going to be in charge shortly.

☐ ☐ ☐ ☐ ☐ ☐ ☐

Hint: Built by professionals, Kate appeared and Celine sang and the story goes on and on.

Q13 Pirates eat in unaccompanied.

☐ ☐ ☐ ☐ ☐ ☐ ☐ ☐ ☐ ☐

Hint: The only person in his house.

Q14 Missile has a strong sense of identity.

☐ ☐ ☐ ☐ ☐ ☐

Hint: Samuel mused 'I think, therefore...'.

Q15 Which square fits in the pattern? A, B or C?

Hint: Inside out or outside in?

How did you get on?

Score 3 for each correct answer.

Score an extra 3 points if you did not use the Hints).

Enter your total here ☐

1 in 2 people can expect to score 10 or less when they start.

1 in 40 people can expect to improve their score to 70+.

Cryptic tip 04

'To eat' can imply 'to go/put inside another word or phrase'. For example:

- *Shortly* **Charles** will get **nothing** *to eat* leading to DISORDER (5)

  Shortly/abbreviated Charles = Chas, gets nothing = O to eat = inside Chas = chaos (= disorder)

The need to take out or extract letters, on the other hand, is commonly indicated by 'ex', or 'some', or 'some of'. For example:

- Ex-draggoons
  Some draggoons   } laugh, telling of fierce attack (9)
  Some of the draggoon

  The answer is 'onslaught', viz *ex*-draggo<u>ons laugh, t</u>elling...

'Belittle' is another way of indicating the need to abbreviate. For example:

- WE will *belittle* **America** *shortly* = US

'Indefinite' indicates 'a' or 'an'. For example:

- *After* **an Juniper drink an indefinite** PAIN IN THE CHEST

  So, after an + Juniper drink + an indefinite = an + gin + a = angina = pain in the chest

A common way to get 'ab' at the beginning of an answer is to refer in some way to seamen – as in able bodied (ab) seamen.

A common way, on the other hand, to get 'able' at the end of an answer word is to anagram 'Elba'.

Cryptic crossword 04

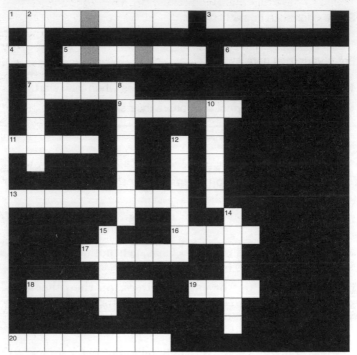

ACROSS

1. Pirates eat one meal unaccompanied in the house (4, 5)
3. Boat succumbed though giant of a man was going to be in charge shortly (7)
4. We will belittle America shortly (2)
5. Samuel asserted that a missile must first have a strong sense of identity (1, 2, 3)
6. Unravel threads – that's most difficult (7)
7. After a Juniper drink an indefinite pain the chest (6)
9. An existential start stays down before rising to make enlarged film title (4, 2)
11. Little Charles will get nothing to eat, leading to disorder (5)
13. Summer on Elba somehow would be timely (10)
16. Three dissolve into sleepy air (5)
17. Danced and staggered after the blow (6)
18. Retrace cooked-up food supplier (7)
19. Eliminate words as the tide turns (4)
20. A carthorse moved a musical group (9)

DOWN

2. Some of the dragoons laugh telling of fierce attack (9)
8. Seamen before usual folk – that's odd (8)
10. Unions reorganize as with one voice (6)
12. The decreed alterations faded into the distance (7)
14. Alterations in density will determine our fate (7)
15. Oyster camouflages paler gem (5)

circuit 05

The publishers of this book are to be congratulated on designing covers that are not too far apart

(Ambrose Bierce)

Q1 Letters have been arranged around the edge of the two circular tables below. The same letter is missing from each table at the positions marked •. When you have inserted the correct missing letter you will be able to discover what your eastern guest is eating by walking around the tables.

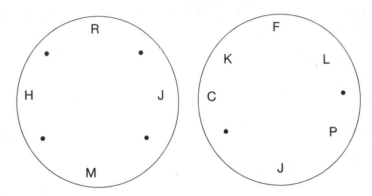

Q2 What would you call a space-travelling wizard?

Q3 Fill in the numbers in the bottom row.

3	3	6	9
15	24	39	63
102			

Hint: Numbers get longer from left to right, and progress similarly from one to the next.

Clue: Last number is > 400.

Q4 The poster of her as a sexy cave woman in a bikini is better known than the film from which it was taken – *One Million Years BC* (1966). Passionate about yoga, a *Cosmopolitan* cover girl in 1978, she is now a successful writer and business woman.

_ _ _ _ _ _ / _ _ _ _ _ (6, 5)

Hint: Sounds like artists suppressing the language of Wales.

Q5 You can rise from a dependent low life to make a go of things on your own.

_____ ?

_____

_____

_____

_____

VICE

Hint: Nasty at first you can make a lot by this kind of dancing, but you can better afford to ride horses once you can go it alone.

Q6 Every block in this pyramid contains a number which is the sum of the two on which it rests. What are the missing numbers?

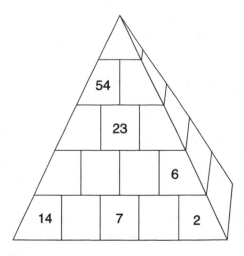

Q7 Complete the Sudoku.

	1	2			8	4	7	6
	4	7	1	2	6	5	8	
	6	8						
1		4	5	3		6	9	
6			8		1	2	4	
7	8	9	2		4	3		5
2					3	8		
4		1	7			9		2
		5	6	1				4

**On every circuit, Questions 8, 9 and 10 will be about numbers –
their significance in nature, mathematics, science, religion,
mythology, art or history – all proven bastions of the 50+ mind.**

Q8 7,000 years ago the Sumerians used the number __ __ __ to
tell us by degree, where on earth we were!

> Hint: It is the smallest number that can be made by multiplying 24
> other numbers together.

Q9 __ __ is the number of characters in a system designed by
Louis Braille in 1821; the number of hexagrams in 1 Ching; the
number of arts (or positions) detailed in an Indian social study
by religious student Vatsyayana called Kama Sutra (for 'when
I'm __ __').

> Hint: The first number to be a square, a cube and sixth power.

Q10 There are numerous references to __ __ rams, lambs, cubits and wives in the Bible, but in February this number is mostly associated with love and with the number of lines in Shakespeare's romantic sonnets, 'Shall I compare thee to a summers day?'; Europe's longest reigning monarch – the Sun King – reigned for 72 years from 1643, he was Louis __ __th of France.

> Hint: There are thought to be this number of stopping places (stations) for Christ's cross on the Via Dolorosa.

When you have worked out the title of the next four films, try to rent, buy, borrow and watch them. They are all a brain work out. They all involve emotional, visual and verbal thinking, plus either logic to aid your critical thinking, or humour to aid your creativity.

Q11 Tom Hanks goes for a rest and swallows gum before parking briefly.

☐ ☐ ☐ ☐ ☐ ☐ ☐ ☐ ☐ ☐ ☐

Q12 Definitely more than one article in France precedes mean person with abilities.

☐ ☐ ☐ ☐ ☐ ☐ ☐ ☐ ☐ ☐ ☐ ☐ ☐

> Hint: A musical with an unhappy French title.

Q13 An existential start stays down before rising to make an explosive title.

☐ ☐ ☐ ☐ ☐ ☐

> Hint: A boxer's upper cut is inflated when photographs are enlarged in this way.

Q14 Erin's surname becomes solid, shortly belonging, in a familiar way to Victoria Hospital, as foretold.

Hint: Try breaking up the surname __ / __ __ __ __ / __ / __ __ __ / __
– Julia Roberts battling against the capitalist powers behind a chemical plant.

Q15 Which square fits in the pattern, A, B or C?

A, B or C?

A   B   C

Hint: How did the pentagon and the square move?

How did you get on?

Score 3 for each correct answer.

Score an extra 3 points if you did not use the Hints).

Enter your total here ☐

1 in 2 people can expect to score 10 or less when they start.

1 in 40 people can expect to improve their score to 70+.

Cryptic tip 05

Phrases along the lines of 'With North, South, East or West' indicate that the letters N, S, E, and W will be used. Phrases along the lines of 'Without North, South, East or West' indicate that the letters N, S, E, and W will not be used. (The word 'point', 'points' or 'pointer' may also be present.) For example:

- PEN POINTS *made about* **Ibsen** *not opposed by West* (4)

  About Ibsen = anagram of Ibsen, not opposed by West = not East = without 'e' (remove 'e' from Ibsen) = nibs (4) = pen points

For down clues, operations like 'climb', 'upside', 'upwards', 'up', 'ascending' etc. indicate that the reverse is required. For example:

- PLACE **to tie boat** *up* (4, down)

  To tie boat up = moor, but 'up' in a down clue gives a reverse = room (4) = place

Also look at:

- BODY BASED IN BELIEF is **prepared**, *including a* **cheer leader** (4)

  Cheer leader gives us a 'c' (lead letter of 'cheer') to include in 'prepared' – but we only have four letters, so prepared must be paraphrased to a three-letter word, e.g. 'set'. When we include 'c', we get 'sect' = a body based in belief (trying to insert 'body' into 'belief' would have needed many more letters than four!).

- BIG *part of* the **devastation** (4)

  The number tells us that we are only looking for four letters, part of devastation = vast (4) = big

Cryptic crossword 05

ACROSS

3. Large part of the devastation (4)
6. Tom Hanks leads search for remainder of the trees one gets stuck up before finding a place to park for a while (7, 4)
7. Space to tie boat backwards (4)
8. Pen points made about Ibsen not opposed by the west (4)
10. Beheaded wizard found in German city (6)
12. I blame Mario about things I remember (11)
13. Repeated shouts of approval confused the district attorney briefly in a show of defiance (7)
14. The backward doctor one knows is menacing (7)
16. Broken wrist can lead to legal issues (5)
17. Several broken cones are served with butter, jam and cream (6)

DOWN

1. Existential start stays down before rising to explode as title for a film (4, 2)
2. Succeeding late in life (7, 2)
4. Neuroscience author is back before Monday (5)
5. Group prepared to include a cheerleader (4)
9. In October lingers a German city (6)
11. Giving out signals indicating time-up followed by a sound sensation (8)
15. The inexperienced intrude clumsily (7)

We would like to thank indexers, Society of, The
(after Waterhouse, K.)

Q1 Every year, Simon takes children with Type 1 diabetes on an outward bound holiday. This year he has organized a barbeque to raise funds. He goes to do the shopping and spends half his budget plus £10 on meat, half of the remainder plus £10 on sugar-free drinks, and half of what is then left plus £10 on fuel. He has £20 left. How much did he have in his budget to start with?

Q2 Abbreviated parent?

M _ _ _ _ _ _

Q3 Each of the following cards has a number on one side and a letter on the opposite side. Which of the following cards must you turn over in order to test a rule that 'if a card has a number one on one side, it has a letter A on its opposite side'?

Hint: 2nd and 4th are not relevant to the rule being tested. If 3rd has a letter other than A on the other side it is irrelevant to the test. If it has an A it does not disconfirm the rule.

Q4 This Nicaraguan beauty was a snake fiend in *Never Say Never Again* (1983). A top model by 17, did she keep her famous promise to do nude scenes forever?

_ _ _ _ _ _ A / _ _ _ R _ _ _ (7, 7)

Hint: After a pub crawl it sounds like motor vehicles here for a time.

Q5 Elevate your word skills so that you rise from the deck to be the captain.

_____ ?

_____

_____

_____

DECK

Hint: Always at his call and reliant on this kind of pay, you can rise to lie in the sun and eat expensive sea fish when you are captain of the ship.

Q6 Every block in this pyramid contains a number which is the sum of the two on which it rests. What are the missing numbers?

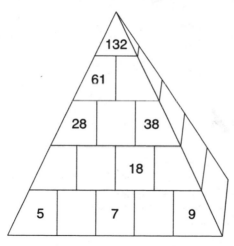

Q7 Complete the Sudoku.

	4		3	5				9
	6		1	2	9	7		5
	7	9	4	6	8	1	2	
2	1	3		8				
4	8		7		6	2	3	
6		7	2	1	3	4	5	
7		1		3				4
9	2		8		5			7
8		4						2

On every circuit, Questions 8, 9 and 10 will be about numbers – their significance in nature, mathematics, science, religion, mythology, art or history – all proven bastions of the 50+ mind.

Q8 For some, this number is the highly regarded product of two cubes, and the sum of three.

Hint: The cube of the number is the result of multiplying the number by itself three times. E.g. $2 \times 2 \times 2 = 8$; $3 \times 3 \times 3 = 27$; $4 \times 4 \times 4 = 64$; etc.

Q9 7,000 years ago, the Sumerians devised a system of doing 'sums' based on __ __ which is still used in today's geometry and timekeeping, and the Chinese used this number of pegs in Chinese Chequers.

Hint: The 19 __ __ s brought the pill, sex, drugs and rock and roll mixed with revolutions, assassinations and men on the moon.

Q10 In the 1957 film __ __ *Angry Men*, Henry Fonda, playing number 8, started as the only one who didn't think the accused was guilty. It is the force of the strongest wind and the number of tribes who descended from Jacob.

Hint: Jesus had this number of disciples and there are this number of days in Christmas and inches in a foot.

When you have worked out the title of the next four films, try to rent, buy, borrow and watch them. They are all a brain work out. They all involve emotional, visual and verbal thinking, plus either logic to aid your critical thinking, or humour to aid your creativity.

Q11 The effect of the sun is fading in the final round of Come Dancing (in Paris).

Hint: The effect of the sun = tan and Marlon Brando's dance is from Latin America.

Q12 When the Bard was In Love, it sounds like he made his weapon more intimidating, by waving it around.

□ □ □ □ □ □ □ □ □ □ □

Hint: In the sixteenth century, this Bard lived in Stratford, England, but his plays were performed at the Globe Theatre in London.

Q13 Before you hear Miss Fitzgerald's first name, you will hear lots of bleating from both the drinking places you pass on the way.

□ □ □ □ □ □ □ □ □ □

Hint: In which Jane Fonda famously stripped under the effect of zero gravity.

Q14 The top and bottom of it is you and I being helped to make another name for Mozart.

□ □ □ □ □ □ □

Hint: Top and bottom = beginning and ending. You and I = US; being = AM.

Q15 The circumference of each of the identical pulleys A, B, C, D, E is twice the diameter of the axles to which they are fitted. If A turns at 200 cycles per second, at what speed will D rotate?

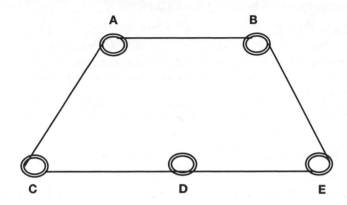

Hint: Since only the axles are connected, the size of the circumferences is irrelevant.

How did you get on?

Score 3 for each correct answer.

Score an extra 3 points for each correct answer obtained without using the hints.

Enter your total here ☐

1 in 2 people can expect to score 10 or less when they start.

1 in 40 people can expect to improve their score to 70+.

Cryptic tip 06

Solve clues in numerical order, working clues across and down in parallel. This maximizes the number of crossovers. The resulting cross letters are all extra clues.

Look for the cross letter in the clues which crossed. This helps to spot anagrams or part words or inserted words.

Present participles – words ending in the suffix 'ing' – are a gift. If the synonym in the clue ends in 'ing', the answer is also likely to. For example:

- **He** *has* **a ring** for LISTENING IN COURT (7)

    He + a + ring = hearing (7) = listening in court

Proper names often indicate an anagram. For example:

- **Stan gets a** *disguise* IN STILL WATER (9)

    Stan is probably part of an anagram of 9 letters, i.e. Stan gets a = stagnates (9) = in still water

Look out for double meanings, like 'Harry' = proper name and verb to attack or chase about. For example:

- *Harry* the **dragon** *with nothing to eat* finds OLD STYLE SOLDIER (7)

    Attacking the word 'dragon' and putting nothing, i.e. 'O', inside it yields dragoon (7) = old-style solider.

Cryptic crossword 06

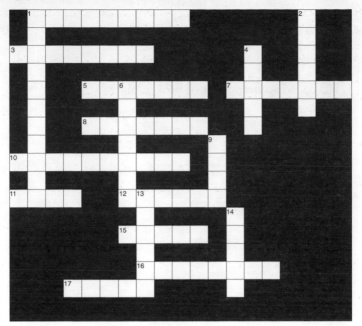

ACROSS

1. Stan gets a disguise in still water (9)
3. The effect of the sun fading is what they are doing in Latin America, or latterly in a film shot in Paris (8)
5. He has a ring for listening in court (7)
7. Crafty afterthoughts about others keep him busy in the garden shed (7)
8. Harry the dragon with nothing to eat finds old-style soldier (7)
10. Bleatings from both holes lead to jazz start in film (10)
11. Sounds like a Welsh vegetable got crushed under the boat (4)
12. Tells a disturbed star female (6)
15. Barristers succeed in causing confusion about brute (5)
16. Snag is backward halfback (8)
17. The causes of the problem were revealed when torso was dissected (5)

DOWN
1. Rattle weapon to hear the Bard (11)
2. Goose flies out of danger (6)
4. Cross word weapon (5)
6. Film about Mozart indefinably made us (7)
9. Avid reversal reveals Prima Donna (4)
14. Gripping books after tea (6)
15. Herbaceous component of broken plate (5)

In Managing Public Services, I estimated that half of all senior managers were asses. I wish to withdraw my statement – half of all senior managers are not asses.
(after Disraeli)

Q1 Fill in the missing consonants below and so clarify the word:

E __ U __ I __ A __ E

Q2 A joint of baby goat?

K __ __ __ __ __

Q3 Put a single digit in each box such that the sum of the digits = the total given in the clue for that row or column (see overleaf for clues). Do not use any digit more than once for the answer to a given clue. Do not use zero. All clue answers end in an odd number (based on 'Adlock' by Gamon and Bragon www.brainwaves.com).

Hint: Work in from the corners.

Clue: 10 down is 46829.

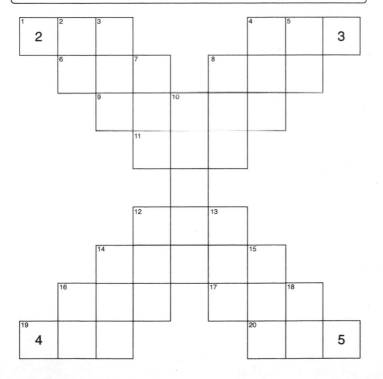

Across Total	Down Total
1. 7	2. 6
4. 8	3. 10
6. 11	4. 13
8. 22	5. 13
9. 25	7. 18
11. 22	8. 20
12. 17	10. 29
14. 34	12. 23
16. 19	13. 18
17. 20	14. 19
19. 20	15. 24
20. 17	16. 11
	18. 12

Q4 Chronically shy as a child, she eventually won a Golden Globe for *LA Confidential* in 1997. Recently voted the sexiest woman ever by *Empire* readers, she first appeared on the cover of *Cosmopolitan* in 1978 and is now president of PETA.

_ _ _ / _ _ _ _ _ _ _ _ (3, 8)

Hint: Surname sounds more appropriate to a pub musician, or a sheep sewing machine!

Q5 Okay you sank to the bottom, but you can still float up again and learn to stay afloat.

_____ ?

_____

_____

_____

_____

SANK

Hint: After you sank you found yourself on the beach and spoke about being on these, but you will take the cream once you learn to stay afloat.

Q6 Use only the numbers given to fill the vacant squares so that every row, column and both of the diagonals each total 219.

13, 15, 108, 43, 42, 20

21, 12, 20, 19, 48, 15

46, 17, 51, 23, 62, 43

78	59			
			69	
63			66	
	80			62

Q7 Complete the Sudoku.

1			2			8		9
6		9	1		8	2	3	4
				4	9	1		
	1		4	8				2
			5		7			8
8			6	1	2			
		5	7					
	6			3	5		2	7
4	7							3

On every circuit, Questions 8, 9 and 10 will be about numbers – their significance in nature, mathematics, science, religion, mythology, art or history – all proven bastions of the 50+ mind.

Q8 What number do a triangle, a Fahrenheit thermometer and the work of the Sumerians in 5,000 BC have in common? __ __ __

> Hint: Music to the ears of dart players.

Q9 The 18 __ __ s saw Darwin's *The Origin of Species*, a war in Crimea and a mutiny in India. One hundred years later saw James Dean, Elvis, Marilyn Monroe, the cold war, the Suez crisis, a war in Korea, the jive, Mods and Rockers and the beehive.

> Hint: Moses received the Torah after wandering round for one day less than this.

Q10 The last minute is the __ __ th hour and the same hour of the same day of the same month commensurates the end of World War I, which claimed the lives of 20 million people. An American airline flight of this number flew into a building that looked like this number, on this day, in September 2001. In 1960, Frank Sinatra, Dean Martin and Sammy Davis Jr made Ocean's __ __ and there were __ __ members of the gang that planned to rob the three biggest casinos in Las Vegas. The film was remade by George Clooney, Brad Pitt and Julia Roberts.

> Hint: Neil Armstrong used Appollo __ __ to land on the moon in 1969.
>
> This triangle will magic the number you require:
>
> ```
>          2
>       3     5
>    6     1     4
> ```

When you have worked out the title of the next four films, try to rent, buy, borrow and watch them. They are all a brain work out. They all involve emotional, visual and verbal thinking, plus either logic to aid your critical thinking, or humour to aid your creativity.

Q11 The Tricolor Triology by Kryslof Kieślowski.

Three Colours...

☐ ☐ ☐ ☐ ☐ ☐ ☐ ☐ ☐ ☐ ☐ ☐

> Hint: Set in France under the French Flag.

Q12 The actors are on holiday, especially Tom Hanks.

☐ ☐ ☐ ☐ ☐ ☐ ☐ ☐

> Hint: Drop some stitches or throw some ropes or tempting flies before you see a route.

Q13 Brando's paternal deity.

☐ ☐ ☐ ☐ ☐ ☐ ☐ ☐ ☐

> Hint: Between God and her there was some surplus.

Q14 Typically, Hitchcock had the shrink cut exactly in half.

☐ ☐ ☐ ☐ ☐ ☐

> Hint: A shrink could be a psychologist.

Q15 The seats A–H on this seesaw are spaced at equal intervals from the pivot. John weights 60 kg and sits at E. Jane also weighs 60 kg and sits at B. Jill also weighs 60 kg. Where should Jill sit to balance the seesaw?

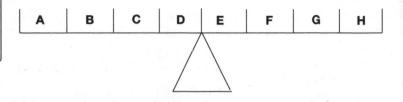

Hint: The turning moments on one side of the pivot must equal the turning moments on the other.

Turning moment = weight × distance from pivot.

How did you get on?

Score 3 for each correct answer and score an extra 3 points for each question where you did not need a hint.

Enter your total here ☐

1 in 2 people can expect to score 10 or less when they start.

1 in 40 people can expect to improve their score to 70+.

Cryptic tip 07

A plural clue must have a plural answer, often giving you an 's' at the end. (But watch out for cunning Latin plurals!) For example:

- BLACKENED SAILORS *of* the **Tsar** = tars (anagram of 'Tsar' with 's' at end)

- **Tsar's** *outstanding* PERFORMERS = stars (anagram of Tsar's with 's' at end)

He (or she) often indicates a profession, or person doing something, and so the answer might well end in '-er'. For example:

- HE PICKS THINGS UP MECHANICALLY scaring **the long-legged birds** (5, 6)

  This is 'crane driver' (5, 6 ending in '-er'), i.e. He who picks things up mechanically and scares long-legged birds (cranes).

The use of '-ly' or '-lly' as a suffix in the synocript often indicates that '-ly' or '-lly' will be the last letters of the answer also. For example:

- GENERALLY there is **Public Land** *plus either end of* **Lindly** (8)

  'Generally' means we are seeking a synonym ending in '-ly' (as found at either end of Lindly). Common (public land) + ly = commonly (8) = generally

If you have a genre or category of things then you may be seeking a specific example of that generic category as your answer. For example:

- 'Beech' is a specific type of the generic category 'trees'

- 'Ling' is a specific type of 'heathers' or 'fish'

- CASUAL WORKERS payment and still *ends up in* **Heathers** (9) = hireling

- KEEPING UP COURAGE in the dark *after* **game of cards** *with* **Heather** (9)

  Game of cards = whist + ling (heather) = whistling (9) = (in the dark) to keep up courage

Cryptic crossword 07

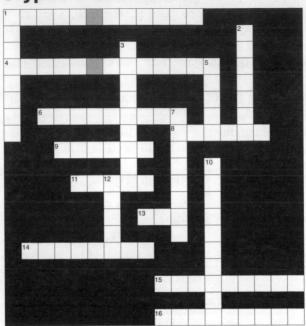

ACROSS

1. He picks things up mechanically shooing the long-legged flies further away (5, 6)
4. Kieślowski's tricolour number before we seize the pass (5, 7)
6. Commonly there is a senior military man and either end of Lindley (9)
8. An alcoholic drink indefinitely does not sound like heart disease. (6)
9. Hitchcock cuts shrink in half. (6)
11. Tsar's outstanding performers (5)
13. Sting by hustling NCO (3)
14. Referred to a ship's haven in a mouthpiece grown in water (8)
15. Casual workers pay rent and still end up at Heather's (9)
16. Keeping spirits up in the dark after game of cards with Heather (9)

DOWN

1. Actors absent, especially Tom Hanks (8)
2. Can I raise a little tax for a Roman Catholic state? (7)
3. Brando's paternal deity (9)
5. Steaming fish was David's weapon
7. Young captain gives brief account of a stormy night sailing (8)
10. Chippies comes in after fish (10)
12. Someone from Scotland is royal place for punters (4)

circuit 08

It was a clash between the will of the workers and the won't of the management.

(adapted from 'Yes Prime Minister')

Q1 Please supply the missing number:

10	12	44
6	14	40
4	6	20
14	12	?

Q2 Is father's function a sell out?

P _ _ _ _ _

Q3 Bill owns 4 working suits – 2 black, 2 blue – and 3 pairs of dark burgundy leather shoes that each go well with each of his suits. He wears his suits and shoes in strict rotation every day of the week so that they 'recover' well in between. Perhaps because he always looks the part, he has been promoted again and celebrates by buying a new grey silk suit and a new pair of Bally shoes – again burgundy in colour. He wore his new combination today, the 1st November. If he continues his former practice, on what date will he next wear his new combination of grey suit and Bally shoes?

Q4 She fronted a new wave band named after her, belting out hits like 'Heart of Glass' and 'Denis'. A *Cosmopolitan* cover girl in 1978, she recently reformed her 1970s band and has an ongoing career as a jazz vocalist.

_ _ _ _ _ _ / _ _ _ _ _ (6, 5)

> Hint: At first the tide ran out between her spotted cubes and then her soiled surname launched a series of successful films for Clint Eastwood.

Q5 At the moment you are only at the foot of the ladder, but if you can get yourself up a few rungs, someone can give you one of these.

_____ ?

_____

_____

_____

_____

FOOT

Hint: The source of all is to be caring and to get close to others, in a group, so that someone can then give this you.

Q6 Use the numbers given to fill the vacant squares so that every row, column and both of the diagonals each total 236. You may use any number more than once.

4, 12, 14, 8, 25, 30, 31, 38

43, 46, 47, 51, 54, 59, 62

63, 66, 69, 74, 81, 130

	43		51	
	47		47	

Q7 Complete the Sudoku.

1	2	4		6	7		8	3
3	5	7	1		8		4	
6	8		2		3	5	7	
	1	6	3		4			9
4				1		6	2	7
		8	6	2		3	1	
8	4	3	9			7		2
9	6				2			5
	7	2	4	3	6	1		8

On every circuit, Questions 8, 9 and 10 will be about numbers – their significance in nature, mathematics, science, religion, mythology, art or history – all proven bastions of the 50+ mind.

Q8 This number – __ __ __ – was first scored on TV by snooker player Cliff Thornton. He started in 1983 but it was nearly 1984 by the time he finished! In 1997, Ronnie 'The Rocket' O'Sullivan achieved the same score in 5 minutes, 20 seconds.

Hint: 15 × red, 15 × black, plus the 6 colours.

Q9 After 7,500,000 years, Douglas Adams's Deep Thought worked out that the secret of life, the universe and all that was __ __, and the Egyptian God Osiris ordered that those who died would then be tried by this number of judges. The first book ever published, *The Gutenberg Bible*, has this number of lines per page.

Hint: On January 30th 1969, the Beatles' last public performance – impromptu from the roof of the Apple Studio in London – lasted for this number of minutes.

Q10 Possession is __ parts of the law, and you can be dressed to these numbers and punished by a cat with this many tails.

Hint: The digits of all multiples of this number always add up to this number (or to a multiple of it). Also, if you invert any 3-digit number and subtract the smaller from the larger, the middle digit will always be the one you are seeking now.

When you have worked out the title of the next four films, try to rent, buy, borrow and watch them. They are all a brain work out. They all involve emotional, visual and verbal thinking, plus either logic to aid your critical thinking, or humour to aid your creativity.

Q11 French girl starts by being unclear about me and ends in deceit.

☐ ☐ ☐ ☐ ☐ ☐

Hint: Unclear, indefinite = A, about = on either side of (ME) and it ends in a three-letter word = deceiving.

Q12 It begins with deception and ends with a charge, after a good car chase.

THE FRENCH

☐ ☐ ☐ ☐ ☐ ☐ ☐ ☐ ☐ ☐

Hint: Deception = CON; electrified chemistry = ions – lots of links.

Q13 Definite start to the times of work that ends up belonging to us.

☐ ☐ ☐   ☐ ☐ ☐ ☐ ☐

Hint: Definite start = THE (definite article), and ends with belonging to us = OURS.

Q14 Although not at all detached, the centre of the title seems separate, though the end sounds like it is seriously intended.

☐ ☐ ☐   ☐ ☐ ☐ ☐ ☐ ☐ ☐ ☐ ☐

Hint: A place to live that's not detached at all, and 'ment' sounds like 'meant' (seriously intended).

Q15 The seats A–F on the seesaw are equally spaced. There is a child at A (30 kg) and an adult at E (60 kg). Where must another child (30 kg) go to balance the seesaw?

| 30 kg | B | C | D | 60 kg | F |

Hint: Calculate the turning moments.

How did you get on?

Score 3 for each correct answer.

Score an extra 3 points if you did not use the Hints).

Enter your total here ☐

1 in 2 people can expect to score 10 or less when they start.

1 in 40 people can expect to improve their score to 70+.

Cryptic tip 08

Reference to a country – e.g. France, or French, or Parisian, or 'à la', or Gallic, or cross channel, or tunnel, or François, or just F – could mean that the answer contains a word, words or bits of words of the language of the country to which reference has been made. For example:

- DESCEND *from* **TGV** (7)

  TGV = from French train = detrain (7) = descend

- **Eric** *is clearly going wild about* **the French** GIRL (6)

  Eric going wild = anagram of Eric, about = on either side of, the French = la = Claire (6) = a girl (clearly!)

- **Exciting** *start* with **Rome five** in a **French street** is A THEATRICAL SHOW (5)

  Exciting is 'e', + V (Roman 5), in rue (French street) = revue (5) = a theatrical show

- **Refering to German conjunction** and **gin**-*based cocktail* is SHOCKING (10)

  Refering to = as to, + und (German conjunction 'and'), + ing (gin-based cocktail) = astounding (10) = shocking

- TIMETABLE for *short-term* **primary education** in **German school** (8)

  Short-term/abbreviated primary education (first letters) = ed, in schule (German school) = schedule (8) = timetable

- **Spanish exclamation** *in* a trance *after tea* requires PATIENCE (9)

  Spanish exclamation = ole, in trance after T = tolerance (9) = patience

Cryptic crossword 08

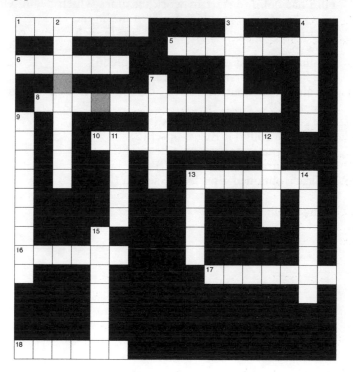

ACROSS

1. Descend from TGV
5. Timetable for short-term primary education in German school (8)
6. She was filmed making an indefinite deception about me in France (6)
8. Film title was not detached though separate and seeming seriously intended in the end (3, 9)
10. Refering to German conjunction and gin-based cocktail is shocking (10)
13. Coastal area spreads disease (7)
16. Eric is clearly going wild about the French girl (6)
17. Fatherly sponsors play no parts (7)
18. Rapped more smartly dressed (6)

DOWN

2. Film has definite start to working times which begin with heavy breathing but which we own in the end (3, 5)
3. Exciting start with Rome five in French street opens show (5)
4. Remnants of past slicer unrecognizable (6)
7. The French waterski on tropical lake (6)
9. Spanish exclamation in a trance after tea requires patience (9)
11. The geyser on the top can talk (5)
12. Sadness all round if Reg is upset (5)
13. Energetic mates can get up a head of this (5)
14. Energetic granny is winning (7)
15. Delicacy obtained after fretful search (7)

Laws on the distribution of wealth ensure that shortages are equally divided among the peasants.
(after John Gaftason)

Q1 The value of dark chocolate:

6 bars of Mora Mora and 5 bars of Sambirano cost £36.00

5 bars of Mora Mora and 6 bars of Sambirano cost £36.60

How much does each type of dark chocolate cost, per bar?

Q2 Should you recycle this weapon?

S _ _ _ _ _ N

Q3 Find word answers to the five clues and overlap them in the squares below; each starting on a numbered square part way through the preceding word.

Clues

1   Something you sit at to eat (6)
4. Brain injury (6)
8. Bordering on New York (7)
14. Possess (3)
16. Brain cell (6)

1	2	3	4	5	6	7	8	9	10	11	12	13	14	15	16	17	18	19	20	21
T																				

Q4 Born in Malibu, she was one of the all-time modelling greats for 20 years, until she crashed her helicopter. A *Cosmopolitan* cover girl in 1980, she is now a successful businesswoman.

_ _ _ _ _ _ _ _ / _ _ _ _ _ _ _ _ (8,8)

Hint: Christine's diminutive first name combined with 'edgy' second name.

Q5 If a life of beer and sandwiches has made you feel low down the ladder, you can easily climb up to enjoy again flowing human kindness.

_____?_____

_____

_____

_____

_____

_____

        BEER

Hint: Sounds like sweeter route, can be driven but a higher toll charged, grates a lot but yields this flowing human kindness.

Q6 Use the numbers given to fill the vacant squares so that every row, column and both of the diagonals each totals 190.

6, 44, 40, 41, 42

24, 32, 33, 10, 16

29, 18, 47, 36, 38

38, 38, 13, 12

		52		59
	60			
	98			
				65
59				

Q7 Complete the Sudoku.

8				4		7		9
	1		7				2	
4			8					
				7		2	6	
7			6		9			4
	4	6		1				
					2			5
	9				1		7	
1		4		3				2

On every circuit, Questions 8, 9 and 10 will be about numbers – their significance in nature, mathematics, science, religion, mythology, art or history – all proven bastions of the 50+ mind.

Q8 A square dozen is a gross number – __ __ __ – which is important to players of mah-jong and which you don't come across until the 12th position in a Fibonacci series.

> Hint: Found by degrees inside a decagon.

Q9 As in WD __ __ and the number of days in Lent, its frequency in Moslem writings may be due to its Arab meaning of 'a lot'. After the American Civil War, General Sherman ordered that this number of acres be given to each freed slave.

> Hint: Ali Baba had this number of thieves.

Q10 There are __ wonders in the world and you can sail that number of seas (many more actually). If you have a child until this age you will have created the person (Xavier, sixteenth-century missionary) who will go on to have this number of ages (*As You Like It*, Act II, scene III) – though Shakespeare's view is now outdated by neuroscience. The Austin __ , Lotus __ , and Caterham __ were popular British cars.

Hint: Britain, Portugal, Prussia and Hanover took on the might of France, Russia, Sweden, Saxony and Spain in the __ years war between 1756 and 1763.

When you have worked out the title of the next four films, try to rent, buy, borrow and watch them. They are all a brain work out. They all involve emotional, visual and verbal thinking, plus either logic to aid your critical thinking, or humour to aid your creativity.

Q11 A mobile army surgical hospital in Vietnam shortly becomes the unlikely title of a smash hit comedy.

Hint: A way of eating potatoes that is popular in the UK with bangers (sausages).

Q12 These Buddhists lived between what sounds like a large town and a sugar plantation.

Hint: A large town could sound like 'city' and a sugar plantation could sound like 'cane' and these kind of Buddhists come between.

Q13 The entrance to this large house is like the first word of Santa Claus's favourite triple word. You then pass many bedrooms like a hospital before you reach the extremity.

☐ ☐ ☐ ☐ ☐ ☐ ☐   ☐ ☐ ☐

> Hint: An extremity is an 'end'.

Q14 The article and the Latin year end, contain a constant lot of keys to playing quietly.

☐ ☐ ☐   ☐ ☐ ☐ ☐ ☐

> Hint: The keys, or ivories, can be black or white and need to be damped by pedals to produce the effect the names implies.

Q15 Which square, A, B or C, fits best?

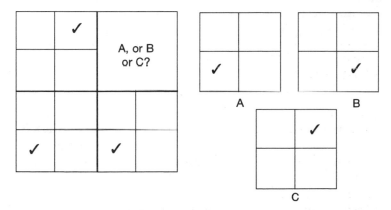

> Hint: Imagine a mirror along each diagonal.

How did you get on?

Score 3 for each correct answer.

Score an extra 3 points if you did not use the Hints).

Enter your total here [ ]

1 in 2 people can expect to score 10 or less when they start.

1 in 40 people can expect to improve their score to 70+.

Cryptic tip 09

When answers involve words from a modern European language it is usually signalled by including a reference to the country (see the Cryptic Tip in Circuit 08). No such reference is usually available when Latin words are used. These commonly include pro = for; re = about or related to; m or mille = thousands; am or ante meridian = before midday or morning; ditto or do = same again; Regina or Rex = queen or king or monarch; ult or ultimo = last; opus = a work; ante = before; ad = to, towards; vide = to see, as seen. For example:

- ONE MANDATED TO VOTE **for 2 algebraic variables** (5)
  Pro (Latin 'for') + XY (2 algebraic variables) = proxy (5) = one mandated to vote
- SAVIOUR **about** to **curse** *erratically* (7)
  Re (Latin 'about') + scuer (eratic anagram of curse) = rescuer (7) = saviour
- **Heavy soil** *contains* **thousands** and is HOT AND STICKY (6)
  Heavy soil = clay, containing thousands = containing Latin Ms = cla + m + m + y = clammy (6) = hot and sticky
- **In the morning** *sort of* **corny** WORD FORMED FROM INITIAL LETTERS (7)
  In the morning = between 'a' and 'm' (am = Latin 'morning'), sort of = anagram of corny = crony = acronym (7) = word formed from initials
- Judge gave **CD** to **monarch** (8) = record to ER = recorder (8)

Cryptic crossword 09

ACROSS

1. TTT is a teasing dance in South America (3, 3, 3)
4. Filmed instrument has mathematical value and plays quietly until the year end (3, 5)
6. One mandated to vote for two unknowns (5)
7. Punt almost disappeared with the wrong load (7)
10. There was a young rhyme in part of Ireland (8)
11. Ground for potters contains thousands and is hot and sticky (6)
12. A film initially entitled mobile army surgical hospital (4)
15. Firefighter about to curse short monarch improperly (7)
16. Applauds the increases even though they all start with a penny (7)
17. Dismiss the military paymaster (7)

DOWN
1. Buddhists live between what sound like a city and a sugar plantation (7, 4)
2. French friends of English writer (4)
3. Howard met his demise in cinema (7, 3)
5. No man is not initially an island in this part of the Middle East (4)
8. Manual transport that prioritizes a familiar Richard before a British philosopher (8)
9. Initial word is corny in the morning (7)
11. Character from Greece caught despite sounding guilty is very smart (4)
13. Folds wind blown petals (6)
14. Judge gave the tapes to the British Monarch (8)

I am a self-made man who worships his creator.
(after Disraeli)

Q1 Jog up a narrow road, leading to less fat.

_ _ _ _

Q2 A sick-sounding symbol of America:

I _ _ _ _ _ _

Q3 Which is the most synonymous saying to: 'There's no such thing as a free lunch'?

(A) All things come to he who waits.
(B) Where there's bees, there's honey.
(C) The only free cheese is in mousetraps.
(D) Too many cooks spoil the broth.
(E) The early birds eat the worms.

Q4 A cover girl for *Cosmopolitan* in 1981, she has since appeared in *Not the Nine O'Clock News*, completed a PhD and married a famous Scottish comedian and actor.

_ _ _ _ _ _ / _ _ _ _ _ _ _ _ _ _ (6, 10)

Hint: Shares a first name with Baywatch's most well-known babe and a surname with the railway's best-known inventor.

Q5 A toad is often at the bottom of the social ladder, but after only six steps, with one final bound you can be just one kiss away from royalty.

_____?

_____

_____

_____

_____

_____

_____
TOAD

Hint: Urge happily that clothing and earthy footwear be sold off before one final bound.

Q6 Use the numbers given to fill the vacant squares so that every row, column and both of the diagonals each totals 142.

44, 24, 23, 36

30, 18, 8, 37, 22

48, 26, 19

		28		22
			28	39
25	32			
25			28	
	30	32		

Q7 Complete the Sudoku.

1	2					6	9	8
	4			6				3
6		8		3			4	
2		5		9	6	4		7
3		6	7					
4						3	6	1
		2	8			9	1	
		1			3			4
9	5	4	6	7		8		

On every circuit, Questions 8, 9 and 10 will be about numbers – their significance in nature, mathematics, science, religion, mythology, art or history – all proven bastions of the 50+ mind.

Q8 _ _ _ is the product of two numbers held in a sacred light. Perhaps that is why there are this number of beads on a Buddhist rosary, this number of girls enamored of Krishna and this number of seats in the Parliament of Nepal.

> Hint: You can count up to this number in the Pentagon, even if they do not believe that 12 and 9 are sacred.

Q9 The Anglican Church has _ _ articles and the old Wembley Stadium had this number of steps up from the pitch to the Royal Box – the title also of a gripping spy novel by John Buchan, made into a film by Alfred Hitchcock in 1935, remade in 1959 and 1978. Jack Benny celebrated this birthday 41 times before he died ('Age is mind over matter – if you don't mind, it don't matter!').

> Hint: The sum of five consecutive prime numbers.

Q10 Punishment was _ of the best but the Birmingham _ were wrongly convicted. The numbers of wives of Henry VIII; the last word of the title of a book of children's poems by A. A. Milne (*Now we are _*); the number of types of 'quark' – one of three fundamental particles of which the universe is composed; the number of legs of the earth's most numerous species; strings on a guitar; points for a touchdown; potting a pink; protons in carbon atoms of which all life is composed.

> Hint: The smallest perfect number, it is the only number that is both the sum as well as the product of its factors. Take coins of any size and arrange them around one at the centre, so that the surrounding coins are touching. The number of surrounding coins will always be the number you are now seeking.

When you have worked out the title of the next four films, try to rent, buy, borrow and watch them. They are all a brain work out. They all involve emotional, visual and verbal thinking, plus either logic to aid your critical thinking, or humour to aid your creativity.

Q11 In this Italian film, sweet Italian girls spend their time between a young boy and a lively foam mattress.

☐☐ ☐ ☐☐☐☐☐ ☐☐☐☐☐

Hint: Young boy = I aD; a lively foam mattress is Vitafoam; the Italian for sweet is dulce.

Q12 She is taught unclean movement to music.

☐☐☐☐☐ ☐☐☐☐☐☐☐

Hint: What is the opposite of clean?

Q13 The unclean lot from a baker's are offered freedom in return for a dangerous deed.

☐☐☐ ☐☐☐☐☐ ☐☐☐☐☐

Hint: For unclean see Q12. The final word finds small imperial measures hidden in their den.

Q14 William the policeman starts by holding in a shout until I end up briefly over the top.

☐☐☐☐☐ ☐☐☐☐☐☐

Hint: The boy dancer finally makes it from Tyneside to Covent Garden but the Oscar should have gone to Dad as well as Julie Walters.

Q15 Which pane is likely to be smashed next?

							*		A	B
	*								C	D
			*						E	F
				*					G	H

Hint: The vandals are moving clockwise in predictably increasing steps.

How did you get on?

Score 3 for each correct answer.

Score an extra 3 points if you did not use the Hints).

Enter your total here ☐

1 in 2 people can expect to score 10 or less when they start.

1 in 40 people can expect to improve their score to 70+.

Cryptic tip 10

'Opus' is the Latin word for 'work' (abbreviated to 'op' or 'ops'). One's opus magnum is one's great work. For example:

- He *accepts* what **little work** there is in THE BELIEF THAT THINGS WILL IMPROVE (4)

  Op = little work, is accepted by He = hope (4) = the belief that things will improve
- **Nothing works!** (4)

  O (nothing) + ops = oops!
- EXPLOIT WORKERS **working** on a **press** (7)

  op + press = oppress (7)
- BEETAMAX **sees nothing** (5)

  Vide (Latin 'sees') + O (nothing) = video (5) = beetamax

Numbers often indicate their Roman letter equivalents: 1 = I, 3 = III, 5 = V, 10 = X, 50 = L, 100 = C, 500 = D, 1000 = M. A bar over the top indicates thousands. For example:

- **Second-class one** *plus different* **sort** makes special CAFÉ (6)

  Second-class = B + I (one) + stro (anagram of 'sort') = bistro (6) = café
- OLD FILES show that *overarching* **search** *was arranged around* **four** (8)

  Four = IV, arranging 'search' around IV = archives (8) = old files
- UNPICK **French one** and find **quintet** in **real** *confusion* (7)

  French one = un, + quintet = V, in anagram of 'real' = unravel (7) = unpick
- **Six for each** SNAKE (5)

  VI (six) + per (Latin 'for each') = viper (5) = snake
- At **five** to **nine** **go back to the North East** to find MATERNAL WOLF (5)

  V (five) + IX (nine) + EN (North East backwards) = VIXEN = female wolf
- **None** out of **ten** for spotting these GIANT BEASTS **back in the North East** (4)

  O (none) + X (ten) + EN (back in North East) = oxen (4) = giant beasts
- HIRED CARS **thankfully** *turned up* **at eleven** (5)

  Ta = thankfully (or turn up 'at' = ta) + XI (eleven) = taxis (5) = hired cars

• RESIDENT OF VILLAGE has **drink** after **6:50** (8)
  Lager (drink), after VIL (6 + 50) = villager (8) = resident of village

Cryptic crossword 10

ACROSS
1. Second-class one plus different sort produces special café (6)
3. Resists work camera shots (7)
9. Beetamax sees nothing (5)
10. Film shows the unclean imperial measures in the den (3, 5, 5)
11. Stella films opening hisses at the sailor and into battles (4, 4)

DOWN
1. Police yell and I go over the top on film (5, 6)
2. My mistakes! (4)
4. Film about recycling books (4, 7)
5. Unpick Parisian one and find quintet in real confusion (7)
6. Sounds like cannibal was pleased to have her on the menu for this film (9)
7. George Bernard is into flesh but redeems himself in great film part (9)
8. Go and overdose briefly on the northern hill as filmed (10)

Minds are brilliant unless they are made up.
(after Bonham Carter)

Q1 Fill in the missing letters to find the basis of religion:

_ _ E O _ O _ Y

Q2 A parrot with its wings clipped?

W _ _ _ _ _ / T _ _ _ _ _

Q3

108	356	496
196	780	292
284	648	?

Hint: Start by comparing (B – A) with C.

Q4 The only one whose halo lasted five years of the show. First appearing as a cover girl in *Cosmopolitan* in 1981, she had a major success in West Side Story on Broadway and is now a writer of best-sellers, like *The American Look*.

_ _ _ L Y N / _ _ _ _ _ (6, 5)

Hint: Introduced in a positive German way to one who attaches good luck to horses.

Q5 Stuck up a gum tree, or out on a limb, sounds like you can still reach upwards to find a couple of fruit and maybe some tasty game in the top branches.

_____ ?

_____

_____

_____

_____

TREE

Hint: Old fashioned and then plural pronouns in large numbers join together to rip these couplets of fruit from branches where game birds might be found on the first day of Christmas.

Q6 Use the numbers given to fill the vacant squares so that every row, column and diagonal totals 118. You can use a number more than once.

3, 27, 6, 24

21, 19, 8, 14

5, 23, 25

			21	43
	41	63		
27				37
	23	37		
39			50	

Q7 Complete the Sudoku.

		4	3			8	7	9
5			1	8	9	2	3	
9	3	8	2	4		1		6
	1			6		5	9	
6	4	5					8	
7				1	3			2
8	9			2	5	6	4	3
	7				1		2	
			6					8

On every circuit, Questions 8, 9 and 10 will be about numbers –
their significance in nature, mathematics, science, religion,
mythology, art or history – all proven bastions of the 50+ mind.

Q8 Signifying completion, __ __ __ is a milestone in sport and
in top compilations. Its various names derive from the Greek
'Kekaton' the Romans 'centum' and a Germanic word for a dog
that can control about this number of sheep.

Hint: The sum of the first: 4 cubes, 9 primes and 10 odd numbers.

Q9 If you lay __ __ coins flat on a table you can make a
hexagon. You then make a star by using 6 coins to create 6
equilateral triangles, one on each of the six sides. If you now
remove the outer layer of coins, you will be left again with your
original number of coins, but this time they will be in the shape

of a six-pointed star – not the original hexagon! (Try drawing round a coin to investigate.)

> Hint: You have odds of __ __ to 1 against winning at Monte Carlo, where the roulette wheels start at 0 and go up to and including 36.

Q10 It is the fifth number in the Fibonacci series; the number of planets visible to the naked eye; the number of pillars of Islam and the number of minutes in a short break, as in 'Take __ '.

> Hint: Genesis, Exodus, Leviticus, Deuteronomy and the Book of Numbers are the __ books of Judaism.

When you have worked out the title of the next four films, try to rent, buy, borrow and watch them. They are all a brain work out. They all involve emotional, visual and verbal thinking, plus either logic to aid your critical thinking, or humour to aid your creativity.

Q11 Not West is Not West.

> Hint: Blocks from this direction in Europe have melted since the fall of the Berlin Wall.

Q12 Also from an Eastern Culture, she wants to play football and *Bend it...*

> Hint: Spicy marriage cooled it with Alex, so moved to where it was really hot and then to LA.

Q13 A medic of peculiar affection.

Hint: Medic = Dr and Peculiar = Strange.

Q14 The first four letters definitely start things forward into art and all the food is finished in the end Mrs Robinson.

Hint: Definitely = The; Gee G starts to get things going forward; in arts = RA; and finished the food = ate.

Q15 What follows next, A B or C?

is to ___ as ___ is to A, B or C?

A   B   C

Hint: Try moving the triangles clockwise.

How did you get on?

Score 3 for each correct answer.

Score an extra 3 points if you did not use the Hints.

Enter your total here ☐

1 in 2 people can expect to score 10 or less when they start.

1 in 40 people can expect to improve their score to 70+.

Cryptic tip 11

More on numbers:

- SPITEFUL WOMAN *stuck* **nine** *into beheaded* **diagram** (5)
  Diagram = Venn diagram, beheaded = VEN, insert IX = VIXEN = spiteful woman
- *After* **51** **were shouted at,** they were FREE TO GO (9)
- Fifty one = LI + berated (shouted at) = liberated (9) = free to go
- The SUBJECT today is the **top 99** (7)
  Top + 99 = top + IC = topic (7) = subject
- PUTS IN **a thousand seedlings** (8)
  A thousand = IM + seedlings (plants) = implants (8) = puts in
- Make deals with **many farm workers** (10)
  Many = C (thousands) + on tractors (farm workers) = contractors (10)
- ANIMAL that's **nothing** like the sound of the one *in* **the pub** (4)
  Nothing = O, in bar (the pub) = boar (4) = animal (The Boar = common pub name) (sounds like the pub bore!)
- I was accepted by the **men** but *after* **tea** we found **nothing** *outside* worth taking home as a SOUVENIR (7)
  I = me + men = memen + t = mement + O (nothing outside) = memento (7) = souvenir
- DISCOVERED **nothing** *in* the **fund** (5)
  O (nothing) + fund = found (5) = discovered
- **The French elected member** with **nothing on** is OPEN TO RIDICULE (7)
  The French = La + MP (elected member) + O (nothing) + on = lampoon (7) = ridicule

- STARCHY PUDDING awaits familiar figure of **Patrick** *returning* before **ten** with his **accountant** (7)

  Pat returning = tap + IO (ten) + ca (accountant abbrev) = tapioca (7) = starchy pudding

- Ex **indefinite number** *devour* **Scottish monster** leaving NOTHING OUT OF PLACE (8)

  Indefinite number = N + eat (devour) + ness (Scottish monster) = neatness (8) = nothing out of place

Cryptic crossword 11

ACROSS
2. The brilliance of the first brother (not the other) is seen before 10 (4)
4. Dark chocolate digestives taken from nearer the back of the freighter (5, 6)
5. Secret French city is home of film (2, 12)
10. The queen goes after five and I go after tea fearing heights (7)

11. Film start requires law briefly relevant to a negative chief executive in the middle east (9)
12. The subject today is the top 99 (5)

DOWN

1. Filmed house had a number 51 (4, 5)
3. Musical film of the male magician of imperial weight (6, 2, 2)
6. 'Not west' is 'not west' reversed the film.
7. Hired cars thankfully turn up at eleven (5)
8. Resident of village has drink after 6:50 (8)
9. Discovered that there was nothing in the fund (5)

Washington couldn't tell a lie.
Nixon couldn't tell the truth.
You need to tell the difference.
(Terry Horne lecture notes, 2006, after Mort Sahl)

Q1 You can get a long way by filling in the missing letters:

T R _ N _ _ O _ _ I _ E _ _ A L

Q2 A frequent exclamation of juvenile indifference.

W _ _ _ E _ _ _

Q3 This crossword (based on Gamon and Bragdon www.brainwaves.com) has only 26 squares. You can use each letter of the alphabet once only.

> Hint: Write out the alphabet and cross out each letter as you use it. Near the end, try anagrams of the unused letters. Try starting with 5 Across or 3 Down.

Clues across
2. Vessel for punch
5. Wound
7. Anno Dominae
9. Host
10. Sleeveless

Clues down
1. Promise or 'the mess we're in'
3. Burdensome beast
4. Not real doctor
6. Short way
8. Turkish hat

Q4 Daughter of Ingrid Bergman. After 14 years she was fired as no longer young enough to be the face of Lancôme. After appearing on the cover of *Cosmopolitan* in 1983, and in *Blue Velvet* (1986), and in *Fearless* (1993), she now, at age 55, markets her own cosmetic and skincare range.

_ _ _ _ _ _ _ _ / _ _ _ _ _ _ _ _ _ _ (8, 10)

> Hint: A short savings account becomes beautiful in Spain and then sounds like it comes in under sail.

Q5 Start by reading those of others then word by word aspire to write one of your own.

_____?

_____

_____

_____

READ

Hint: The way is measured in the old way, past the black bird, to your literary goal.

Q6 Use the numbers given to fill the vacant squares so that every row, column and both of the diagonals each totals 111. You can use numbers more than once.

3, 14, 20, 23, 6

22, 15, 13, 26,

17, 9, 38, 8

		28		26
	30	36		
	50		24	
29			22	
36				26

		3	4	7		6		8
4		6	9					
7		9		6			5	
	1	4	8	3		7		
	6			5	2	4	8	
		8						
6		2				9		
	7		3	2	1	8	4	6
8	4		7		6			

On every circuit, Questions 8, 9 and 10 will be about numbers –
their significance in nature, mathematics, science, religion,
mythology, art or history – all proven bastions of the 50+ mind.

Q8 The right tangential number, __ __ is square and its decade
saw more WWW, DVD, DNA, extreme sport, human cloning
and global warming, and no more Soviet Union, East Germany,
Czechoslovakia or Freddie Mercury.

> Hint: Thomas Edison patented 100s of inventions, including the
> light bulb. Said creative thinking involved __ __ per cent
> perspiration and only 10 per cent inspiration.

Q9 We have the Babylonians to thank for being able to combine __ __ with 7 in our daily lives. The Greeks used this number for their alphabet and Homer divided his *Odyssey* and *Iliad* into this number of books.

> Hint: This number of carats denotes gold in its purest form, i.e. 14 carats indicates a proportion of 14 parts gold to 10 parts other metal.

Q10 __ time is the most common rhythm in music, and there were __ Horseman of the Apocalypse; __ cardinal points; __ seasons; __ Greek elements; __ apostles in Christianity; the __ Tops sang 'I'll be there' in 1966; after Mao's death, his wife Jiang Qwing, together with Zhang Chanqiao, Yao Wenguan and Wang Hong Wen were arrested as the Gang of __ who caused the cultural revolution of the 1960s.

> Hint: __ letter word; __ poster bed; __ minute warning; __ suits of playing cards; __ movements in a classical symphony.

When you have worked out the title of the next four films, try to rent, buy, borrow and watch them. They are all a brain work out. They all involve emotional, visual and verbal thinking, plus either logic to aid your critical thinking, or humour to aid your creativity.

Q11 Life is a taxi ending with tea, my friend.

☐ ☐ ☐ ☐ ☐ ☐ ☐

> Hint: A variety show at which you sit at tables.

Q12 A cream cheesy state film in which lawyer Tom Hanks is discriminated against because he has AIDS.

☐ ☐ ☐ ☐ ☐ ☐ ☐ ☐ ☐ ☐ ☐ ☐

circuit 12

Hint: Phil goes to find the Greek oracle but it ends indefinitely in a state in America.

Q13 To put an end to being laughed at by a parrot, it is necessary.

TO KILL A

Q14 Sounds like a male driver of a horse and carriage is needed during a severe drought.

Q15 What's next, A, B or C?

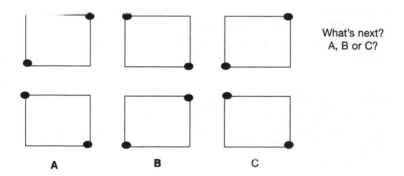

What's next?
A, B or C?

A   B   C

Hint: Try moving dots clockwise, maintaining the spacing.

How did you get on?

Score 3 for each correct answer.

Score an extra 3 points if you did not use the Hints).

Enter your total here ☐

1 in 2 people can expect to score 10 or less when they start.

1 in 40 people can expect to improve their score to 70+.

Cryptic tip 12

Do not leap to numerical answers until you have first checked out if it's an anagram. If it's an anagram, the number is a red herring. For example:

- One real messed up girl (7)
  This is an anagram of 'one real', so no need to be looking for '1' in the answer = Eleanor (7) = girl
- Varieties of nine great fruit (9)
  = tangerine (not a word with 9, ix)
- About 10 of the new trains were shortlived (8)
  Beware as there are two anagrams here. New trains = transi, + about ten = ent = transient (8) = shortlived

Sometimes the clue indicates that the answer contains a specific example of numbers:

- Numerical alternatives to three voices (6)
  Ten (numerical) + ors (alternatives) = tenors (6) (as in The Three Tenors)
- Encourage as you listen to a song (7)
  Listen = hear + song (is a number) = hear + ten = hearten (7) = encourage
- A large number enquire about real beer (4)
  Large number = C + ask (enquire) = cask (4) = real beer
- Actual number in the region (5)
  Actual = real + M (a number) = realm (5) = a region
- Although a great number was included by the trio, they shook with nerves (7)
  Trio = treble, including M (a great number) = tremble (7) = shook with nerves

- We hear that a number had a meal (5)
  = eight (5) (we hear 'ate')
- Many hurried to the fruit (9)
  Many = C + ran (hurried) + berry = cranberry (9) = fruit
- Many make a row (6)
  Many = M + align = malign (6) = row

Cryptic crossword 12

ACROSS
1. Southern fruit is a weapon (5)
4. Many hurried to the fruit (11)
6. A number had a meal, we hear (5)
7. A musical like a taxi by mistake before tea, my friend (7)
8. Fisherman starts by finding a corner (6)
10. One real messed up girl (7)
14. Supervision above vision (9)
15. Artist briefly in male film (4, 3)

16. American uncle leads bachelor a merry dance (5)
17. Sounds like removing the sign again will change the law (6)
18. Encourage as you listen to a song (7)
19. Numerical alternatives to three voices (6)

DOWN

2. A cheesy film state in which Phil finds in oracle before it ends indefinitely (12)
3. Many make a row (6)
5. Former writers I have found to be costly (9)
9. Accountant to steal poor substitute for dark chocolate (5)
11. Believed in canine mother briefly (5)
12. Of course Aunt is in a mess before the race (9)
13. Variations of nine great fruit (9)
16. Reversing fruit layer produces the rest (5)

My conversation has occasional flashes of delightful silence.

(Simon Wootton, 2007)

Q1 It might take you a while to find the following five letters at this pace.

The first letter is in stars and a seventh heaven,
The second is in none and also in eleven,
The third is in any and inside of play,
The fourth is in kind and also in weigh,
You'll find the fifth one hot, if from heaven you stray.

Q2 Image makers used to come in sun-tanned cartons:

B _ _ / B _ _ _ _ _ _

Q3 Rearrange each of the following letter groups to form a word. Place the words in a 5 x 5 grid, vertically and horizontally.

1. A E H S V
2. A E H N V
3. A E R T V
4. E E R S V
5. E E R N T

Hint: 1 = shave.

1	2	3	4	5
2				
3				
4				
5				

Clues

1. requires razor or plane
2. place of safety
3. avoid
4. poetry
5. sign of welcome

Q4 Born in Australia and known as 'The Body', she became an 80s supermodel. She appeared on the cover of *Cosmopolitan* in 1985. Now over 40, she is still modelling and is also a successful business woman.

_ _ _ _ / _ _ _ _ _ _ _ _ _ _ (4, 10)

Hint: Lady in France goes to get unhealthy food for her male child.

Q5 At the bottom you have only one coin, but a philosophical word at a time, you can turn it into something better proofed against inflation.

_____ ?

_____

_____

_____

COIN

Hint: Trade up for this staple and tie up with the next until the temperature drops, then exchange for that which glitters and belongs not to a fool.

Q6 Use the numbers given to fill the vacant squares so that every row, column and both of the diagonals each totals 91. You can use a number more than once.

4, 10, 9

23, 19, 18, 11

12, 17, 13

31				21
23				29
	38		22	
	24	27		
		21	21	

Q7 Complete the Sudoku.

	9		3	4	5	6	7	
		5	6		8			
6			1			3		5
5	3		4	8	6	1	9	
2			7		3	5		
							6	3
	2						5	
	6			1		8		
	5					2		

On every circuit, Questions 8, 9 and 10 will be about numbers – their significance in nature, mathematics, science, religion, mythology, art or history – all proven bastions of the 50+ mind.

Q8 With this number, __ __ , Abe so began a two-minute address dedicated to the proposition that 'all men are born equal'. The world will little note nor long remember what was said, but will not forgive what we do not do to complete the work of those who gave their lives to ensure that government of the people, by the people, for the people, shall never perish from this earth. 'Four score years and ten...'

Hint: Sum of the squares of the first four primes.

Q9 History says they stabbed Caesar __ __ times, but Shakespeare's Octavius added 10 cuts for good measure in Act 5, Scene 1. The axis of the earth is so tipped and the tropics move the same north and south of the equator. Worn by Michael Jordan in Chicago, Shane Warne in Australia and David Beckham in Madrid.

Hint: A favourite psalm at funerals.

Q10 'Now there are __ steps to heaven' according to Eddie Cochrane (1960) and that appears to be borne out by Christianity (father, son and holy spirit); Islam (Mecca, Medina, Jerusalem); Taoism (Yin, Yang and Man); Hinduism (Brahma, Shiva and Vishnu); Buddhism (Buddha, Dharma, Sangho).

Hint: __ little pigs; __ billy goats gruff; __ blind mice; __ wise men.

When you have worked out the title of the next four films, try to rent, buy, borrow and watch them. They are all a brain work out. They all involve emotional, visual and verbal thinking, plus either logic to aid your critical thinking, or humour to aid your creativity.

Q11 The Austrian hills are alive with the...

☐ ☐ ☐ ☐ ☐ ☐ ☐ ☐ ☐ ☐ ☐ ☐

Hint: Julie Andrews helps the Von Trapp family to climb every mountain to escape the Nazis.

Q12 Who hummed the Harry Lyme theme? Not the first, not the second, but...

☐ ☐ ☐ ☐ ☐ ☐ ☐ ☐ ☐ ☐

Hint: Black and white grainy Cold War spy film is a bit of a *ménage a trois*.

Q13 Was in the tale of two con men in the West, memorable for the piano piece that is still one of the best-selling music sheets for the piano.

☐ ☐ ☐   ☐ ☐ ☐ ☐ ☐

> Hint: A risk around bees, wasps and scorpions – its in the tail!

Q14 Humphrey Bogart on a jungle river near Victoria Falls, the regal boat was called the...

☐ ☐ ☐ ☐ ☐ ☐ ☐   ☐ ☐ ☐ ☐ ☐

> Hint: If Freddie Mercury's band had been out of Africa...

Q15 Which of the following, A, B, C and D, can be folded into a complete cube without overlapping the faces?

A   B   C   D

> Hint: To achieve a full wrap around you must have a run of at least four faces.

How did you get on?

Score 3 for each correct answer.

Score an extra 3 points if you did not use the Hints.

Enter your total here ☐

1 in 2 people can expect to score 10 or less when they start.

1 in 40 people can expect to improve their score to 70+.

Cryptic tip 13

- Zero – zero has only been in Western mathematics for about 800 years. Atkwarizmi, the Arabian mathematician, had used it 400 years earlier, based on work by Indian and Mayan mathematicians, nearly 5,000 years earlier. It can turn up in cryptics as love (after the French for egg), none, nothing, etc.
- One – can turn up as ace, once, unity, unitary or the letter i or I.
- Two – can turn up as deuce, twice, pair, twin, twain, duel or dual, couple, double, bi, binary, ii or II.
- Three – try, thrice, trio, triplets, trinity, iii or III. Or as fates, furries, graces, muses, denials, dimensions.
- Four – quartet, IV, elements, humours, cardinal points of the compass, quarters, corners of the world/earth, winds, rivers of paradise, or IIII on some clocks (Big Ben is wrong) and Einstein's dimensions.
- Five – quintet, quins, quintuplets, V.
- Six – half a dozen, sextet, sextuplets.
- Seven – septet, week, lucky.
- Eight – crew, octet, octane (as in notes in music).
- Ten – decimal, fingers, toes, X.
- Eleven – players, palindromic number.
- Twelve – months, signs (zodiac), hours, ides.
- Thirteen – unlucky, cards in a suit, baker's dozen.
- Fourteen – stone (14 lbs), a fortnight.
- Fifteen – team, 15 red balls in snooker triangle.
- Twenty – a score.
- Twenty-four – hours.
- Twenty-eight – lunar month, dominoes in a set.
- Thirty-two – freezing point in degrees Fahrenheit.
- Thirty-seven – body temperature.
- Forty – long time, days in wilderness, rain, desert.

Cryptic crossword 13

ACROSS

1. Film about the bronze medal male is one of a ménage (3, 5, 3)
5. Number one in the community (5)
6. The whole lot is covered and the fat lady sings (3, 4)
7. Insensitive start confused deer and made it difficult to get them counted (8)
8. Many left initially to go back (3)
10. Flexible relatives (9)
11. Confusing caution results in lots being knocked down (7)
16. Girl reversing can list a lot of dates (7)

DOWN

1. Film about the snake leader sounding like a bell (3, 5)
2. Line of argument (3)
3. Film about a Friday initially reorganized African National Conference and Freddie's band. (7, 5)
4. Sleeping plants a lot of short bullets a long way away (9)
9. Fill a lot randomly to launch a small fleet (8)

Alas poor Yorlik, I know him backwards.

Q1 The same three letters will complete the following four words:

_ _ _ E P, _ _ _ E N, _ _ _ _ L L, _ _ _ A T H

Q2 It can produce a ceiling corner untouched:

W _ _ S _ _ _

Q3 Create a string of 23 letters containing overlapping words to which the numbered clues apply:

1	2	3	4	5	6	7	8	9	10	11	12	13	14	15	16	17	18	19	20	21	22	23

Clues
1. French wine
3. Pertaining to Norway?
6. Confidence trick
8. Can't remember!
14. Reply
16. Short direction
17. A neuroscientist in a well-known area
20. A police verb (hopefully!)

Q4 She appeared on the cover of *Cosmopolitan* in 1990. By 2001, she had won a Golden Globe for best actress and was also the most successful female songwriter of all time. Now in her 50s, three of her video recordings are banned as too sexy by MTV ('Justify', 'Erotica' and 'What it feels like for a girl').

_ _ _ _ _ _ _ (7)

Hint: Normally thought of as with child, she is crazy above and briefly not available.

Q5 Start at the bottom by finding somewhere to pitch your tent, then rise slowly by stages, until you need this for your new factory or office.

_____?_____

_____

_____

_____

CAMP

> Hint: Past tense come, become similar and then satisfy what sounds like your place for sore eyes.

Q6 Use the numbers given to fill the vacant squares so that every row, column and both of the diagonals each totals 78.

15, 5, 3

16, 19, 4, 22, 11

14, 7, 13

23				17
	15		25	
		8	38	
33	15			
		24		27

Q7 Complete the Sudoku.

			6	5				
1	5							
	9	8	1					
	1		4		6		9	
	7	9	3			1		
4		6	5				2	
			9		3	4		5
	6	5		4	2			1
9	4						7	

On every circuit, Questions 8, 9 and 10 will be about numbers – their significance in nature, mathematics, science, religion, mythology, art or history – all proven bastions of the 50+ mind.

Q8 Pareto made a rule of it and Phileas too, __ __ days to do what Ellen did in 8 days fewer, what the US air force did in 94 hours (and 1 minute) in 1949 and what Australian Dave Kunst did on foot, in 1974, taking 1568 days and 21 pairs of shoes.

Hint: In the __ __ s, out went Iron Curtains, Berlin Walls, apartheid, LPs and hippies and in came solidarity, yuppies, PCs, CDs, crack, AIDS and mobile phones for keeping score.

Q9 Joseph Heller's Yossarian was caught in this catch, along with players of American football and field hockey. __ __ yards in a chain, stops in an aperture and bones in a skull, it is a Frenchman's warning that the 'cops are coming'.

Hint: Needed at one time to play soccer.

Q10 Woody Allen said he felt at __ with nature. In old English, Mark __ never allowed school to interfere with his education.

Hint: __ for one is a supermarket offer. These heads are better than one because they have company.

When you have worked out the title of the next four films, try to rent, buy, borrow and watch them. They are all a brain work out. They all involve emotional, visual and verbal thinking, plus either logic to aid your critical thinking, or humour to aid your creativity.

Q11 Clint Eastwood has never been pardoned, he remains...

☐ ☐ ☐ ☐ ☐ ☐ ☐ ☐ ☐ ☐

Hint: No mercy shown in this classic western.

Q12 A great collie favorite gave his name to a brand of dog food.

☐ ☐ ☐ ☐ ☐ ☐

Hint: Begins as a lady from Lancashire, that is.

Q13 A short extra terrestrial wanted to go home.

☐ ☐

Hint: 'Short', like 'brief' or 'contracted', often refers to the use of an abbreviation.

Q14 In numerical incarnations, Simba, head of the jungle was a favorite with kids and songs went into the charts.

☐ ☐ ☐ ☐ ☐ ☐ ☐ ☐ ☐ ☐ ☐

Hint: Sounds like this jungle monarch was not telling the truth – lyin 'sounds like'...

Q15 What comes next, A, B or C?

△	☐	△
△	☐	☐
⬡	☐	A,B or C

⬠ A   △ B   ⬡ C

Hint: Count the number of sides in each column.

How did you get on?

Score 3 for each correct answer.

Score an extra 3 points if you did not use the Hints.

Enter your total here ☐

1 in 2 people can expect to score 10 or less when they start.

1 in 40 people can expect to improve their score to 70+.

How does your score compare to Circuit 01?

Cryptic tip 14

'First' is usually telling you which parts of the clue refer to the start of the answer word. For example:

- After first confusing alternative, it comes to be a cloak (4)
  Alternative = or, confusing = ro + be = robe (4) = cloak
- Freud had most luck first before getting his idea clear (5)
  Most of luck first = luc + id (Freud's idea) = lucid (5) = clear
- Thrifty girl first messed up her fur (6)
  Starting with messed up fur = fru + gal (girl) = frugal (6) = thrifty
- Try to tease at first (7)
  At first = at + tempt (tease) = attempts (7) = try
- To protect watch over vault first (9)
  vault first = safe + guard (watch over) = safeguard (9) = protect

Examples of handy cryptic jargon:

- Stay second (7) = support
- Fractional district (7) = quarter
- First person coins a lady (5) = penny
- Second eleven collapse (7) = subside (7)
- Went first round the snake and climbed the staking (8)
  Went first = led; round the snake (adder) = laddered (8) = climbed up
- Graduates before long get first wind player (10)
  Graduates = BAs + soon (before long) + ist (first) = bassoonist (10) = wind player

- Being was first in French church (9)
  Was = ex + ist (first) + en (French for in) + ce (churche) = existence (9) = being
- Again allowed to rent (5)
  Re (again) + let (allowed) = relet (5) = rent again
- Second-class one plus different sort of eating place (6)
  Second-class = B + I (one) + anagram of sort = bistro (6) = eating place
- Deleted record on other sort of unit ends up fifth rated (12)
  Record = disc + on + unit (anagram – other sort of) + e (fifth rated) = discontinued (12) = deleted
- Troubled masters sense second marking (12)
  anagram of masters sense = reassessment (12) = second marking

Cryptic crossword 14

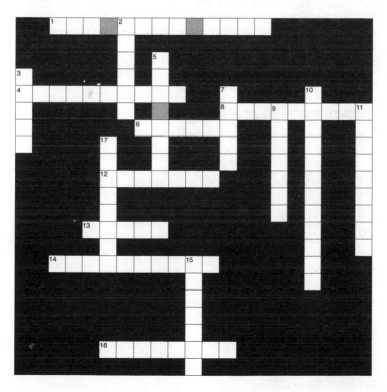

ACROSS
1. Sounds like this jungle monarch did not tell the truth in the film (3, 4, 4)
4. Film lacking mercy has different fun optionally donated (10)
6. Thrifty girl from the south first messed up her fur (6)
8. Survival was first in French church (8)
12. Try to tease at first (7)
13. First past the post coined a lady (5)
14. Graduates before long get first wind player (10)
16. Led round the snake it still ruined her stocking (8)

DOWN
2. The dog filmed in Los Angeles briefly has the secret service first before the fifth grade (6)
3. Mainly luck before getting Freud's idea clear (5)
5. The first confused alternative came to be a cloak in the film (3, 4)
7. Renting must be allowed again (5)
9. Second eleven collapsed (8)
10. Troubled masters sense need for second marking (12)
11. Neat prose translates into international language (9)
15. Second corset
17. Four areas of town produce the four half pints for the Monarchs (8)

Recommended reading

Glynne-Jones T (2007) *The Book of Numbers*. London: Arcturus

Age only matters when one is concerned about aging.
Now that I am finally old, I might just as well be twenty.
(Pablo Picasso, aged 80+)

Old myths die hard and myths about the old die harder.

You have only to review the 'humour' section of your local book shop to see how cliché-ridden is the image of old age: 'So you're 50!', 'So you're 60!', ' A Jubilee of over 60s Jokes', 'Old Wreck Jokes' and so on. People who would think twice, or even three times, before making remarks about people who are 'female' or 'coloured', appear to have no compunction about making gratuitous remarks at the expense of the 50+, who are routinely mocked, trivialized, patronized or simply ignored. Unjust and unjustified remarks undermine the self-image and self-confidence of the 50+ and this, in turn, can lower mental performance (Chapter 01). In this way, the gratuitous remarks can become self-fulfilling.

Yet such remarks are neither justified nor substantiated by our study of the ten components of applied thinking. With the exception of only one aspect, of only one of the ten components of applied thinking, we have found older brains to be superior to younger brains. Instead of mocking, society would be better harnessing the burgeoning brain power of the 50+ to aid its economic development.

In the UK, the 60+ already represent over 20 per cent of the population, rising rapidly to 30 per cent by 2030, but 60+ people appear in less than 8 per cent of media advertisements. Western media perpetuate insidious, belittling remarks like 'on the wrong side of 50', 'even though he is in his sixties he still…', '56 and still going strong'. The likely cumulative effect of such remarks is self-evident. Yet such belittling remarks about the 50+ are not universal. Travelling in Asian and African countries, such remarks are not evident.

This is not to be unrealistic about the limitations and cracks that appear with age. The Japanese treatment of old objects might provide a helpful metaphor: 'where possible, fill in cracks with gold'! To the Japanese, something that has age, experience and history is to be valued and enhanced, even when it has suffered some damage and the cracks are beginning to show. Given that one day we will all be old, to allow ageist remarks and jokes to go unchallenged is like Western turkeys voting for Christmas!

Perhaps, in the former Age of Brawn, or even in the more recent Age of Machine Minding, we were deeply afraid of becoming physically frail. Perhaps the sight of an elderly person reminded us of the inevitability of our own ageing, and maybe this made us anxious. One way to dispel anxiety is to joke or poke fun. But in the Age of the Brain, neuroscience equates age with increased thinking skill and increasing brain power. We no longer feel quite so anxious about getting old. We no longer need to manage our anxieties by poking fun at the elderly.

That is great news for our millennium babies, because they are expected to live to 120+. What would have been the point of them living an 30 extra years, if those 30 years were to be filled with derision and discrimination? There is far more to life than just staying alive.

So power up your 50+ brain and shine the light of your 50+ thinking skills on the problems that face us. Do not wait for great visions from great leaders. These are few. Put your faith in the light of your own thinking. Maintain the power of your 50+ brain and keep your thinking skills switched on. No darkness can ever extinguish light.

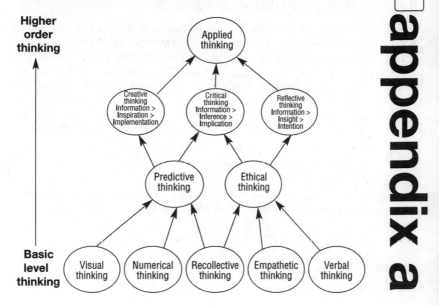

The hierarchy of applied thinking skills

(from *Teach Yourself Training Your Brain*, Horne and Wootton, 2007, Hodder Education)

The model of applied thinking (the nine Is)

Process / Types of thinking	Inform *from*	Infer *via*	Imply *to*
Critical thinking	Information	Inferences	Implications
Creative thinking	Incubation	Inspiration	Implementation
Reflecting thinking	Incidents	Insights	Intentions

(based on *Teach Yourself Training Your Brain*, Horne and Wootton, 2007, Hodder Education)

The process of applied thinking

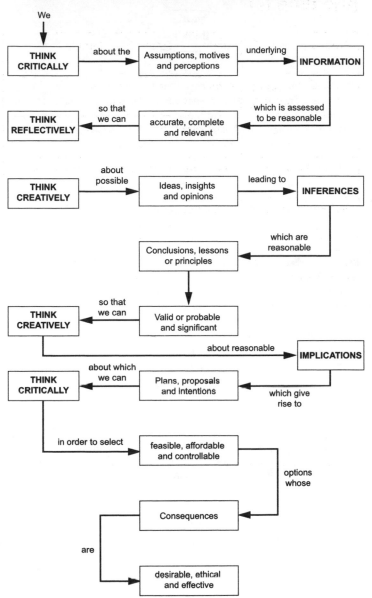

The process of applied thinking

(from *Teach Yourself Training Your Brain*, Horne and Wootton, 2007, Hodder Education)

Unpacking critical thinking

Verbal thinking

What does this assume? Do I accept this? Is it reasonable? Is it fair? Is it logical? Is it consistent? Under what conditions is it valid? Is it useful or reliable? Is it flawed – partially or fatally? By what criteria and who says? Who is trying to achieve what and why? What are the key questions here? What do we actually know? Are the options reasonable?

Recollective thinking

What principles might be helpful? Is it economic? Is it best use of these resources? Is it efficient? What are we trying to achieve? Does this make a worthwhile contribution? What will be the consequences for others affected? Is it equitable? Is it ecological? Is it ethical?

Numerical thinking → **Ethical thinking** ← **Empathetic thinking**

Is it economic? Is it efficient? Is it effective?

Is it the greatest benefit for the greatest number? Does it do the least harm? Does it waste least resources?

What are the likely thoughts and feelings of beneficiaries unintended victims, participants, observers?

Critical thinking

Critique, judgement, opinion, view, evaluation, scepticism.

(from *Teach Yourself Training Your Brain*, Horne and Wootton, 2007, Hodder Education)

Unpacking creative thinking

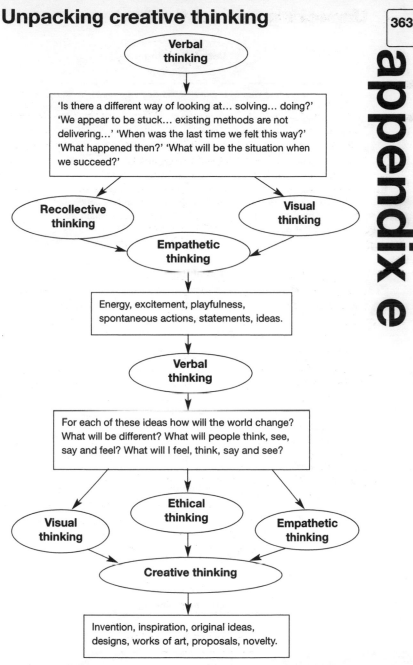

Verbal thinking

↓

'Is there a different way of looking at... solving... doing?' 'We appear to be stuck... existing methods are not delivering...' 'When was the last time we felt this way?' 'What happened then?' 'What will be the situation when we succeed?'

Recollective thinking   Visual thinking

Empathetic thinking

↓

Energy, excitement, playfulness, spontaneous actions, statements, ideas.

↓

Verbal thinking

↓

For each of these ideas how will the world change? What will be different? What will people think, see, say and feel? What will I feel, think, say and see?

Visual thinking   Ethical thinking   Empathetic thinking

Creative thinking

↓

Invention, inspiration, original ideas, designs, works of art, proposals, novelty.

(from *Teach Yourself Training Your Brain*, Horne and Wootton, 2007, Hodder Education)

Unpacking reflective thinking

Verbal thinking

'I wonder what that was all about?' 'What does it mean?' 'What really happened and so what?' 'What can we learn from this and where do we go from here?'

Recollective thinking

What was seen, heard and by whom? Who felt and thought what? What actually was said at the time and in what sequence? What else do we know? What was the picture?

Visual thinking

Verbal thinking

'Remembering all that, here and now, what do I feel and think?' 'What feelings, thoughts and association occur?' 'Is there a pattern here?' 'Has this happened before?' 'What insights are there?' 'What might I infer?'

Recollective thinking   **Empathetic thinking**   **Visual thinking**

Verbal thinking

'What are the implications for some future situations: how might this cause me to feel, think, behave differently?' 'What could I do to ensure this?'

Predictive thinking   **Critical thinking**

Reflective thinking

Insight, learning

(from *Teach Yourself Training Your Brain*, Horne and Wootton, 2007, Hodder Education)

Do you think like a man (TMB) or do you think like a woman (TFB)?

Men score			Women score
	1	At the end of hard day you prefer to:	
3		• talk to someone about your day	4
2		• listen to other people talking	2
0		• not talk at all	0
2		• None of the above	2

Men score			Women score
	2	Thinking about your spelling and writing:	
3		• You find both easy	4
2		• One is okay but not the other	2
0		• Both are weak	0
2		• None of the above	2

Men score			Women score
	3	In arguments you are most upset by:	
3		• a lack of response, silence or sulks	4
2		• a refusal to agree with you	2
0		• being contradicted or questioned	0
2		• None of the above	2

Men score			Women score
	4	On the question of routines, you prefer to do things:	
3		• whenever you feel like it	4
2		• according to a general but flexible plan	2
0		• about the same time every day	0
2		• None of the above	2

Men score			Women score
	5	When shopping you tend to:	
3		• buy special offers, frequently on impulse	4
2		• sometimes buy, sometimes don't	2
0		• purchase only what you went for	0
2		• None of the above	2

Men score			Women score
	6	You prefer to read:	
3		• fiction	4
2		• newspapers or general magazines	2
0		• specialist magazines or non-fictional information	0
2		• None of the above	2

Men score	7	You prefer to work:	Women score
3		• with a group of people you like	4
2		• on your own task but in the company of others	2
0		• in solitude	0
2		• None of the above	2

Men score	8	A friend has a personal problem:	Women score
3		• You can generally understand and sympathize	4
2		• You can usually explain why it's not so bad after all	2
0		• You usually give advice or suggestions on how to solve the problem	0
2		• None of the above	2

Men score	9	Today you meet more than seven new people. Tomorrow:	Women score
3		• you can picture at least seven of the new faces	4
2		• you could put some names to some faces	2
0		• you could remember names but not many faces	0
2		• None of the above	2

Men score	10	You cannot find your keys:	Women score
3		• You do something else until they turn up	4
2		• You try to do something else, but you're distracted by the loss	2
0		• You keep retracing your movements until you find them	0
2		• None of the above	2

Men score	11	When predicting what is going to happen:	Women score
3		• you use your intuition	4
2		• you rely on gut feelings to interpret relevant information	2
0		• you use trends based on historical statistics or other data	0
2		• None of the above	2

Men score	12 When you have heard a song:	Women score
3	• you can sing some of the words next time you hear the tune	4
2	• you can remember the tune but not the words	2
0	• you can vaguely remember the tune	0
2	• None of the above	2

Men score	13 You are listening to the radio or TV and the phone rings. Do you:	Women score
3	• just take the call and talk	4
2	• turn down the radio /TV and talk	2
0	• turn off the radio/TV, tell others to be quiet and talk	0
2	• None of the above	2

Men score	14 You need to reverse a vehicle into a tight spot to park it. Would you:	Women score
3	• look for another parking spot	4
2	• attempt to park, preferably with assistance	2
0	• just try to reverse in	0
2	• None of the above	2

Men score	15 In a place you are visiting for the first time:	Women score
3	• you would not know which way was north	4
2	• you could have a good guess which way was North	2
0	• you would know which way was north	0
2	• None of the above	2

Men score	16 A child's mechanical toy won't work:	Women score
3	• You can sympathize with the child and discuss how they feel about it	4
2	• You can find somebody else to fix it	2
0	• You will usually try to fix it	0
2	• None of the above	2

Men score			Women score
	17	After a good film you prefer:	
3		• to picture the scenes in your own mind	4
2		• to describe it to someone else	2
0		• to relate ideas or themes or lines from the film	0
2		• None of the above	2

Men score			Women score
	18	When explaining or defining something:	
3		• you often use a pencil, pen, paper or gestures	4
2		• you rely on verbal and non-verbal communication only	2
0		• you could define it clearly without repeating yourself	0
2		• None of the above	2

Men score			Women score
	19	Asked to read a map:	
3		• you would prefer some help	4
2		• you would have to turn it to face the way you were going	2
0		• you find it straight forward	0
2		• None of the above	2

Men score			Women score
	20	When thinking about your forthcoming day:	
3		• you often write a list	4
2		• you think about what you want to achieve that day	2
0		• you run through places and activities in your mind	0
2		• None of the above	2

If you are a man, add up your score under the men score column.

If you are a woman, add up your score under the women score column.

Most men we have tested scored less than 44.

Most women we have tested scored more than 40.

People with lower scores tended to use typically male brain (TMB) thinking skills. People with low scores were more likely to rely on logic, deduction, analysis and disciplined organization. The closer they were to zero, the more likely it was that they were good at making detailed plans. They tended to be less easily swayed by emotions and more objective when making decisions.

People with high scores tended to make more use of the thinking skills more frequently used by women. People with a higher score were more likely to be creative or artistic. They made greater use of intuition or gut feelings. They could think inductively, recognize patterns and identify and solve problems on the basis of less information. Men who scored closer to zero had great difficulties when in relationships, especially with women who scored nearer 80 and vice versa.

Mid range scores indicated people who had the ability, under many circumstances, to think either like a typically male brained (TMB) man, or like a typically female brained (TFB) woman. Such people seemed to perform well when working in groups, or when working as managers, especially where there were multi-factor problems to be solved and where novel solutions were needed.

Since we began our research in 1982, knowledge about the structure and working of the brain has exploded. This has helped us to infer that brain differences might account for the differences in the thinking and behaviour that we encountered. In turn, this has allowed us to examine some implications for the way we might behave more effectively when talking to, relating to, working with, or working for people of the opposite sex.

If you are interested in the implications of our gender-based findings, look for *Brain Training for Women* and *Brain Training for Men*, Horne and Wootton (forthcoming).

Oxytoxic Indices

Baking

Victoria sponge	24
Crumble	28
Marzipan	30
Wholemeal pastry	32
Shortcrust pastry	35
Flaky pastry	38

Beans and lentils

Baked beans in tomato sauce	5
Broad beans	5
Cannellini beans	5
Chilli beans	5
Marrow fat peas	5
Tofu	5
Lentils	6
Mung beans	6
Red kidney beans	6
Aduki beans	8
Blackeye beans	8
Chickpeas	8
Couscous	8
Cracked wheat	8

Biscuits

Orbit sugar free gum	10
Bubble gum	17
Ryvita	22
Jelly babies	22
Matzo	22
Jaffa	26
Fig rolls	26
Heinz Stem Ginger	26
Wagon wheel	28
Carrs Water	29
Nice	30
Cream cracker	30
Ginger nut	31
Cracker wheat	31
Rich Tea	32
Jammy Dodgers	32
Smarties	32
Custard creams	33
Croutons	33
Ritz	33
Cadbury Choc Chip	33
Chocolate digestives	33
Gypsy Cream	33
Club Biscuit	33
Hobnob	33
Shortbread	34
Dinky wafers	35
Milky Bar Buttons	36
Penguin	36
Cheddars	36
TUC	36
Cadbury Fingers	36
Yo-Yo Mint	36
Boasters	37
Cadbury Snack	37

appendix h

Bread and cakes

Rye bread	10
Wholemeal roll	10
Soda scone	10
Pikelet/crumpet	13
Wholemeal bread	14
White roll	19
Swiss roll	19
Chapatis	20
Hot cross buns	20
Naan	22
Garlic bread	24
Jam tart	24
Chocolate roll	24
Treacle tart	24
Tortilla	25
Danish pastry	25
Cadbury gateau	25
Mince pie	25
Scotch pancake	25
Carrot cake	25
Almond slice	26
Chocolate chip	26
Lemon slice	26
Crunchy Bar cake	26
Frozen éclair	27
Iced cakes	27
Lemon curd tart	27
Brownies	28
Bakewell slice	30
Croissant	30
Battenburg	30
Éclair cake	32
Caramel shortcake	32
Flapjack	33
Fried bread	35
Milky Way cake	35

Breakfast cereals and bars

Porridge (water)	2
Porridge (milk)	6
All Bran	19
Muesli	19
Weetabix	22
Branflakes	22
Alpen (no sugar)	24
Fruit and Fibre	24
Nutrigrain	24
Cornflakes	25
Nutflakes	26
Alpen Cereal	28
Coco Pops bar	30
Jordan's Maple Bran	30
Harvest Crunch	31
Rice Krispies bar	32
Tracker Chip bars	36

Burgers, chips, fries and sauces

Cider vinegar	1
Tabasco	1
Coleman's Mint Sauce	1
Wine vinegar	1
Soy	3
Ross Chip Shop Chips	5
Heinz Tomato	7
Balsamic vinegar	7
Horseradish sauce	7
McCain's Oven Chips	8
HP Sauce	8
Dijon mustard	8
Veggie burger	9
Coleman's Mustard	12
McCain's Hashbrown	13
McCain's Microchips	14
Croquet potatoes	14
Baxter's Mint Sauce	19
Frozen chips	20
Meat burger	21
Lea and Perrins	22
Tartare sauce	34
BBQ sauce	40

Butter/Margarine

Olivio spread 20%	18
Olivio olive oil	35
Vitalite	40
Flora	41
Clover	43
Willow	47
Stork	48
Lurpack	50
Olivio spread 50%	50

Cheeses

Cottage, low fat	5
Ricotta	9
Philadelphia, light	11
Philadelphia, full	17
Feta	17
Mozzarella	17
Cheddar, half fat	18
Camembert	19
Gorgonzola	20
Heinz, reduced	20
Processed slices	20
Stilton, white	23
Goat, soft	23
Roquefort	23
Jarlsberg	24
Danish blue	24
Edam	25
Gouda	25
Wensleydale	25
Red Leicester	26
Lancashire	26
Gruyere	26
Cathedral City	27
Cracker Barrel	27
Shropshire blue	27
Parmesan	27
Stilton, blue	27
Boursin	28
Cambozola	28
Double Gloucester	28
Mascarpone	28
Sage Derby	29

Chutney/pickles

Sauerkraut	1
Piccalli, Heinz	6
Tomato pickle, Heinz	7
Branston	10
Mango, Burgess	19

Cook-in sauces/marinades

Ross, casserole	1
Sharwood's, soy	1
Dolmio, chicken and vegetable	2
Dolmio, herb and red wine	2
Homepride, Indian tomato	2
Ragu, basil and oregano	2
El Paso, fajita	3
Homepride, balti	3
Homepride, red wine	3
Homepride, tarragon	3
Knorr, wine and onion	3
Uncle Ben's, blackbeans	3
Lea and Perrin, chilli	4
El Paso, burrito	5
Homepride, sweet and sour	5
Knorr, Moroccan	5
Sharwood's, oyster	5
Batchelor's, cheese	25
Coleman's, korma	30
Bisto, cheese	33
Bisto, parlsey	33
Bisto, white	34
Knorr, fajita	40
Knorr, five spice	40
Knorr, Californian chicken	44
Knorr, creamy ham	45
Knorr, Jamaican jerky	45
Knorr, tandori chicken	46
Knorr, herb chicken	51

Crisps and nibbles

Poppadoms	24
Trail mix	29
Golden Rights	30
Twiglets	30
Walkers lite	30
Low-fat crisps	32
Kettle, cheddar	32
Golden Wonder	32
Doritos	33
Yogi peanuts/raisins	33
Quavers	34
El Paso tortilla chips	35
Walkers cheese and onion	36
Peanuts, roasted	40
Popcorn, plain	40

Dairy products

Soya milk	2
Skimmed milk	2
Fat-free yoghurt	3
Provamol rice	3
Fromage frais, fruit	3
St Ivel Shape 0%	3
Muller Light	3
Whole milk	4
Goat's/sheep's milk	4
Greek low-fat yoghurt	4
Plain, whole yoghurt	4
Goat's yoghurt	4
Greek sheep's yoghurt	6
Jersey milk	6
Yoplait drink	6
Muller Fruit Corner	7
Muller Thick and Creamy	7
Greek cows yoghurt	9
UHT Elmlea single	10
Half cream	11
Sour cream	13
Single cream	13
St Ivel smoothie	13
Nestlé condensed milk	19
UHT Elmlea	23
Crème freche	25
Whipping cream	26
Nestlé evaporated milk	28
Double cream	33
Clotted cream, fresh	40

Desserts/Puddings

Tropical Juice Bar, Lyons	2
Jelly (water)	4
Sago, Ambrosia	5
Muller rice	5
Semolina, Ambrosia	5
Muller rice, fat free	5
Rice, Heinz	5
Tapicoa, Ambrosia	5
Lemon sorbet, Carte D'or	5
Soft scoop, Walls	5
Custard, low-fat	5
Tapioca, semi-skimmed	6
Chocolate ice, Lyons	6
Semolina, semi-skimmed	6
Chocolate mousse, Heinz	6
Cornish ice, Lyons	6
Sago, semi-skimmed	6
Rice, Ambrosia	6
Napoli coffee	6
Light choc mousse, Cadbury	8
Trifle, Heinz	8
Rice pudding	9
Cheesecake, Heinz	10
Chocolate mousse, Cadbury	12
Trifle, Cadbury	18
Bread pudding	19
Cheesecake, McVities	20
Christmas pudding	21
Tiramisu, McVities	22
Sponge, Heinz	22
Bounty ice cream	22
Blancmange, B&P	22
Tapioca, Whitworth	23
Profiterols	24
Semolina, Whitworths	24
Spotted dick, McVites	24
Ice cone mints, Lyons	24
Sago, Whitworth	24
Magnum, Walls	24
Meringue	24
Rice, Creamola	25
Galaxy ice cream	25
Snickers ice cream	25
Trifle, Mr Kiplings	26
Twix ice cream	27
Nestlé Smarties ice cream	28
Nestlé Milky Bar ice cream	30
Angel Delight	30
Dream Topping	46

Dips/Dressed salads

Primula, spicy mexican	21
Primula, mango curry	22
Primula, garnishers	23
Sour cream dips	24
Taramosalata	35

Dressings

French Kraft 3%	3
Blue cheese, Heinz	4
1,000 Island, Kraft 5%	5
Caesar, Kraft 4%	6
Mayonnaise light, Heinz	8
Salad cream, Heinz	21
1000 Island, Kraft	24
Blue cheese	29
Helmann's Basil	30
French dressing	32
Baxter's Seafood	35
Mayonnaise, Helmann	50
Mayonnaise, Heinz	50

Drinks (alcoholic)

Dry wine	4
Wine white, sparkling	5
Wine white, medium	5
Lager, Heineken	6
Martini brandy	6
Wine white, sweet	6
Beer (500 ml)	9
Lager, bottled	10
Sherry Bristol Cream	10
Lager, Tennents	10
Newcastle Brown Ale	11
Bacardi Breezer	12
Bacardi Breezer Twist	12
Cider, dry	12
Malt whiskey	14
Brandy	14
Teachers Whisky	14
Vodka	15
Cherry brandy	16
Baileys	20
Grand Marnier	21
Cognac, Courvoisier	24
Cointreau	24
Strong ales	26
Cider, strong	37

Drinks

Special R, Robinsons	1
Diet cola	1
Fruit Break (no sugar)	1
Dietade	1
Libby R (no sugar)	1
7 Up Diet	1
Dandelion Topdeck	1
Pepsi Max or Diet	1
Tango light	1
Lucozade, low-calorie	1
Tea, PG Tips	1
Lemonade, Corona	1
Ribena Spark low	1
Lipton Tea	2
Cranberry, Britivic	3
All Juice lemonade	3
Citrus Spring	3
Grape Schloer	3
Tonic water, Schweppes	3
Lemonade 250, R Whites	3
Apple and Blackcurrant, Quosh	5
Lemonade 250, Barrs	5
Ovaltine	5
Apple juice, Robinsons	6
Coca Cola 200	7
Tango	7
Nescafé Gold Blend	7
Ginger ale, Britvic	7
Nescafé Decaffeinated	7
Ironbru	7
Pepsi 250	7
Nescafé Instant Expresso	7
7 Up 250	8
Horlicks	8
Ribena Spark	8
Bovril, chicken	8
Lucozade	12
Bovril, beef	12
Horlicks, skimmed milk	12
Nestlé Cocoa	20
Coffee syrups, caramel	21
Nesquick, chocolate	25

Nescafé Instant
Cappuccino 26
Horlicks chocolate 26
Nesquick, strawberry 26

Eggs, Fish, Seafood

King prawn, Lyons 3
Tuna Italiana, Heinz 4
Prawn stir fry, Ross 4
Prawns, boiled 4
Seafood, Youngs 4
Smoked haddock, Ross 5
Shrimps 5
Cod steak in butter, Ross 6
Fish pie 6
Tuna pasta Napolina 6
Cod in cheese, Birds 6
Salmon and Broccoli,
Heinz 6
Fish steak with parsley 6
Cod, grilled 6
Eels, jellied 6
Mussels 6
Plaice, steamed 6
Tuna in brine 6
Cod, baked 6
Cod, poached 6
Haddock, smoked 6
Sole, steamed 6
Trout, Youngs 6
Fish in tomato, Ross 8
Seafood lasagne, Ross 8
Pilchards 8
Swordfish, grilled 9
Cod and chips, Ross 10
Boiled egg 10
Salmon, canned 10
Poached egg 10
Salmon, salted 10
Fish and Potatoes, Ross 12
Kedgeree 12
Omelette 12
Herring, grilled 12
Sole goujons, baked 12

Sardines 12
Tuna in oil 12
Fried egg 12
Mackerel 12
Fish fingers, Birds Eye 12
Haddock, breaded 13
Cod Crispy Crunch,
Heinz 14
Skate in butter 14
Kippers 14
Salmon, grilled 14
Plaice, breaded 14
Fish cakes, Ross 16
Fish fingers in oil 16
Haddock Steak Crispy,
Birds Eye 16
Cod in batter, fried 16
Cod, breaded 16
Fish fingers, Ross 16
Prawns Hot, Lyons 18
Omelette with cheese 18

Fast foods/Snacks

Toffee low-fat yoghurt	4
Skate, fried in batter	11
Chips, fried in oil	16
Cod, fried in batter	16
Bacon bun	20
Egg salad sandwich	20
Tuna sandwhich	22
Pizza Express tortellini	23
Cheese sandwich	23
Pretzels, low-fat	26
Burger King Fries	27
Wimpy Bacon cheeseburger	30
Quarter pounder and cheese	31
Chargrilled chicken crisps	32
Cheese and onion crisps	32
McDonald's Big Mac	33
McDonald's Kingsize	37
Jacket skins	38
McDonald's Big Breakfast	40
Pizza Hut garlic bread	41
Pizza Hut tomato bake	44
Pizza Express mushroom	44
Pizza Hut lasagna	44
Pizza Express salad nicoise	48
Pizza Express American hot	50
Pizza Hut meat feast	64
Pizza Hut mixed grill	64

Fruit

Raspberries	1
Cranberries	1
Rhubarb	1
Strawberries	1
Blackcurrants	2
Melon	2
Pawpaw	2
Apricots	2
Peaches	2
Plums	2
Blackberries	2
Damsons	2
Grapefruit	2
Guavas	2
Oranges	2
Apples	3
Grapefruit, tinned	3
Kiwi	3
Pineapple	3
Mandarins, tinned	3
Nectarines	3
Clementines	3
Grapes	4
Mango	4
Gooseberries, stewed	5
Prunes	5
Bananas	6
Dates	8
Figs	8
Figs, dried	14
Bananas, dried	14
Dates, dried	16
Apricots, dried	16
Cherries	32
Coconuts	44

Jams and spreads

De Ville spread, Heinz	7
Raspberry spread	8
Pineapple and ginger	9
Diet strawberry	10
Blueberry spread	10
Diet marmalade	11
Diet raspberry jam	11
Blackberry jelly	14
Apricot jam	17
Blueberry jam	17
Blackberry jam	17
Honey	18
Nutella	36
Chocolate nut spread	36
Cashew butter	40
Peanut butter	41
Hazelnut spread	45

Meat and poultry

Gammon, boiled	13
Beef topisde, roast	16
Sausages	20
Rabbit, stewed	24
Turkey breast, grilled	25
Pheasant, roast	26
Bacon, grilled	28
Venison, roast	32
Duck, roast	33
Rump steak	33
Lamb leg, roast	35
Chicken liver, fried	35
Lamb chops, grilled	35
Calf liver, fried	36
Stewing steak	37
Bacon, fried	40
Chicken breast, fried	41
Bacon, microwaved	41
Bacon streaky, grilled	46
Beef rib, roasted	50
Goose, roast	50
Large steak	60

Oils and fats

Suet	35
Coconut	60
Palm	60
Vegetable	60
White Flora	60
Corn	60
Sunflower	60
Wheat germ	60
Olive	60
Soya	60
Crisp and dry	60
Lard	60

Pasta

Fresh tomato and basil	3
Fresh pesto	3
Heinz spaghetti	3
Heinz spaghetti hoops	4
Heinz ravioli	5
Heinz spag. bolognaise	6
Wholemeal spaghetti	7
Fresh spaghetti	9
Fresh lasagne	10
Ravioli	11
Pesto in jar	28

Pizza and pies

Veggie sausage roll	17
Cheese and tomato thin	18
Fray Bentos chicken and mushroom	20
Napolina bases	20
Steak pie	20
Pork and vegetable pie	23
Pork pie	24
Quiche, cheese and egg	24
Sausage rolls	26
Tyne steak and kidney	30
Fray Bentos steak and mushroom	30
Fray Bentos steak and ale	32
Tyne meat and veg	38
McCain's cheese and veg	40
Tyne meat and potato	40
Yorkshire pudding	40
Ross chicken and veg	50
Ross beef and onion	50
Ross giant pastie	50
Ross vegetable pie	50
Bentos steak and kidney	60
Game pie	70

Ready meals

Ross sizzling prawn	2
Tyne vegetable curry	4
Heinz tortellini	4
Heinz vegetable hot pot	5
Tyne chicken stew	5
Heinz chicken tikka	5
Ross vegetable bake	5
Heinz chilli pots	5
Tyne beef casserole	6
Tyne cheese and potato	6
Heinz bolognaise	6
Findus spicy lasagna	6
Tyne beef curry	6
Ross Caribbean chicken	6
Ross paella	6
Heinz chicken korma	7
Tyne stew	7
Tyne chilli con carne	7
Birds vegetable rice	7
Findus chicken curry	8
Uncle Ben's wholegrain rice	9
Egg fried rice	14
Birds spicy chicken	16
El Paso burrito	19
Birds glazed chicken (0% fat)	22
Birds roast pork	22
Dolmio five cheese tortellini	22
Heinz beef lasagna	22
Birds roast lamb	24
Birds chicken curry	31
Birds chicken and rice	32
Birds chilli chicken	32
Samosa, vegetable	32
Birds spaghetti bolognaise	35
Birds beef curry	35
Birds roast turkey	36
Birds chicken tandoori	37
Birds mustard chicken	40
Samosa, meat	40
Heinz chicken mexicano	67

Snacks

Knorr cheese & ham snackpot	6
Chicken & prawn snackpot	6
Knorr Tikka masala pasta break	6
C&B spicy tomato snackpot	6
C&B curry pasta snackpot	6
Findus chicken & broccoli snackpot	7
Heinz chicken tikka sandwich	12
Chicken & sweetcorn pot noodle	24
Nice and cheesey pot pasta	25
Kraft cheese lunchable	27
Chicken & mushroom pot noodle	29
Batchelors beef supernoodles	30
Batchelors chicken supernoodles	30
Chow mein supernoodles	30
Batchelors curry supernoodle	30
Sausage & tomato pot noodle	30
Sweet & sour supernoodles	30
Batchelors mushroom supernoodles	30
Batchelors balti supernoodles	30
Chow mein pot noodle	31

Soups

Baxter's beef consommé	1
Baxter's French onion	1
Campbell's mushroom	1
Heinz chicken noodle	1
Heinz parsnip and carrot	1
Baxter's carrot and chicken	2
Baxter's cock-a-leekie	2
Baxter's garden soup	2
Heinz lentil soup	2
Baxter's royal game	3
Baxter's highland broth	3
Baxter's spring parsnip	3
Campbell's asparagus	3
Heinz big beef broth	3
Heinz cream of chicken	3
Heinz leek and bacon	3
Heinz thick soups	3
Baxter's cajun	4
Campbell's cream of mushroom	4
Heinz cream of tomato	4
Knorr French mushroom	4
Knorr chicken noodle	20
Knorr French onion	20
Knorr chinese tomato	22
Knorr potato and leek	24
Knorr golden vegetable	26
Knorr carrot and coriander	26
Knorr tomato and red pepper	27
Knorr cream of tomato	29
Crofter's chicken and leek	30
Knorr cream of chicken	37

Sugar and sweets

3 squares dark chocolate (75% cocoa)	4
Meridian maple syrup	18
Tate & Lyle golden syrup	21
Boiled sweets	21
Refreshers	25
Polo mints	26
Tunes	26
Cravens limes	26
Mint imperials	26
Murray mints	26
Tate & Lyle demerara	27
Tate & Lyle granulated	27
After Eights	27
Creme Eggs	29
Double Decker	30
Milky Way	30
Mars Bar	30
Aero	31
Crunchie bar	31
Rolo	31
Walnut Whip	32
Bounty bar	32
Fruit and nut chocolate	32
Maltesers	33
Snickers	34
Blue Riband	34
Cadbury Buttons	35
Galaxy	35
Yorkie bar	35
Toblerone	35
Terry's Chocolate Orange	35
Flake	36

Stock cubes/Stuffing

Tomato purée	5
Burgess gravy	5
Paxo, sage/onion stuffing	8
Paxo, thyme stuffing	10
Bovril	11
Knorr, chicken	15
Bisto, original	16
Marmite	16
Oxo, vegetable	17
Oxo, beef	21
Paxo, golden crumbs	24
Bisto, chicken gravy	26
Whitworth, sage/onion	26
Oxo, lamb/mint	27
Knorr, basil	32
Perfect garlic	37

Toppings

Heinz chicken and mushroom	3
Heinz cheese, ham and pepper	6
Primula pizza cheese top	30

Vegetables

Artichoke, globe	1
French beans	1
Cabbage	1
Celeriac	1
Fennel	1
Leeks	1
Mushroom, boiled	1
Okra (lady's finger)	1
Onions, boiled	1
Peppers	1
Spinach	1
Turnip	1
Cherry tomato	1
Tomato, tinned	1
Runner beans	1
Broccoli	1
Spring greens	1
Celery	1
Courgettes	1
Lettuce	1
Swede	1
Carrots	1
Chicory	1
Cucumber	1
Radish	1
Beetroot	2
Corn, canned	2
Ginger root	2
Water chestnut	2
Cauliflower	2
Kale	2
Aspargus	2
Mange tout	2
Broad bean	3
Peas frozen	4
New potatoes, boiled	4
Parsnips	4
Peas	5
Sweet potato	5
Garlic	6
Potatoes and milk, mashed	7
Yam	7

Corn, boiled	7
Olives in brine	7
Peas, mushy	7
Potatoes, baked	9
Cassava	10
Mushroom, fried	10
New potatoes, roasted	10
Avocado	12
Sun dried tomato	14
Okra, stir fried	18
Aubergine in oil	20
Onions, fried	20
Mushrooms, dried	20
Artichoke, Jerusalem	23
Garlic paste	28

Vegetarian

Rice dream	4
Quorn	6
Burgers, Linda McCartney	8
Soya milk	12
Cornish pasty	14

The figures in these tables are a relative index and intended only to inform your own choices. They are based on UK government data published by HMSO (the Composition of Foods Summary). In European countries consumers can check latest manufacturers labels for up-to-date values of the energy (joules) content of processed foods.

ORAC scores

The US Department of Agriculture compared the ORAC scores of well-known brain foods like spinach, blueberries and broccoli, with dark chocolate. (ORAC scores measure the concentration of flavonoid anti-oxidants in foods.)

Broccoli	890
Sprouted alfafa	930
Plums	949
Sprouts	980
Raspberries	1,220
Spinach	1,260
Strawberries	1,540
Kale/Cabbage	1,770
Blackberries	2,036
Blueberries	2,400
Dark chocolate	13,120

Eat 4 oz of fish a week, either as one meal or keep snacking on, for example, a smoked mackerel.

appendix i

appendix j

Some brain recipes

1 Brain booster morning drink (Oxytoxic Index – 4 per drink)

Ingredients:

    2 cups of blanched sliced almonds
    2 cups of soya milk
    3 drops of vanilla essence
    8 peaches (fresh if cheap and in season,
      if not then tinned in juice not syrup)
    1 tablespoon of honey (e.g. Manuka)
    4 tablespoons of low-fat yoghurt (preferably Greek)
    8 ice cubes

Method: Blend from chilled ingredients and serve cold.

2 Beef up your brain stew (Oxytoxic Index – 6 per portion)

Ingredients:

    500 g stewing beef, diced (solid white fat removed)
    130 g chopped onion
    1 tablespoon of olive oil (less if using a non-stick pan)
    30 g wholemeal flour
    500 ml water or stock
    150 g carrots, chopped, plus any other left over
      root vegetables
    $1/2$ teaspoon of salt, $1/2$ teaspoon of pepper,
    1 teaspoon of turmeric

Method: Brown and seal the meat and onions. Add the flour
and stir for 1 minute. Add water (or stock), vegetables and
seasoning and put in the oven for 2 hours at 180°.

3 Cognitive cauliflower cheese (Oxytoxic Index – 6 per portion)

Ingredients:

25 g olive oil
1 small cauliflower (700 g)
100 g strong cheese (preferably soft not solid)
100 ml water
20 g wholemeal flour
250 ml skimmed milk
$1/2$ level teaspoon of salt
black pepper to taste

Method: Boil the cauliflower until it will just break into florets. Drain, and save 100 ml of the water. Make a white sauce from the oil, flour, milk and water. Add three-quarters of your cheese to the white sauce and pour over the cauliflower. Top with the remaining cheese and brown under a grill or in a hot oven at 220°.

4 Cerebral casserole (Oxytoxic Index – 3 per portion)

Ingredients:

240 g potato plus 120 g each of carrot, onion, swede, parsnip – all diced
90 g tinned sweetcorn
90 g frozen peas
90 g chopped tomatoes
450 g tinned tomato
1 teaspoon of Marmite

Method: Stir into a casserole dish, cover and cook for 1 hour at 190°.

5 Neuronal fish pie (Oxytoxic Index – 6 per portion)

Ingredients:

200 g cooked white fish, e.g. coley
100 g mashed potato
150 g semi-skimmed milk
15 g olive oil
15 g wholemeal flour
$1/2$ level teaspoon of salt

Method: Make a white sauce and mix it with the flaked fish. Put the mashed potato round the edge of the casserole dish and pour in the fish and sauce. Brown in the oven at 200° for 30 minutes.

6 A fresh-ideas fruit salad (Oxytoxic Index – 2 per portion)

Ingredients:

2 tablespoons of lemon juice
1 small apple, cored and cubed
1 medium pear, cored and cubed
1 can/220 g grapefruit segments, in grapefruit juice
1 can/298 g mandarin orange segments, in natural juice

Method: Pour the lemon juice into a bowl, add the apple and pear and swirl to coat. Add the grapefruit and mandarin segments (including all juice), gently stir to mix. Pop in the fridge until ready to serve.

(Thanks to HMSO and Sayaka Mitsuhashi of the Okinawa Centenarian Centre.)

Circuit 01

Q1 fear, pear, peas, peps, pops, hops, hope
Q2 When it's ground.
Q3 A = 2, B = 0, C = 4, D = 6, E = 1, F = 8, G = 7
Q4 Maud Adams
Q5 laze, daze, doze, done, dons

Q6

Q7

2	5	6	3	4	7	8	9	1
8	1	9	2	5	6	7	3	4
4	3	7	1	9	8	2	6	5
1	2	3	4	6	9	5	7	8
6	4	8	5	7	2	3	1	9
7	9	5	8	1	3	6	4	2
3	6	1	9	2	5	4	8	7
5	8	4	7	3	1	9	2	6
9	7	2	6	8	4	1	5	3

Q8 1,000,000
Q9 12
Q10 20
Q11 Apollo (13)
Q12 Pay It Forward
Q13 The Pianist
Q14 Ghandi
Q15 A

Cryptic crossword 01

Circuit 02

Q1

1	3	4	0	2
4	0	2	1	3
2	1	3	4	0
3	4	0	2	1
0	2	1	3	4

Q2 Use a spirit level!

Q3

6	6	12	18
30	48	78	126
204	330	504	834

Q4 Beverly Johnson

Q5 eggs, ergs, errs, ears, bars, bard

Q6

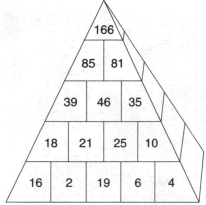

Q7

1	2	3	4	6	5	7	8	9
4	5	7	8	2	9	1	3	6
6	8	9	1	3	7	2	4	5
5	1	2	3	7	4	9	6	8
7	3	8	5	9	6	4	1	2
9	4	6	2	8	1	3	5	7
2	6	4	7	1	8	5	9	3
3	9	1	6	5	2	8	7	4
8	7	5	9	4	3	6	2	1

Q8　1984 (rework of '1948'; title of last novel by George Orwell)
Q9　69
Q10　19
Q11　Dead Poets' (Society)
Q12　On Golden Pond
Q13　Quills
Q14　Cool Runnings
Q15　18
Cryptic crossword 02

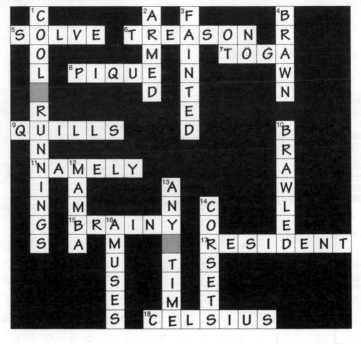

Circuit 03

Q1 Think Twice Cut Once
Q2 A night mayor?
Q3 Just check that the right-hand sides compute to 10.
Q4 Farrah Fawcett
Q5 quit, suit, spit, spin, span, spar
Q6

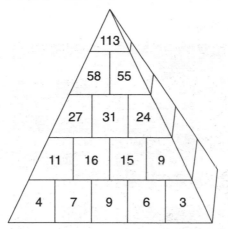

Q7

1	2	3	5	4	6	7	8	9
4	6	7	9	1	8	2	3	5
5	8	9	2	3	7	1	4	6
2	1	4	3	6	5	8	9	7
3	5	6	7	8	9	4	1	2
7	9	8	1	2	4	6	5	3
6	3	1	4	5	2	9	7	8
9	4	2	8	7	3	5	6	1
8	7	5	6	9	1	3	2	4

Q8 04.07.1776
Q9 68
Q10 16
Q11 You Got Mail
Q12 Dr Who
Q13 Blue Velvet
Q14 Pretty Woman
Q15 C

Cryptic crossword 03

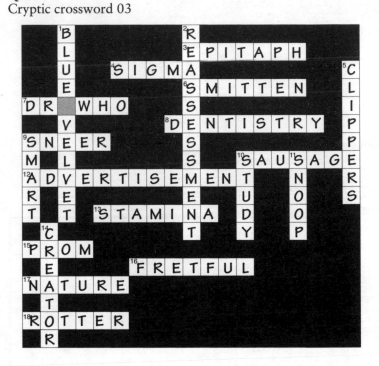

Circuit 04

Q1   aloft, float

Q2   If he had a left ear, a right ear and a final front ear.

Q3   (A) TIRES becomes RITES
      (B) RESET becomes TERSE
      (C) LASTED becomes SALTED
      (D) NEAR IT becomes RETAIN
      (E) LAST TEE becomes SEATTLE

Q4   Rachel Ward

Q5   cute, cuts, cats, vats, vans, fans

Q6

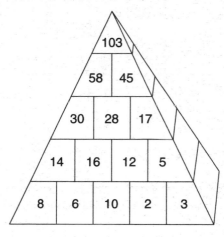

Q7

1	2	3	5	7	8	6	9	4
4	5	7	1	9	6	2	3	8
8	9	6	2	3	4	1	7	5
2	4	9	3	1	5	7	8	6
3	6	1	4	8	7	5	2	9
5	7	8	9	6	2	3	4	1
6	1	2	7	4	9	8	5	3
7	3	4	8	5	1	9	6	2
9	8	5	6	2	3	4	1	7

Q8   1,000 (1,000 island dressing, Millennium Dome, Roman
       mile = 1,000 paces)
Q9   15
Q10 65
Q11 Chocolat
Q12 Titanic
Q13 Home Alone
Q14 I Am Sam
Q15 B

Circuit 05

Q1 A (maharaja, flapjack)
Q2 A flying sorcerer
Q3

3	3	6	9
15	24	39	63
102	165	267	432

Q4 Raquel Welch
Q5 vice, vile, pile, pole, polo, solo
Q7

Q6

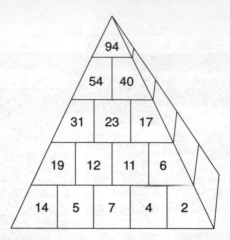

9	1	2	3	5	8	4	7	6
3	4	7	1	2	6	5	8	9
5	6	8	4	7	9	1	2	3
1	2	4	5	3	7	6	9	8
6	5	3	8	9	1	2	4	7
7	8	9	2	6	4	3	1	5
2	7	6	9	4	3	8	5	1
4	3	1	7	8	5	9	6	2
8	9	5	6	1	2	7	3	4

Q8
360
Q9   64
Q10 14
Q11 Forrest Gump
Q12 Les Miserables

Q13 Blow Up
Q14 Erin Brockovich (B.Rock.O.Vic.H)
Q15 A
Cryptic crossword 05

Circuit 06

Q1 £300 i.e. 300 minus (150 + 10) leaves £140, minus (70 + 10) leaves £60 minus (30 + 10) = £40, leaves £20 from original £300.

Q2 Minimum

Q3 Only the 1st

Q4 Barbara Carrera

Q5 deck, beck, back, bask, bass, boss

Q6

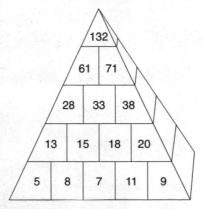

Q7

1	4	2	3	5	7	6	8	9
3	6	8	1	2	9	7	4	5
5	7	9	4	6	8	1	2	3
2	1	3	5	8	4	9	7	6
4	8	5	7	9	6	2	3	1
6	9	7	2	1	3	4	5	8
7	5	1	6	3	2	8	9	4
9	2	6	8	4	5	3	1	7
8	3	4	9	7	1	5	6	2

Q8   216
Q9   60
Q10 12
Q11 Last Tango (In Paris)
Q12 Shakespeare (In Love)
Q13 Barbarella
Q14 Amadeus
Q15 200 cycles per second
Cryptic crossword 06

Circuit 07

Q1 Elucidate
Q2 Kidney
Q3

2	4	1

	2	4	5

| | | 5 | 6 | 4 | 3 | 7 |

| | | | 7 | 6 | 9 |

| | | | | 8 |

| 1 | 4 | 3 |
| 8 | 5 | 9 |

| 6 | 2 | 9 |

| 4 | 8 | 9 | 6 | 7 |

| 2 | 8 | 9 | | 3 | 8 | 9 |

| 4 | 9 | 7 | | 9 | 3 | 5 |

Q4 Kim Basinger
Q5 sank, sand, said, skid, skim, swim
Q6

78	59	15	21	46
13	17	108	69	12
63	20	19	66	51
23	43	62	43	48
42	80	15	20	62

Q7

1	3	4	2	5	6	8	7	9
6	5	9	1	7	8	2	3	4
7	2	8	3	4	9	1	5	6
5	1	6	4	8	3	7	9	2
2	4	3	5	9	7	6	1	8
8	9	7	6	1	2	3	4	5
3	8	5	7	2	4	9	6	1
9	6	1	8	3	5	4	2	7
4	7	2	9	6	1	5	8	3

Q8   180
Q9   50
Q10 11
Q11 (Three Colours) Red, White (and) Blue
Q12 Castaway
Q13 Godfather
Q14 Psycho
Q15 F

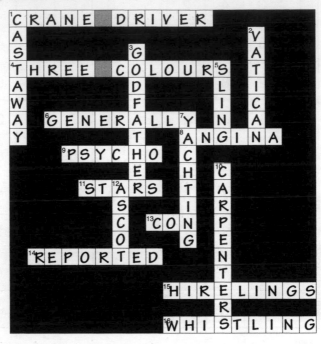

Circuit 08

Q1 52 (double the sum of the first two numbers in the row)
Q2 Parole
Q3 On the 21st November
Q4 Debbie Harry
Q5 foot, font, fond, bond, band, hand
Q6

46	59	12	38	81
4	43	130	51	8
74	25	14	69	54
46	47	66	47	30
66	62	14	31	63

Q7

1	2	4	5	6	7	9	8	3
3	5	7	1	9	8	2	4	6
6	8	9	2	4	3	5	7	1
2	1	6	3	7	4	8	5	9
4	3	5	8	1	9	6	2	7
7	9	8	6	2	5	3	1	4
8	4	3	9	5	1	7	6	2
9	6	1	7	8	2	4	3	5
5	7	2	4	3	6	1	9	8

Q8 147
Q9 42
Q10 9
Q11 Amelie
Q12 (The French) Connection
Q13 The Hours
Q14 The Apartment
Q15 C

Cryptic crossword 08

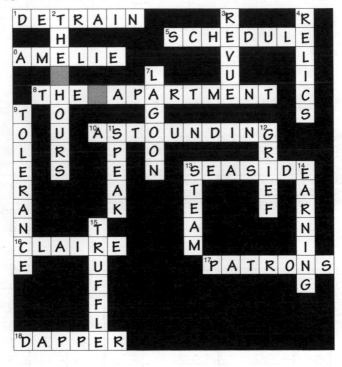

Circuit 09

Q1   Mora Mora £3.00, Sambirano £3.60

Q2   Shotgun

Q3

1	2	3	4	5	6	7	8	9	10	11	12	13	14	15	16	17	18	19	20	21
T	A	B	L	E	S	I	O	N	T	A	R	I	O	W	N	E	U	R	O	N

Q4   Christie Brinkley

Q5   beer, beet, belt, bell, bill, mill, milk

Q6

33	10	52	36	59
32	60	47	38	13
24	98	18	38	12
42	16	29	38	65
59	6	44	40	41

Q7

8	6	2	1	4	5	7	3	9
5	1	3	7	9	6	4	2	8
4	7	9	8	2	3	5	1	6
9	5	8	3	7	4	2	6	1
7	2	1	6	5	9	3	8	4
3	4	6	2	1	8	9	5	7
6	3	7	9	8	2	1	4	5
2	9	5	4	6	1	8	7	3
1	8	4	5	3	7	6	9	2

Q8 144
Q9 40
Q10 7
Q11 Mash
Q12 Citizen Kane
Q13 Howard's End
Q14 The Piano
Q15 B
Cryptic crossword 09

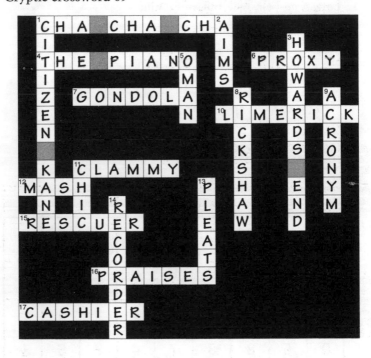

Circuit 10

Q1 Lean ('jogging up' the word 'lane' produces 'lean' (anagram) meaning reduced fat)
Q2 Illegal
Q3 C
Q4 Pamela Stephenson
Q5 toad, goad, glad, clad, clod, clog, flog, frog
Q6

44	24	28	24	22
30	8	37	28	39
25	32	26	36	23
25	48	19	28	22
18	30	32	26	36

Q7

1	2	3	4	5	7	6	9	8
5	4	9	1	6	8	2	7	3
6	7	8	2	3	9	1	4	5
2	1	5	3	9	6	4	8	7
3	8	6	7	1	4	5	2	9
4	9	7	5	8	2	3	6	1
7	3	2	8	4	5	9	1	6
8	6	1	9	2	3	7	5	4
9	5	4	6	7	1	8	3	2

Q8   108
Q9   39
Q10 6
Q11 La Dolce Vita
Q12 Dirty Dancing
Q13 The Dirty Dozen
Q14 Billy Elliot
Q15 H

Cryptic crossword 10

Circuit 11

Q1 Theology
Q2 walkie talkie
Q3 Missing number is 728. (648 – 284) × 2 = 728.
Q4 Jaclyn Smith
Q5 tree, thee, them, teem, team, tear, pear
Q6

25	24	5	21	43
6	41	63	5	3
27	27	8	19	37
21	23	37	23	14
39	3	5	50	21

Q7

1	2	4	3	5	6	8	7	9
5	6	7	1	8	9	2	3	4
9	3	8	2	4	7	1	5	6
2	1	3	4	6	8	5	9	7
6	4	5	9	7	2	3	8	1
7	8	9	5	1	3	4	6	2
8	9	1	7	2	5	6	4	3
4	7	6	8	3	1	9	2	5
3	5	2	6	9	4	7	1	8

Q8   100
Q9   37
Q10 5
Q11 East Is East
Q12 (Bend It) Like Beckham
Q13 Dr Strangelove
Q14 The Graduate
Q15 C
Cryptic crossword 11

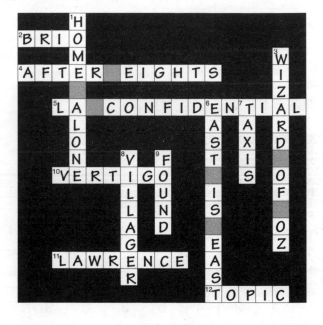

Circuit 12

Q1 Transcontinental
Q2 Whatever
Q3

			P					Q		
B	O	W	L					Q		
	X		I	N	J	U	R	Y		
			G				A	D		
	F		H		M	C				
V	E	S	T			K				
	Z									

Q4 Isabella Rossellini
Q5 read, road, rood, rook, book
Q6

20	14	28	23	26
17	30	36	22	6
9	50	13	24	15
29	14	8	22	38
36	3	26	20	26

Q7

1	2	3	4	7	5	6	9	8
4	5	6	9	1	8	2	3	7
7	8	9	2	6	3	1	5	4
2	1	4	8	3	9	7	6	5
3	6	7	1	5	2	4	8	9
5	9	8	6	4	7	3	1	2
6	3	2	5	8	4	9	7	1
9	7	5	3	2	1	8	4	6
8	4	1	7	9	6	5	2	3

Q8 90
Q9 24
Q10 4
Q11 Cabaret
Q12 Philadelphia
Q13 (To Kill A) Mockingbird
Q14 Rain Man
Q15 C

Across:
1. SPEAR
4. CRANBERRIES
6. EIGHT
7. CABARET
8. ANGLER
10. ELEANOR
14. OVERSIGHT
15. RAIN MAN
16. SAMBA
17. REPEAL
18. HEARTEN
19. TENORS

Down:
1. SHELDEPHI
2. MALIGN
3. EXPENSIVE
5. CARB
9. DOM
11. TAI
12. NATURALLY
13. TANTEGE
16. SIREEP

Circuit 13

Q1 The five letters can make S N A I L (as in 'at a snail's pace').

Q2 Box Brownie

Q3

S	H	A	V	E
H	A	V	E	N
A	V	E	R	T
V	E	R	S	E
E	N	T	E	R

Q4 Elle MacPherson

Q5 coin, corn, cord, cold, gold

Q6

31	4	23	12	21
23	12	9	18	29
10	38	11	22	10
10	24	27	18	12
17	13	21	21	19

Q7

1	9	2	3	4	5	6	7	8
3	4	5	6	7	8	2	1	9
6	7	8	1	2	9	3	4	5
5	3	7	4	8	6	1	9	2
2	1	6	7	9	3	5	8	4
4	8	9	2	5	1	7	6	3
7	2	1	8	3	4	9	5	6
9	6	4	5	1	2	8	3	7
8	5	3	9	6	7	4	2	1

Q8 87
Q9 23
Q10 3
Q11 (The) Sound Of Music
Q12 The Third Man
Q13 The Sting
Q14 (The) African Queen
Q15 D

Cryptic crossword 13

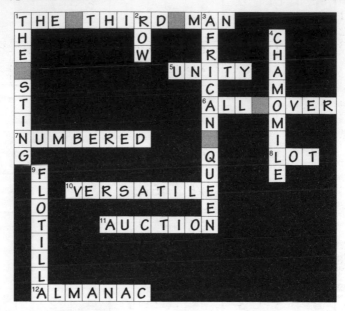

Circuit 14

Q1 sheep, sheen, shell, sheath

Q2 A website

Q3

1	2	3	4	5	6	7	8	9	10	11	12	13	14	15	16	17	18	19	20	21	22	23
V	I	N	O	R	S	C	A	M	N	E	S	I	A	N	S	W	E	R	N	I	C	K

Q4 Madonna

Q5 camp, came, same, sate, site

Q6

23	15	16	7	17
4	15	19	25	15
5	22	8	38	5
33	15	11	5	14
13	11	24	3	27

Q7

2	3	4	6	5	7	8	1	9
1	5	7	2	8	9	3	4	6
6	9	8	1	3	4	2	5	7
3	1	2	4	7	6	5	9	8
5	7	9	3	2	8	1	6	4
4	8	6	5	9	1	7	2	3
7	2	1	9	6	3	4	8	5
8	6	5	7	4	2	9	3	1
9	4	3	8	1	5	6	7	2

Q8 80
Q9 22
Q10 2
Q11 Unforgiven
Q12 Lassie
Q13 ET
Q14 The Lion King
Q15 A
Cryptic crossword 14

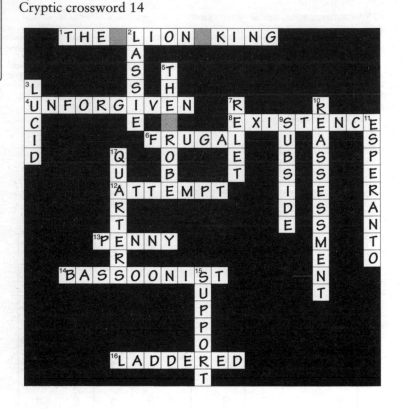